Exploring Art at the National Gal

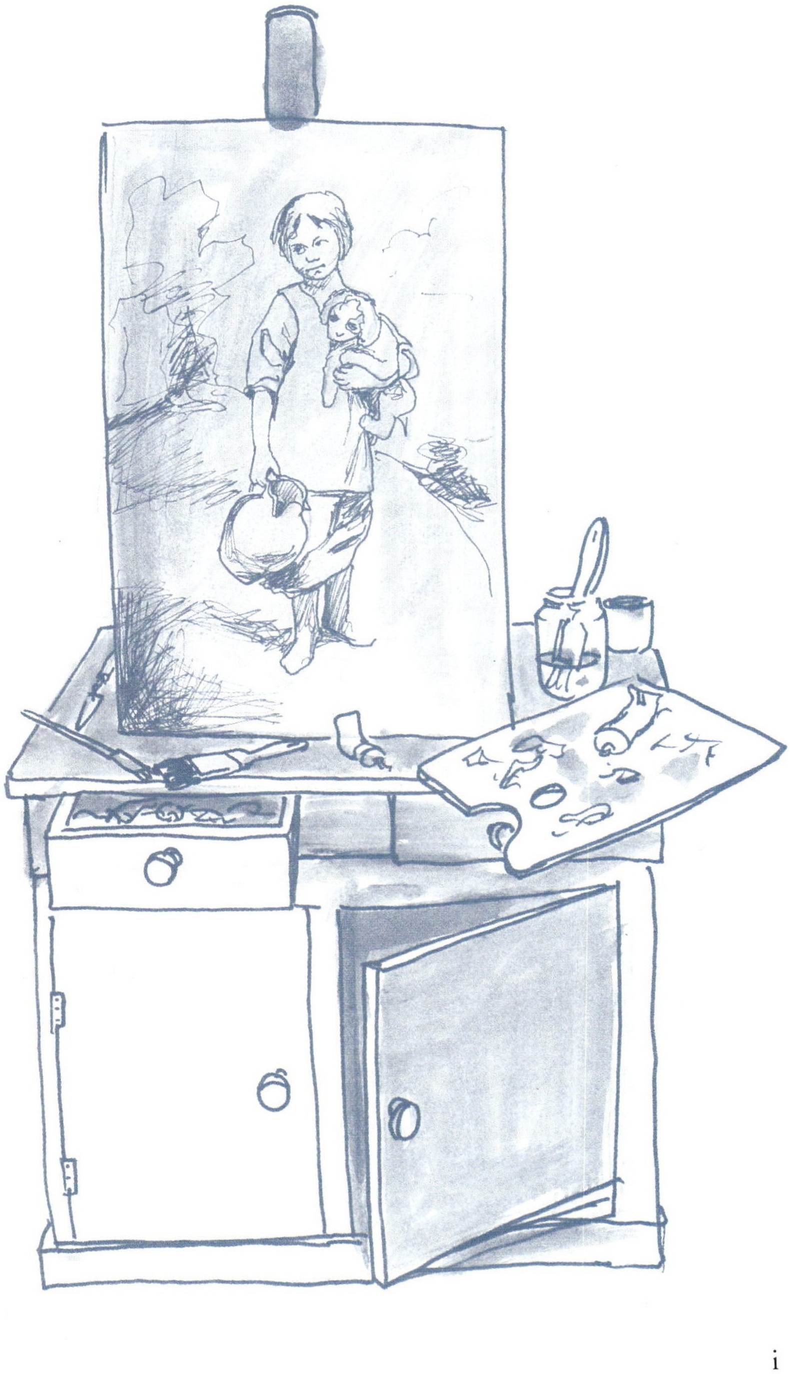

EXPLORING ART AT THE NATIONAL GALLERY

A HANDBOOK FOR PARENTS, TEACHERS AND YOUNG PEOPLE

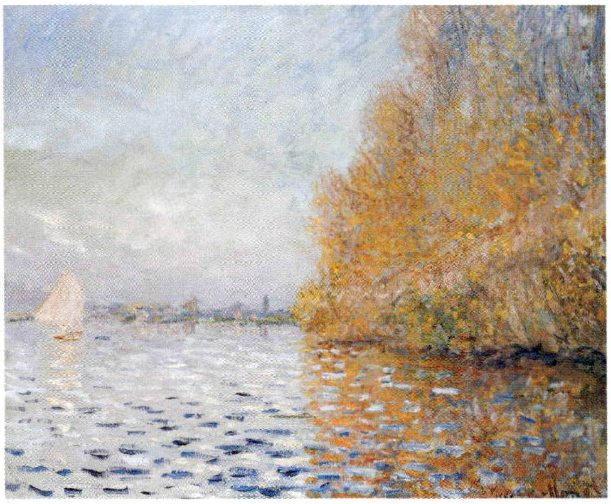

Marie Bourke

National Gallery of Ireland
Gailearaí Náisiúnta na hÉireann

Published in 1997 by
The National Gallery of Ireland
Merrion Square West
Dublin 2

Sponsored by Bord Gáis

Supported by The Gulbenkian Foundation

The paintings and photographs are the property of the National Gallery of Ireland, unless credited otherwise.

British Library Cataloguing in Publication Data available

ISBN: 0-903162-34-2

Front cover: **Argenteuil Basin with a single sailboat**, 1874
Claude Monet (1840-1926)
Back cover: **Eucharistic Symbols**, 1947/8
Evie Hone (1894-1955)

Text editor: Elaine Campion
Designer: Bill Bolger
Line drawings: Geraldine O'Neill
Photography: Roy Hewson
Printed in Ireland by βetaprint

Contents

Illustrations

Author's acknowledgements

Exploring Art has been written to answer just a few of the many queries about paintings, techniques and museums that I have been asked over the years. The book has emerged as a result of experience gained from several years working in art galleries, and it has benefited from a slow gestation process. I hope it will prove useful to parents, teachers and young people and that it will go some way towards demystifying the world of museums. In so doing, it might also explain the quiet passion that motivates people who work in galleries and museums.

I am most grateful to National Gallery of Ireland staff who helped in the preparation of this book, particularly Raymond Keaveney, the Director, Brian P. Kennedy, Maighread McParland and Andrew O'Connor (conservation), Dr Michael Wynne, Sergio Benedetti, Fionnuala Croke and Dr Hilary Pyle (curatorial). My sincere thanks to Tina Roche (development), Marie Fitzgerald (shop), Marie McFeeley (reproductions) and Roy Hewson (photography), Bill Maxwell and Valerie Keogh (press). A special word of thanks to the hard-working and good-humoured education team: Jackie Ryan for the slide pack, Catherine Bates for the theme worksheets, Jim O'Callaghan for the art competition, and Jenny Siung for the outreach talks. Thanks also to the education volunteers for their continued assistance, to Pat Reenan, and to the attendants' working party. A special word of appreciation to Carmel Naughton, for her enthusiastic support of the project.

Mo bhuíochas d'achan duine a chuidigh liom.

For discussion on aspects of the themes and practical projects, my sincere thanks to Alison Fitzgerald and Helen Beaumont. Thanks also to the teachers who were consulted, Caroline Bond, Naomi Cassidy and Germaine Murphy, and other colleagues who were helpful, Joe McDonnell, Catherine Marshall, Yvonne Scott, Mary Pat O'Malley, Anne O'Connor and Patsy McCabe.

A huge debt of gratitude is owed to Bord Gáis for generously sponsoring the book, the slide pack, the themesheets, the art competition and the exhibition. It was a pleasure to work with Paul O'Shaughnessy, Catherine Lovett, Miriam Farrelly, Kathleen O'Sullivan and Michael Boyle.

A word of appreciation to the Gulbenkian Foundation, in particular Ben Whitaker, the Director.

To Bill Bolger, Head of Visual Communications at the National College of Art and Design, for his superb work in designing this book.

A final note of thanks to Barry Drinan, Aoife and Sinéad, three of the most special people in the world.

Mo bheannacht libh a scríbhinn.

Foreword

One of the key functions of the National Gallery of Ireland is to introduce young people to art and to educate them as to its history and significance. The first and most critical element is to provide free access to the marvellous collections of Irish and European art which range in date from the fourteenth to the twentieth centuries. The second element is to provide young visitors with a variety of aids to help them better appreciate and understand what it is they are viewing.

Most young people have their first introduction to art and museums either in the company of their parents or through their school programmes. Such programmes involve not only the teaching of art as a skill, but also visits to museums and galleries. Planning museum trips and achieving the maximum benefit from them makes particular demands on parents, teachers and children. This publication, written by Marie Bourke, Head of Education at the Gallery, will help people to understand museums better and assist them in using the National Gallery as an educational resource. It is an informative and enjoyable introduction to the National Gallery of Ireland.

Exploring Art provides parents teachers and young people with background information about the Gallery, its history and operation. It tells them about the pictures and how one can analyse and discuss them from various points of view, most notably by way of themes. It includes a useful glossary of art terms, a comprehensive schedule of artists and their contribution to the development of art, and tables charting the social and political background to the various periods in the history of art. In addition, the text deals with how the teacher can use the experience of visiting the Gallery to initiate activities in the classroom. It is worth noting that Gallery visits are made all the more stimulating and enjoyable when they are organised in conjunction with the helpful and supportive staff of the Education Department.

The publication of *Exploring Art at the National Gallery*, together with the children's art exhibition and teacher's pack, has been made possible by the generous and enlightened support of Bord Gáis, with some assistance from the Gulbenkian Foundation, to whom we are most grateful.

Raymond Keaveney
Director
National Gallery of Ireland

Preface

Exploring Art at the National Gallery provides a fascinating and informative introduction to the Gallery and its extensive collections. It will help people to develop a greater understanding of art, encourage them to visit their local museums and educate young people on the importance of their National Gallery.

Bord Gáis has enthusiastically embraced this project because the text is specifically aimed at parents, teachers and young people. I am sure that this enlightening and well-illustrated book will allow the National Gallery to reach a much wider audience, as it provides a first opportunity for many readers to learn something about themes in art, techniques and art movements, and to find out more about their favourite artists. Teachers will find that visiting the Gallery has been made easy for them through the helpful guidelines and the many practical projects provided in the book. Bord Gáis is particularly pleased to support the provision of an *Exploring Art* teacher's pack for schools, comprising copies of this book, a set of slides and theme worksheets.

An added feature of our support for this project is the art competition on the theme of the environment. Several of the winning pictures will be displayed in the 1998 Bord Gáis calendar, and all the winning entries and many more will form a children's art exhibition at the National Gallery in September–October '97. In this way Bord Gáis reinforces its strong commitment to the environment. We are delighted, through our association with the National Gallery of Ireland, to highlight the work of young Irish people at primary and post-primary level, who through their pictures demonstrate their concern and feelings about the natural environment in a colourful and refreshing manner.

This is not our first association with the National Gallery of Ireland, but part of what we see as an ongoing support of cultural and environmental projects nationwide. Bord Gáis is proud of the highly professional and creative way our National Gallery presents art and provides year-round programmes for the public. *Exploring Art* is just one example of this excellence.

Michael Conlon
Chairman
Bord Gáis

About this book ...

Exploring Art is designed to encourage adults and young people to discover the fun and excitement of looking at pictures in the National Gallery's wonderful collection.

It is a handbook written for parents, teachers and young people who have an active interest in but not an in-depth knowledge of art, and is based on meetings with and listening to visitors of all ages to the National Gallery of Ireland. At different stages they indicated a desire to know more about works of art and their background. Most have already discovered that even a basic knowledge of paintings and sculpture enhances the enjoyment of a visit.

Exploring Art introduces you to a new way of looking at works of art which will help you to understand them better. It can be used as a guide to the works of art in the National Gallery and how to 'read' them. The selected works include oil paintings, watercolours, panel paintings and drawings, chosen to show the enormous variety of techniques artists have employed to represent their world. Many of the paintings are hundreds of years old and contain fascinating details, like *pentimenti*, inscriptions, coats of arms and preliminary drawings, all of which are explained here.

The book has been structured so that teachers can easily access the information they require. For example, they may view the collection through themes, such as portraits, still life, scenes from the life of Christ, landscapes and narratives. With each thematic exploration, there are suggestions for practical projects, suitable for primary and post-primary schoolchildren, together with ideas to help young people get started on some practical art and design work. Questions about where works fit in the chronology of art can easily be researched by looking at the chapter 'Art through the Centuries', which catalogues all the major phases in the history of art, including Irish art, in addition to outlining the social, political and cultural background of each period. Structures are set out to help teachers arrange visits to the Gallery, organise follow-up work and projects in the classroom, and write their own activity sheets.

There is a glossary of art terms, and a chapter explaining the various art styles and periods represented in the collection, all explained in simple language.

Exploring Art will not tell you everything there is to know about works of art, or about all the pictures in the National Gallery of Ireland. It will, however, tell you more about your favourite pictures, and looking at the reproductions will encourage you to seek out other original works in the National Gallery.

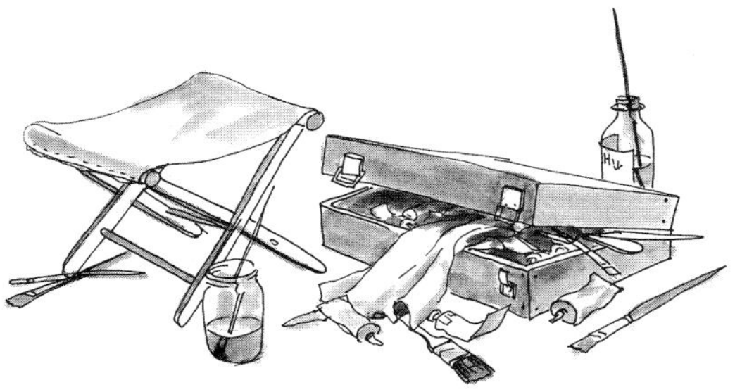

1

The National Gallery of Ireland

The idea of establishing a permanent public collection of Old Master paintings became a reality in Ireland following the Irish Industrial Exhibition which was held in 1853 on the grounds of Leinster Lawn, Dublin, funded by William Dargan (1799-1867), the railway magnate. The exhibition was surprisingly successful, and to commemorate Dargan's generosity, a committee was set up which joined with the Irish Institution in having as its sole aim the founding of an Irish National Gallery.

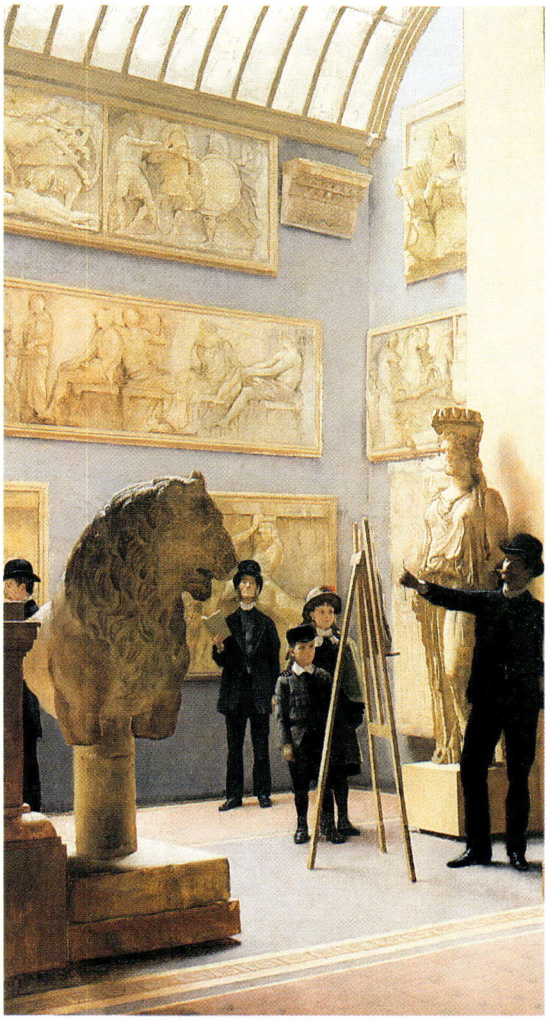

Taking Measurements: the artist copying a cast in the Main Hall of the National Gallery of Ireland, 1887 by Richard T. Moynan

Established in 1854 by an Act of Parliament, the National Gallery of Ireland opened its doors to the public ten years later. The new building, designed by the Irish architect Francis Fowke, was modern for its time, boasting top-lit galleries illuminated by gas burners in the winter months. As a fire-safety measure, the floors were built of iron and concrete, a revolutionary concept that anticipated twentieth-century pre-stressed, reinforced concrete. The original building was extended in 1903, when Thomas Newenham Deane designed a wing, and there was a further extension in 1968, designed by Frank du Berry of the Office of Public Works. During the intervening years the collection has grown, and once again the National Gallery is expanding, with a new wing to be built fronting onto Clare Street in the year 2000.

When first opened to the public, the collection consisted of some 125 works of art. Through gifts, donations and a wise purchasing policy, the collection has gradually been broadened to include Italian, Dutch, French, German, Early Netherlandish, Flemish, Spanish, English and Irish paintings. Today the Gallery houses close to thirteen thousand works of art, including paintings, watercolours, drawings, prints, sculpture and *objets d'art*, ranging in date from the fourteenth to the twentieth centuries. These works comprise the national collection of European Old Master paintings, Irish paintings and national portraits.

The National Gallery is state funded, but it has also been the recipient of many gifts from notable benefactors such as the Countess of Milltown, Sir Hugh Lane and Sir Alfred Chester Beatty. George Bernard Shaw, in gratitude to the Gallery for the part it played in his education as a young boy in Dublin, bequeathed to it a third of his estate. Recent outstanding benefactors include Máire MacNeill Sweeney, the Irish Jesuit Community, Sir Denis Mahon, and Sir Alfred and Lady Beit who presented the Gallery with seventeen masterpieces from Russborough House. The generosity of such benefactors has greatly enriched and enhanced the national collection as the National Gallery of Ireland enters the twenty-first century.

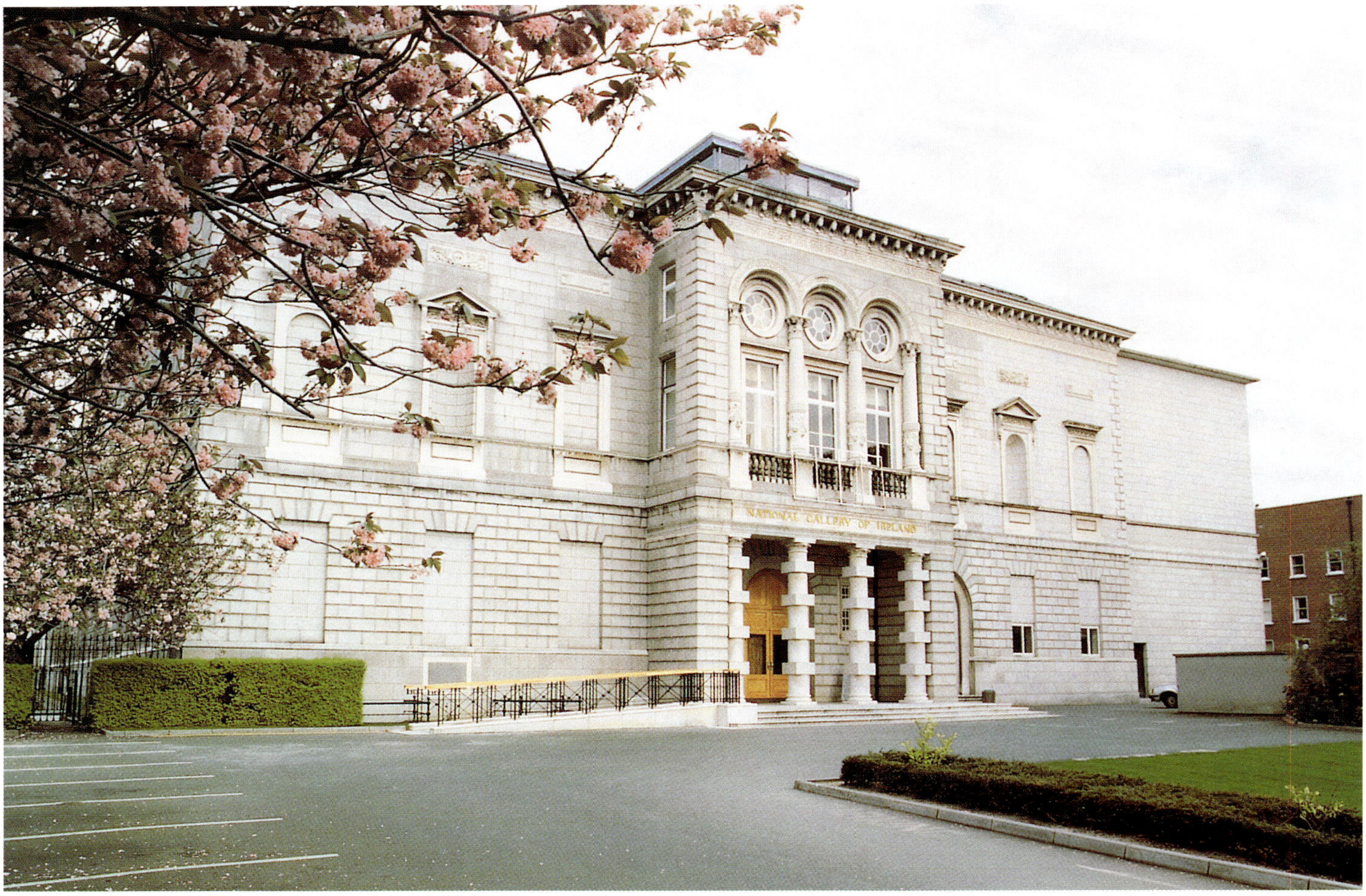

The façade of the National Gallery of Ireland, showing the 1864 Dargan Wing (left), the 1903 Milltown Wing (centre), and the North Wing (right)

Paintings are for everyone

The Universal Declaration of Human Rights (Article 27) states: 'Everyone has the right freely to participate in the cultural life of the community, to enjoy the arts, and to share in scientific advancement and its benefits'. Though the pictures in this book hang in the National Gallery of Ireland in Merrion Square in Dublin, they belong to everybody and are enjoyed by visitors from all over the world. The National Gallery works to make its collections accessible, so that all visitors feel welcome and find the level of information they require. In the main, the paintings are grouped according to their date and place of origin, for example, the Irish School, seventeenth-century Dutch School, etc, and are labelled clearly with the title, the name of the artist (if known) and the date the work was acquired by the Gallery. The design of the labels, which are bilingual, takes into account people with impaired sight. Sometimes information about the subject or the historical context is provided on separate panels. Security attendants, who are present in the rooms to protect the exhibits, will also answer visitors' queries and help with directions.

People visit the National Gallery for all kinds of reasons, apart from looking at the paintings. For instance, they may just want to have lunch or meet friends, they may come to hear a seminar or a lecture, to listen to a concert or to try the multimedia room, to take part in a children's project, to colour a worksheet, follow a tour, join a family activity or visit the shop. Whatever their reason for visiting, everyone is equally important at the National Gallery of Ireland.

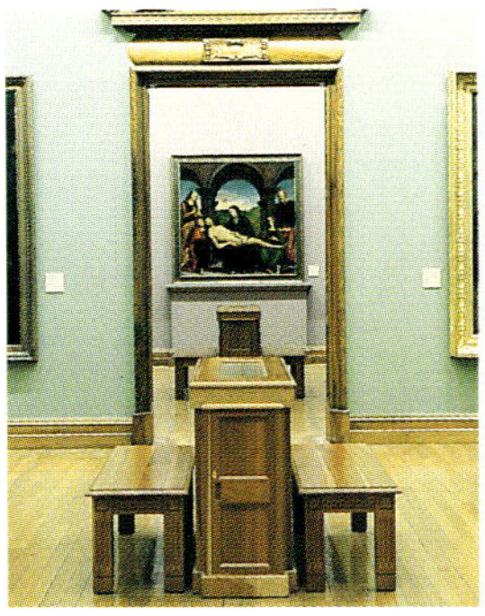

Some Facts about the Gallery

- The paintings in the National Gallery belong to the Irish nation – everyone is welcome to visit and view them. Each year the Gallery has over one million visitors.

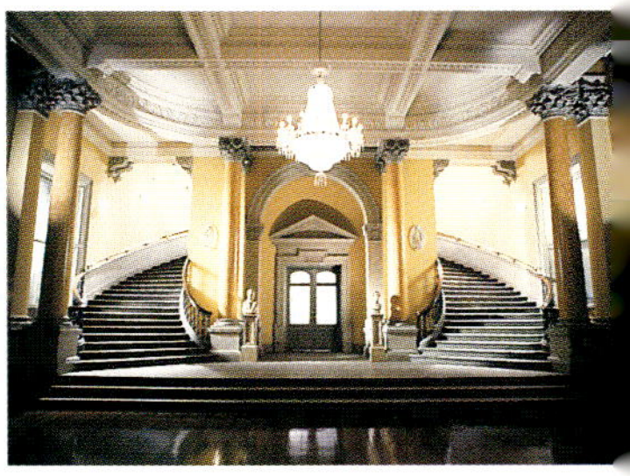

- Admission to the Gallery is free.

- Opening hours are: Monday to Saturday 10am - 5.30pm, Thursday 10am - 8.30pm, Sunday 2pm - 5pm. The Gallery is closed on Good Friday, and 24, 25 and 26 December.

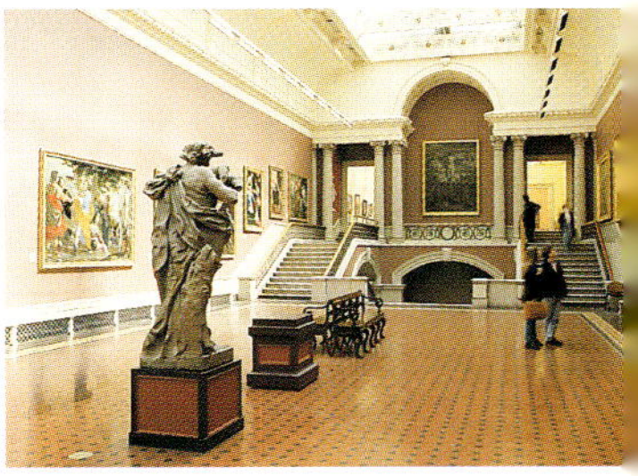

- The National Gallery seeks to provide a service that is equally accessible to all its visitors. Details of its programmes and activities are published quarterly in *Gallery News*, which is available from the Gallery Information Desk.

- Visitor aids include an information service, guidebooks, floor-plans, multimedia and audio guides.

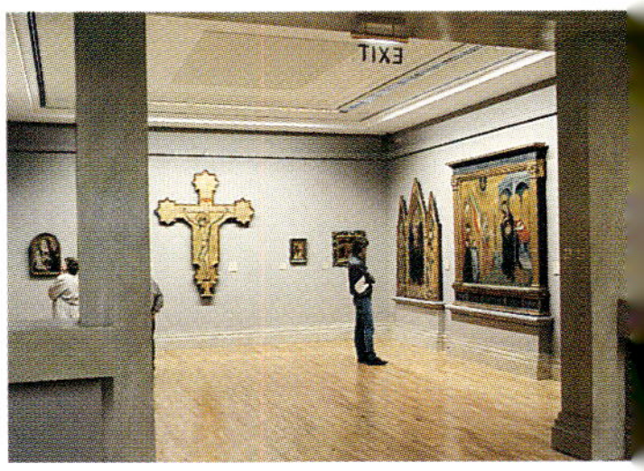

- The National Gallery encourages families to visit, by putting on special projects for teenagers, children and tiny tots.

- Ramps, lifts, wheelchairs, induction loops, toilets, phones and other facilities are provided for people with disabilities and special needs. There are also tours using Tactile Picture Sets for people with impaired sight, and tours with an interpreter for people with impaired hearing. The Gallery's *Access Guide* highlights these services.

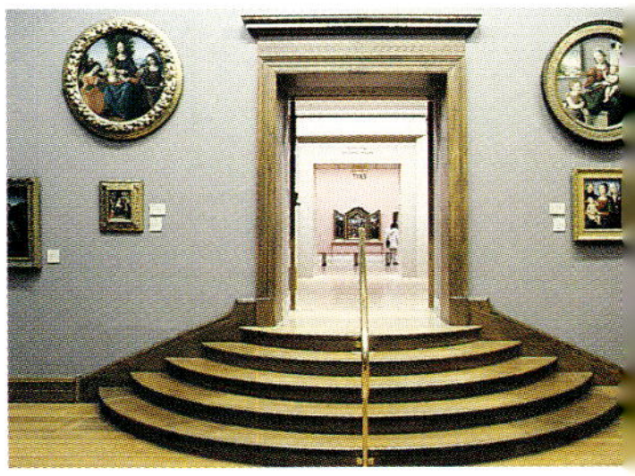

Snapshots of the National Gallery of Ireland

- The Gallery Shop and Restaurant, located on the ground floor, are open during Gallery hours.

- The National Gallery of Ireland's comprehensive Education Service includes:

  The Public Programme: Public lectures and tours, and the Family Programme.

  Continuing Education: Drawing and art appreciation classes for adults.

  Young People's Activities: Schools programme of art lectures, portfolio days, transition-year class, spring study days, theme worksheets and school tours. Other events include the Teenagers' Drawing Course, the Children's Summer Club and the Christmas Art Holiday. Publications include the children's art exhibition catalogue, Artists' Profile workbook, activity sheets and several colouring books.

Community Awareness and Outreach Programme: This includes the disability service and annual Family Day. The Outreach Programme brings the Gallery to a wider public throughout the country by means of access initiatives, including talks on art and children's workshops, provided at venues such as hospitals, prisons, libraries, museums and regional arts centres. A number of pilot outreach projects are also taking place in disadvantaged areas.

An Education/Information Pack is available free of charge from the Education Department (Phone 01-661 5133). Write three weeks in advance if you wish to book a tour. The address of the National Gallery of Ireland is: Merrion Square West, Dublin 2.

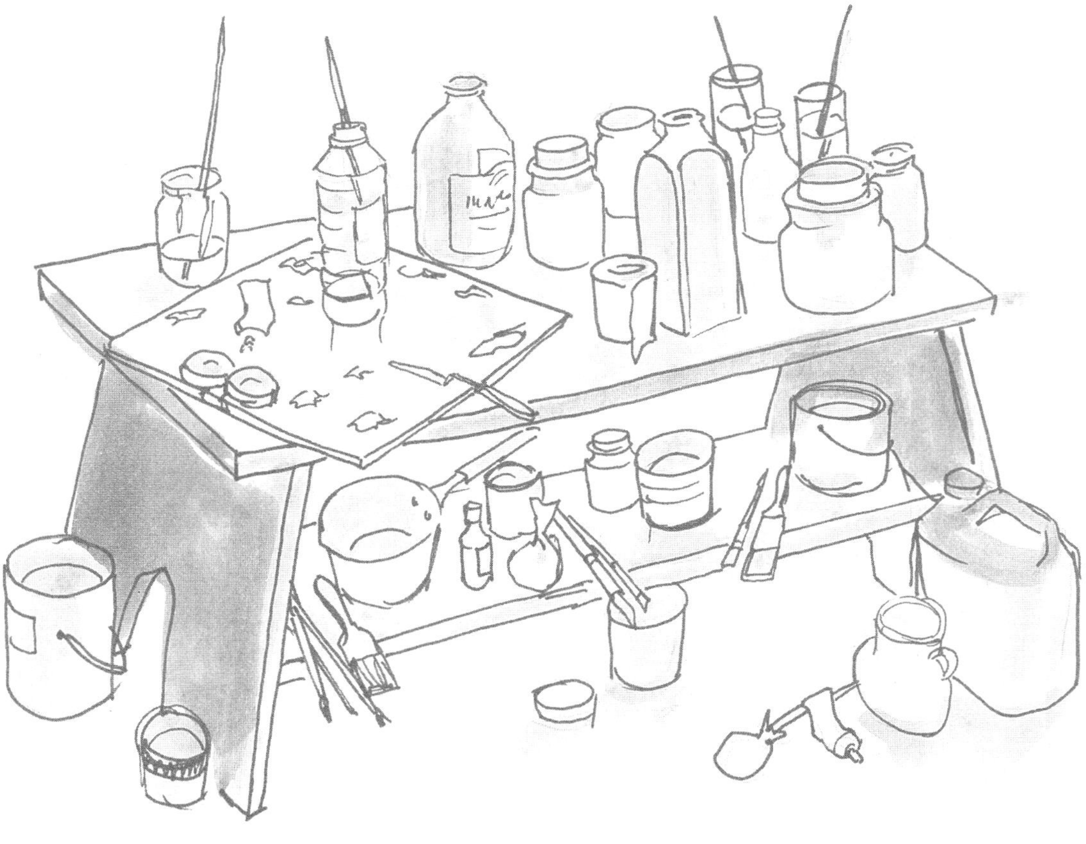

2

Museums and Galleries – an Introduction

What is a museum or an art gallery?

A simple definition of a museum or an art gallery is 'a place where works of art or items of other interest are collected, cared for, researched, interpreted and displayed for everyone to visit and enjoy'. Old objects, whether paintings or sculpture, archaeological artefacts, stuffed animals, costumes, photographs, toys or whatever, become more delicate and fragile as they age, and as a result they can be easily damaged and destroyed. Museums house collections of special objects that are beautiful, interesting, irreplaceable, of historical interest and, most important of all, because people get pleasure from looking at them. Public museums are relevant to today's world because they are storehouses of knowledge where everyone can learn to interpret the past, relate it to the present and create for the future.

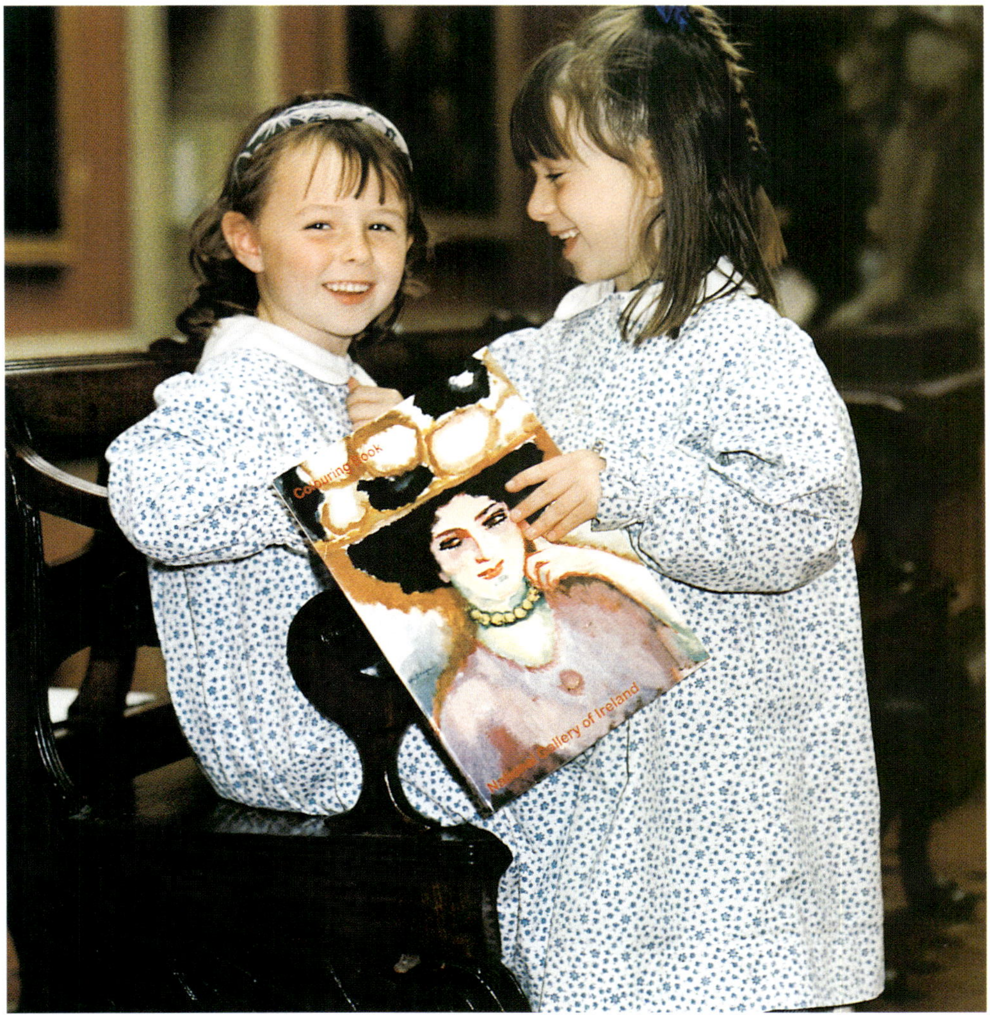

Young enthusiasts sharing a joke during a visit to the Gallery

What are its functions?

A gallery is an immensely stimulating, satisfying and enjoyable place in which to work. It demands diverse skills ranging from administrative to curatorial, from scientific to security. The major functions of a gallery include: acquiring and conserving objects, caring for the collection and mounting exhibitions, researching and interpreting the collection. These tasks are carried out by the various departments involved in the day-to-day work of the gallery: conservation and restoration, curatorial, education, library, publications, photography and exhibitions. All the individual departments are essential to the efficient working of a gallery. A Board of Governors and Guardians who rely on the specialist skills and advice of the director and staff, for instance, govern the management of the National Gallery of Ireland.

Acquisition

A key feature of the role of a public gallery is to acquire works for the collection; this is done by purchasing new works of art, and by attracting gifts and bequests to the gallery. Each object in the collection, particularly new acquisitions, is photographed and given an identification number. In this way the gallery has a record for all time of everything in its care. The history and facts about each work of art are kept in special archival files.

Conservation

An important part of any gallery's job is to protect and conserve its collection. The care and safekeeping of the collection is in the hands of conservators and restorers who, understanding that works of art grow old and fragile, use their knowledge to treat the

A conservator using a powerful microscope to assist in the process of restoring a painting (Photograph courtesy of Eric Luke, *The Irish Times*)

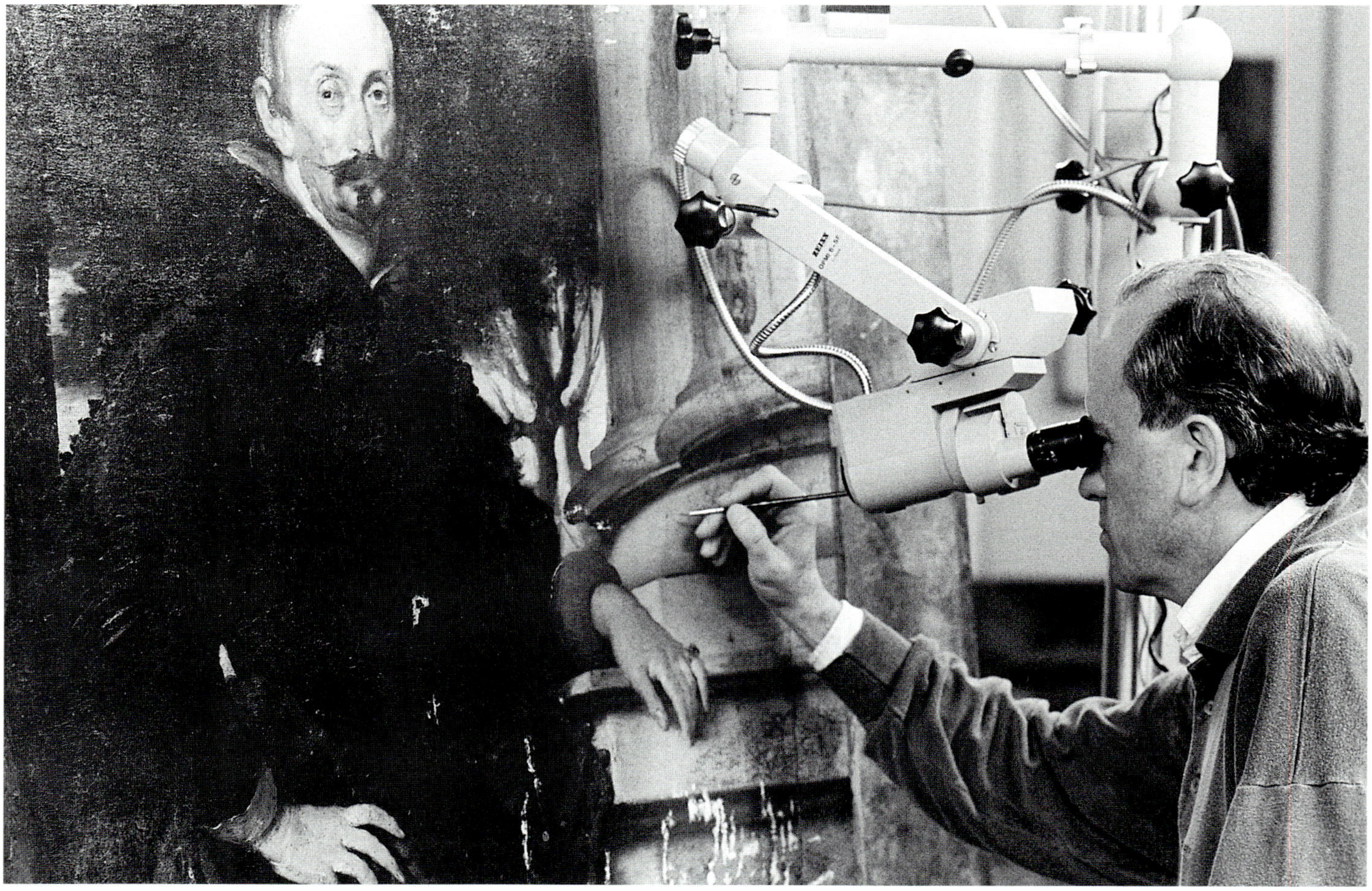

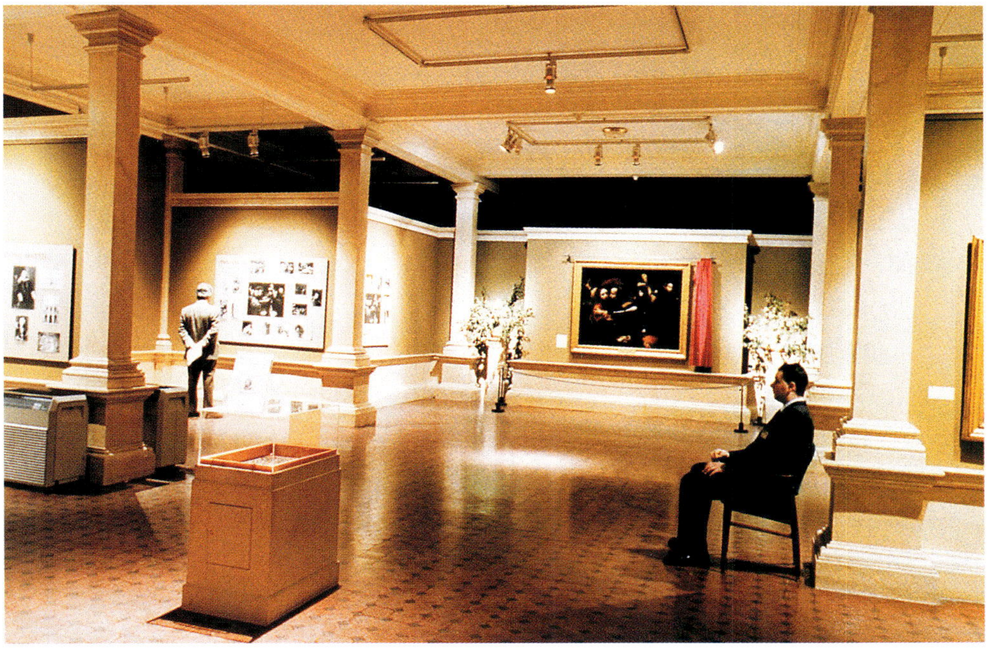

Organising temporary exhibitions such as 'The Master Revealed' is an important aspect of the Gallery's work

works and to preserve the collection for future generations. Conservators are experts in the different materials and techniques that are used to make works of art. A gallery employs conservators expert in different areas to deal with oil paintings, works on paper, and frames. While conservators and restorers are trained to use scientific equipment in the course of their work, they primarily use their hands skilfully and patiently to clean and repair works of art that can never be replaced.

Sophisticated scientific equipment is used to control the environment of a gallery, in addition to variations in lighting. Conservators sometimes work in collaboration with scientists, monitoring a gallery's elaborate systems of air conditioning, including temperature and humidity. Rapid changes from hot to cold or dry to damp can cause untold damage to works of art, and so it is vital to be able to control the climate inside the building. Located throughout most major galleries are small sensors that measure the temperature and the amount of moisture in the air. Their function is to alert the staff so that steps can be taken to avoid a situation whereby the air heats up, cools down, dries out or becomes too damp. Air pollution also needs to be monitored and controlled.

Caring for the collection and mounting exhibitions

Curators use their training to care for the collection and look after its wellbeing, in addition to answering queries about the collection and about works of art in general. Managing and monitoring displays of the collection is another part of the curators' work. They decide which objects go on display in the public galleries and arrange each display so as to help people understand and appreciate what they see. Many galleries organise temporary exhibitions, and the planning, research and mounting of such displays are largely the responsibility of the curators. Sometimes designers make scale models of the rooms to assist the curators in planning the layout of the exhibition.

Curators also arrange to have the works photographed, write the labels and compile the catalogues. They may organise a touring programme for some exhibitions. As part of managing a gallery's collection, they frequently have to monitor paintings going on loan to overseas galleries, for example, supervise packing, travel and security arrangements. The knowledge gathered by curators, who are constantly researching their particular area of interest, is an invaluable source of reference when acquiring new works for the collection.

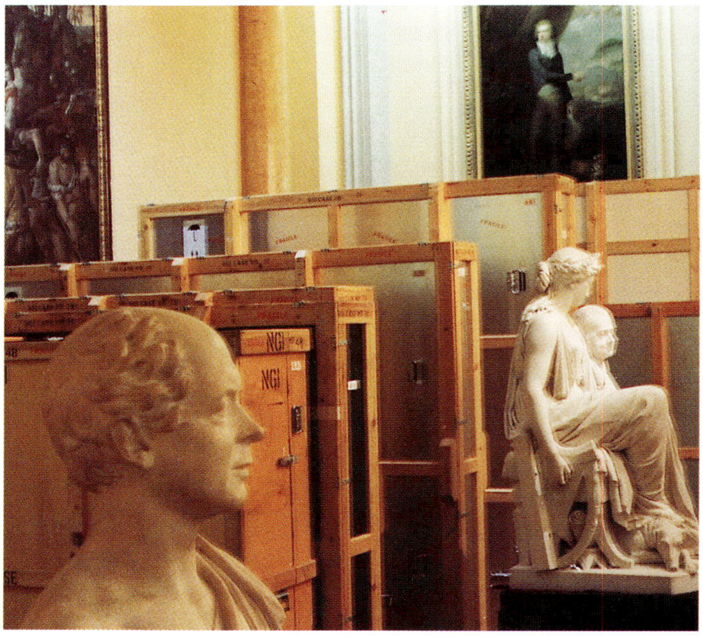

An exhibition, packed and ready to travel to an overseas gallery

Research

An important aspect of a curator's job is to research works of art in the collection and learn more about them. Curators do this by looking carefully with a fresh observant eye at each work in question, in order to determine how it was made, why it was made, what is its subject matter and meaning, and what other works the artist created. By consulting catalogues, books, articles, documents or other archival material, usually located in the gallery's library, and by communicating with colleagues around the world, curators seek to create a body of knowledge regarding the author and period of each work, tracing its history from the time it was painted down to the present day. The results of their research are compiled in detailed catalogues. Through their education and training, curators can provide an intelligent, thoughtful and informed appraisal of a collection.

Interpretation and education

The task of imparting information about the collection to the general public is carried out by people specially trained in museum education. The information can be conveyed in a variety of ways: through different kinds of publications and processes aimed at students, children and the general visitor, through lectures given by art historians and other experts, on topics ranging from simple art themes to specialist subjects, and through guided tours of the collection, organised for the general public, school groups and for the visually and the hearing impaired. Information may also be conveyed through exhibitions revealing the work of an artist, a group of artists or a period in art, ranging from major shows to minor in-focus displays, as well as seminars and conferences on art-related themes. Young people's activities include teenagers' art appreciation and portfolio classes, school programmes and summer art adventures for tiny tots, activity sheets for all ages, and also slides, videos or films of the collection. An important aspect of the museum educator's job is to ensure that a comprehensive education service is equally accessible to all sections of the community, including families, children, adult groups, schools, and people with disabilities and special needs.

Museum educators are required to integrate with every facet of gallery life. Their background involves training in art history or fine art, coupled with museum studies or arts administration. They may also have acquired teaching experience and skills in information technology, graphic design and librarianship, combined with organisational ability and good public relations. The key challenge for the museum educator is to explore ways in which the institution can create new opportunities to help people understand, appreciate and enjoy the collections.

3

Visiting the National Gallery

Forward planning and preparation

The National Gallery of Ireland provides education staff and facilities, welcomes school and adult groups and encourages teachers to take part in courses. This is supported by Department of Education policy and the school curriculum, which encourages the use of resources such as museums and galleries to help develop the expressive and creative abilities of young people. We hope that integrating a well-planned Gallery visit with classroom activities will provide the potential for learning and making connections in a most rewarding way.

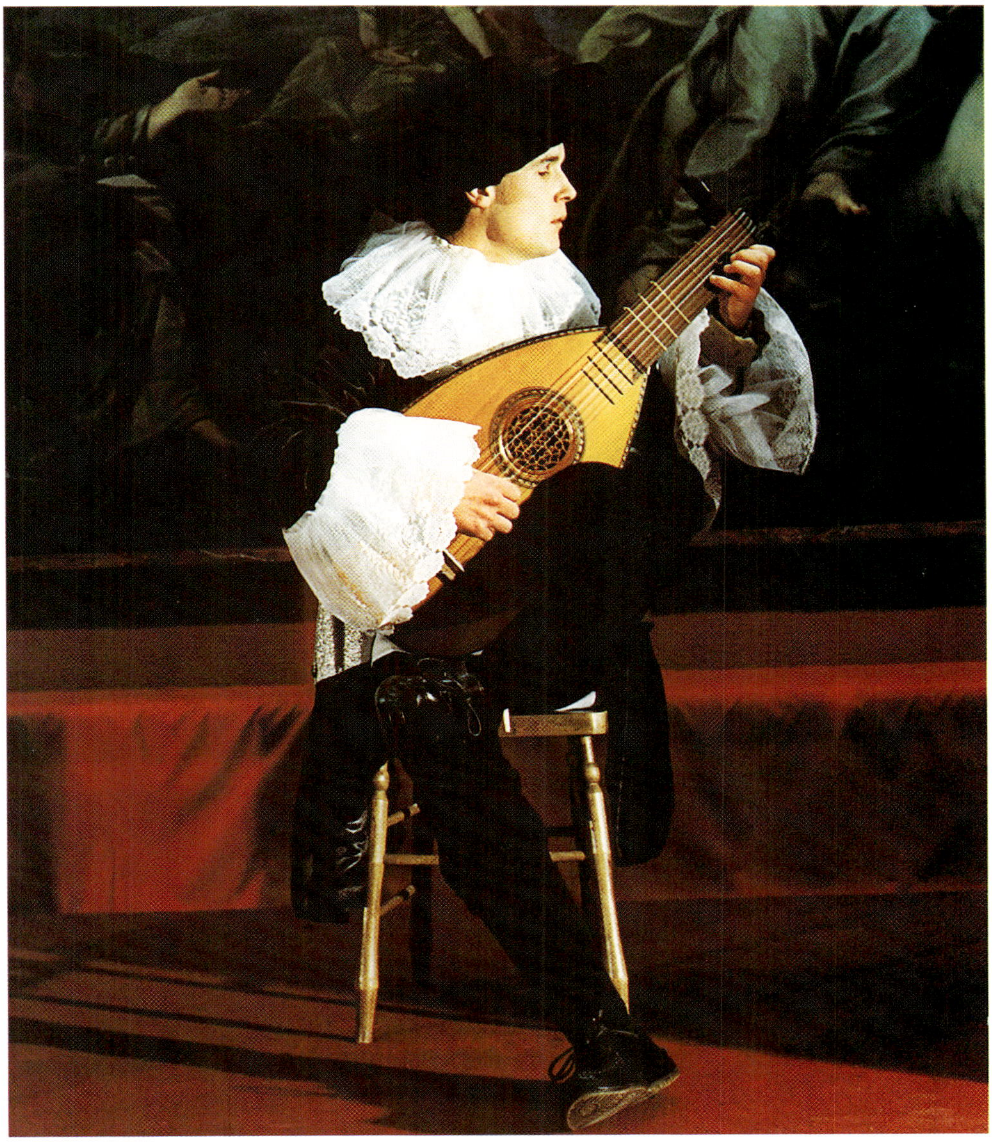

Bringing pictures alive – a young musician posing as **The Lute Player** in the Baroque Gallery

Phone and discuss the proposed visit with education staff. Ask for an Education/ Information Pack to be forwarded to you.

Write to the Gallery's Education Department three weeks in advance of the tour. Indicate the date and time you wish to come, the number and ages of the students, and specify if you would like worksheets or themesheets. Let us know in advance if the group has special needs or if assistance is required. The National Gallery is completely accessible to people with disabilities and an *Access Guide* outlining the services and facilities is available from the Information Desk. Tours are available for people with impaired sight using Tactile Picture Sets (raised reproductions in plastic of ten paintings in the collection), and tours with interpreters are available for people with hearing impairments.

Before the visit give the students an idea of what to expect. Indicate that the National Gallery is a large building with many beautiful displays. Explain why the objects on display cannot be touched. Mention that good behaviour includes being considerate towards other visitors. Encourage the students to bring sketching pads and drawing equipment to learn from the Old Masters.

Discuss the projected visit with the students, as they may wish to make suggestions of their own. Prepare the students using slides, reproductions and catalogues (but do not overdo it); they will enjoy recognising the works and it will enhance the Gallery visit.

Punctuality is essential for pre-booked tours.

Leave before the students tire. Approximately one to two hours maximum.

A successful outcome will depend on whether the students enjoyed themselves and want to go back for more.

The visit

Guidelines for a pre-booked tour

On arrival at the Gallery, register with Reception and let the attendants know the name of the party so that they can inform the guide. Ask about arrangements for coats and bags and find out the location of the toilets.

Assemble. Conducted tours of the Gallery are about exploring and developing a sense of discovery. When showing visitors around the Gallery, the guide will invite questions and initiate discussion. The works of art will be looked at from several different aspects, including the subject, the artist, the period and technique, together with compositional details such as line, shape, form, colour, tone and texture. The guide will try to let every child talk about some aspect of the painting and will listen and help where necessary. Above all, the guide will encourage the students to express their own thoughts and experiences about the works of art on display.

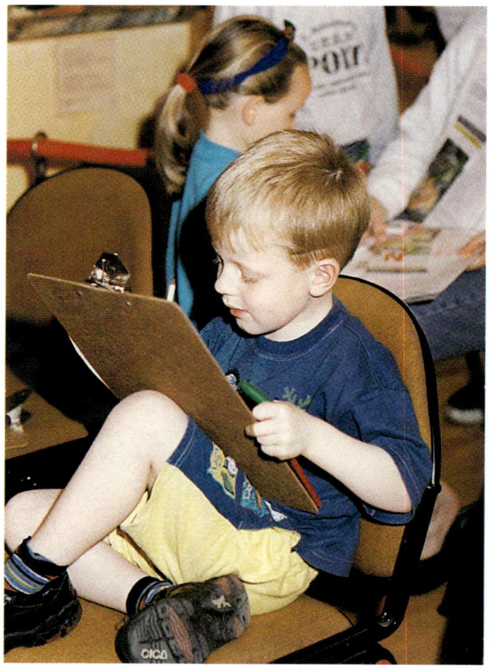

A little master at work

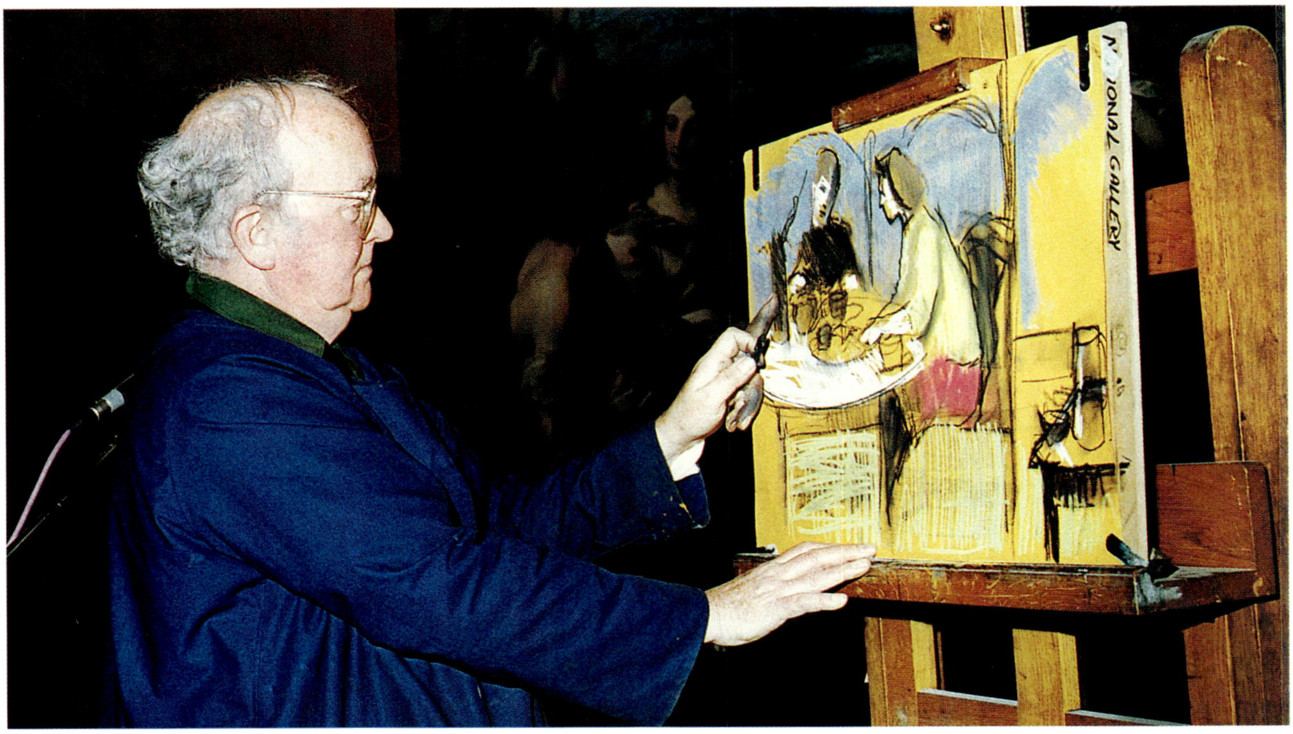

A demonstration during a teenagers' drawing course by the artist John Coyle RHA

Practical work. Sketching and taking notes from the paintings is recommended. There are also many Gallery worksheets, themesheets and activity sheets available. Make sure groups are small and spread throughout the rooms.

Teachers may wish to answer the students' questions by referring to some of the following National Gallery of Ireland/NGI catalogues and books:

NGI illustrated summary catalogue of paintings, 1981
NGI illustrated summary catalogue of drawings, watercolours and miniatures, 1983
NGI illustrated summary catalogue of prints and sculpture, 1988
NGI comprehensive colour illustrated guide. Scala, 1990
NGI colour illustrated guide, 1996

Using the summary catalogues and other catalogues published on the individual schools of painting, you could look up information on the name, date and nationality of an artist, the title of the work, details of its past history and the medium on which it was painted, e.g. canvas, wood panels, paper or board, or further in-depth details about the artist and the painting.

Other information may be found in the following reference books:

Cambridge Introduction to Art Series, of books ranging from the art of Ancient Greece and Rome to twentieth-century art, published by Cambridge University Press
E. H. Gombrich, *The Story of Art,* Phaidon, 1995
E. Grimal, *Dictionary of Classical Mythology,* Penguin, 1990
J. Hall, *Dictionary of Subjects and Symbols in Art,* John Murray, 1996
M. Levey, *From Giotto to Cézanne,* Thames and Hudson, 1990
E. A. Livingstone (Ed), *Concise Oxford Dictionary of the Christian Church,* Oxford University Press
P. & L. Murray, *Penguin Dictionary of Art and Artists,* 1991
N. Stangos, *Thames and Hudson Dictionary of Art and Artists,* 1994

Curriculum. Class projects can extend beyond the collection to investigating the architecture of the building. Cross-curricular projects should be encouraged, as well as the disciplines directly served by the collections.

Looking at the paintings

You do not have to be an art historian or an expert to look at works of art. By looking, thinking and asking questions, you can discover a lot. You might ask yourself what is the story of the picture? Why did the artist create it? Where was it meant to hang – in a palace, a monastery or a house? Does it fall into any of the themes in the history of art – portraits, landscapes, history painting, narratives, the nude? When was it made and what was going on in the world at that time? What is it painted on? Does it seem well crafted?

Consider your own experience of the work of art. How does it make you feel: happy, sad, angry, calm, frightened or uplifted? Feel free to judge the work – do you like it? Could you live with it?

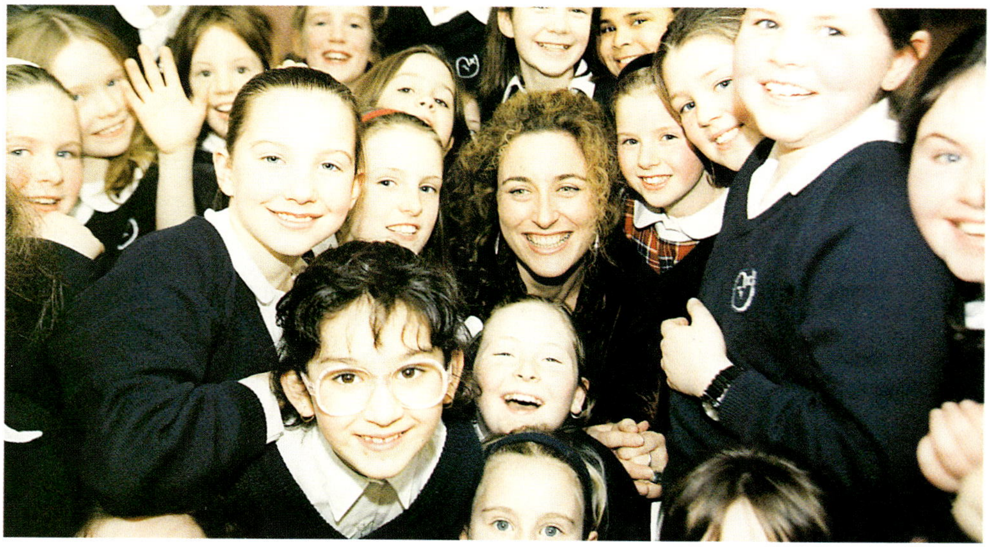

Primary-school children enjoying their visit to the National Gallery (Photograph courtesy of Jim Walpole, *The Star*)

Try a different approach with young people. Be a detective – try to work out what kind of people are in the pictures and what jobs they had. Look at a few of the portraits. Would you want any of the sitters to be your friend? Compare happy works with sad ones, mysterious pictures with unusual ones.

Encourage children to view the Gallery as a treasure trail. Tell them to hunt for pictures showing hats or shoes, jewellery or animals. Explore the pictures and try to find odd, curious and amazing details. Ask questions and listen to the children's answers. Invent stories about the pictures. Obtain activity sheets from the Information Desk and spend time with the children seeking out the answers and colouring the drawings. Help the children to look and learn from what they see.

Spend some time in the shop before you leave. The Gallery Shop sells a wide variety of books and catalogues about the collections. You might also want to buy a poster, slide, greeting card or book as a memento of the visit.

Helpful hints

- Ask at the Information Desk for a floor-plan and programme of events.
- Take your time – you don't have to see everything on display.
- It helps to wear comfortable shoes.
- Take a break for lunch or coffee – that way you won't get tired.
- Make a head count.
- Know when it's time to stop. You can always come back.

Follow-up in the classroom

The positive outcome of a Gallery visit depends on careful planning. The process can be continued later with classroom activities, enabling the students to make surprising and unexpected connections. The visit may help develop a greater understanding of some of the major themes in art, the work of an artist or a period in history. Some of these practical suggestions should help reinforce the experience of the Gallery visit.

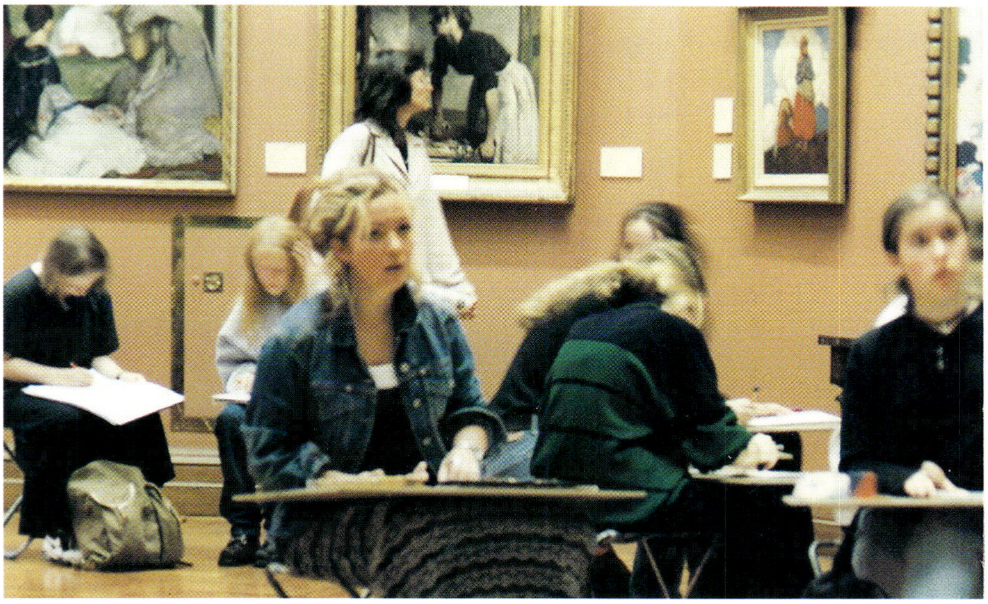

Young people drawing during one of the Portfolio Courses run by the Gallery

Gallery worksheets, themesheets and activity sheets: Teachers often encourage children to make a start on the worksheets while they are in the Gallery, and then complete them later in the classroom, because they help strengthen the experience of the visit. Observe the children's ability to recall the detail and colour of the paintings and use this exercise to explore further their own ideas about the Gallery.

Discussion: Encourage the students to discuss and share the information they gathered in the Gallery. This will help them revive the experience of the visit, listen to others and compare perceptions. What was the highlight of the visit? Did they have a favourite work of art? Was there any work they really hated and why did it not appeal to them? Through discussion and debate, let them explain their likes and dislikes, and in so doing give expression to their thoughts about art. The excitement felt by students after a visit is a measure of its success. Teachers need to evaluate the visit to ensure that it met the needs of the students.

The students can extend the process of discussion and evaluation in a concrete way by compiling reports or writing accounts of the visit, using library and other school resources to find out more about the works of art. The notes and sketches the students made in the Gallery could be used to create a display.

Drama: Use a slide or reproduction of one of the children's favourite Gallery paintings as the basis for role-play. Children love acting and dressing up. They can create the story, write out the words and make up costumes. By acting out the image, they will enjoy recreating the story of the painting.

Poetry: Select one of the Old Master paintings that the children liked on their Gallery visit. Does it illustrate a story? Is it calm or dramatic, pale or colourful? How does it make them feel? When the group have talked about the picture, encourage them to try and distil their ideas in a poem. It is not an easy exercise but it will help them to think carefully about the work of art and perhaps use words in a more accurate and descriptive way.

Visual/Writing exercise: Post-primary students might bring their drawing equipment and make notes and sketches of the paintings, the rooms and the architecture of the Gallery. Back in the classroom these can be worked up and used as the basis for exam project work, or display or portfolio work. Another exercise they could tackle is to make a record of their thoughts and observations in the Gallery and to type these up as descriptive, factual or imaginative essays.

An artist encouraging discussion during the Children's Summer Club

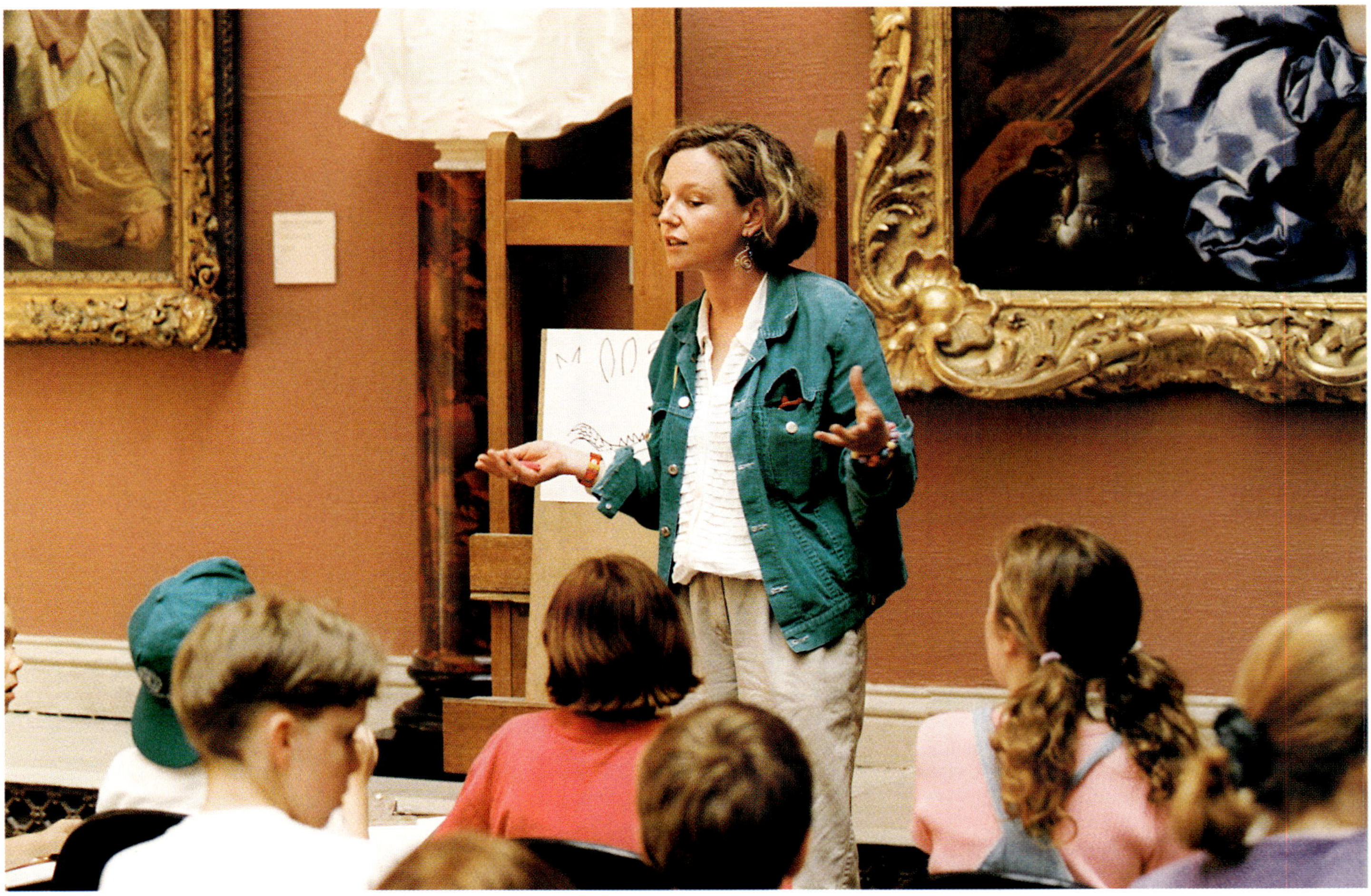

Design: Set the students a design exercise. Ask them to create a floor-plan of one of the rooms in the Gallery, noting public access, lighting and colour scheme, the hanging of the paintings and display of sculpture. Exhibit all the floor-plans in the classroom. Discuss the plans and allow the students express their own perceptions and ideas. Did they like the decoration of the rooms? Were the paintings well hung and displayed to their best advantage? Did the lighting influence the hanging of the paintings? Were the labels clear and legible, too brief or about right? Were people with special needs catered for? Was the sculpture well positioned? Do they mind some objects being placed behind glass – do they know of any other way to protect them against damage? Conclude the discussion by encouraging each student to explain his or her own design.

Practical projects

The following practical projects, for primary and post-primary students, use paintings from the national collection in an unusual and imaginative way. Find one that particularly suits you, your friends or your class and enjoy the process of creating the project and seeing how it emerges. These activities will help you enhance your understanding of art.

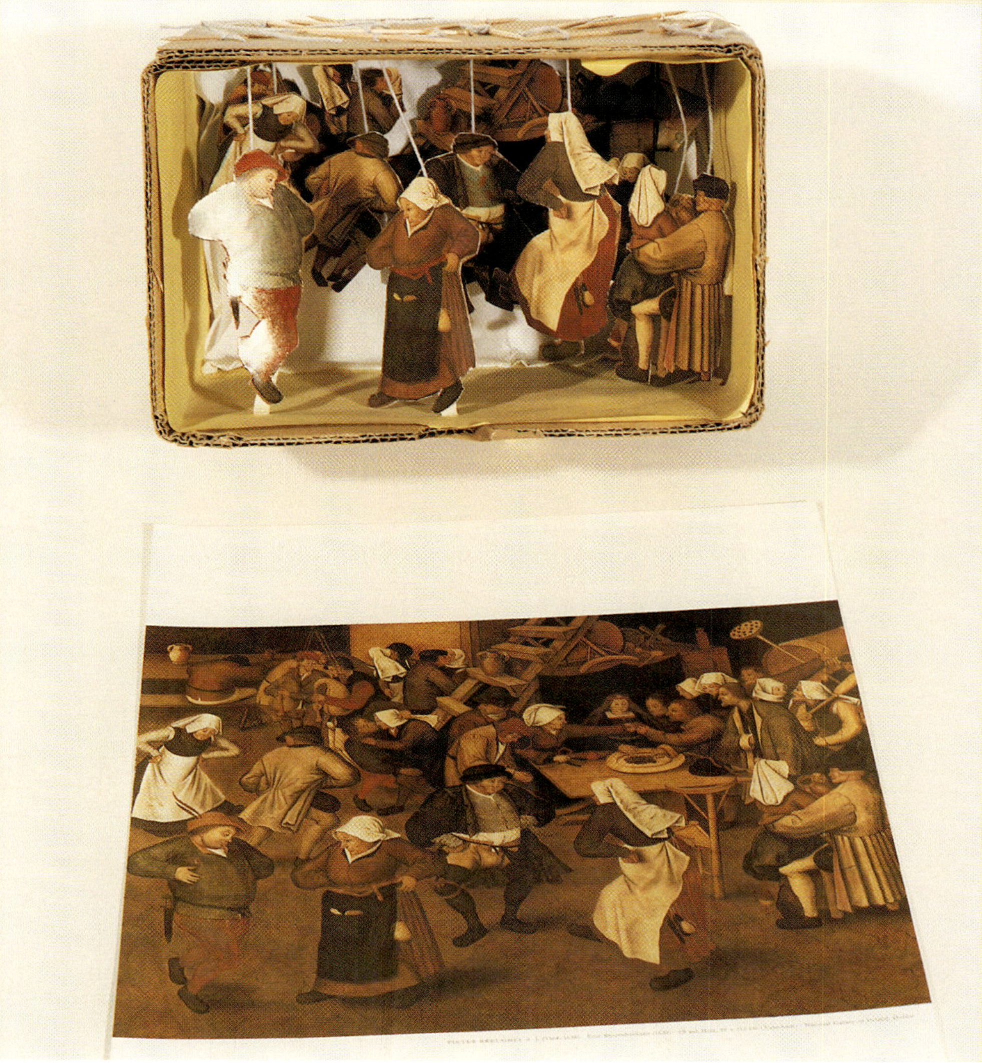

Brueghel's **The Peasant Wedding** adapted as a puppet show

1. Strongbow and Aoife's puppet show

Obtain a print of *The Marriage of Strongbow and Aoife* by Daniel Maclise or Brueghel's *The Peasant Wedding* from the Gallery Shop. Allocate one figure to each child in the class. Cut out all the main figures in the picture and paste each one onto a sheet of hard paper. Take a cardboard box and imagine it is a stage setting. Leave one side open and paint the inside green.

Using adhesive tape, attach a piece of fine cord or wool to the back of each figure, draw the cord up through the cardboard roof and tie it around a cocktail stick. When all the figures have been suspended with cord, the project is completed. Talk to the children about the story of the painting, about the Normans and this period in Irish history. Encourage the children to invent their own story about the wedding – and let them have some fun enacting it.

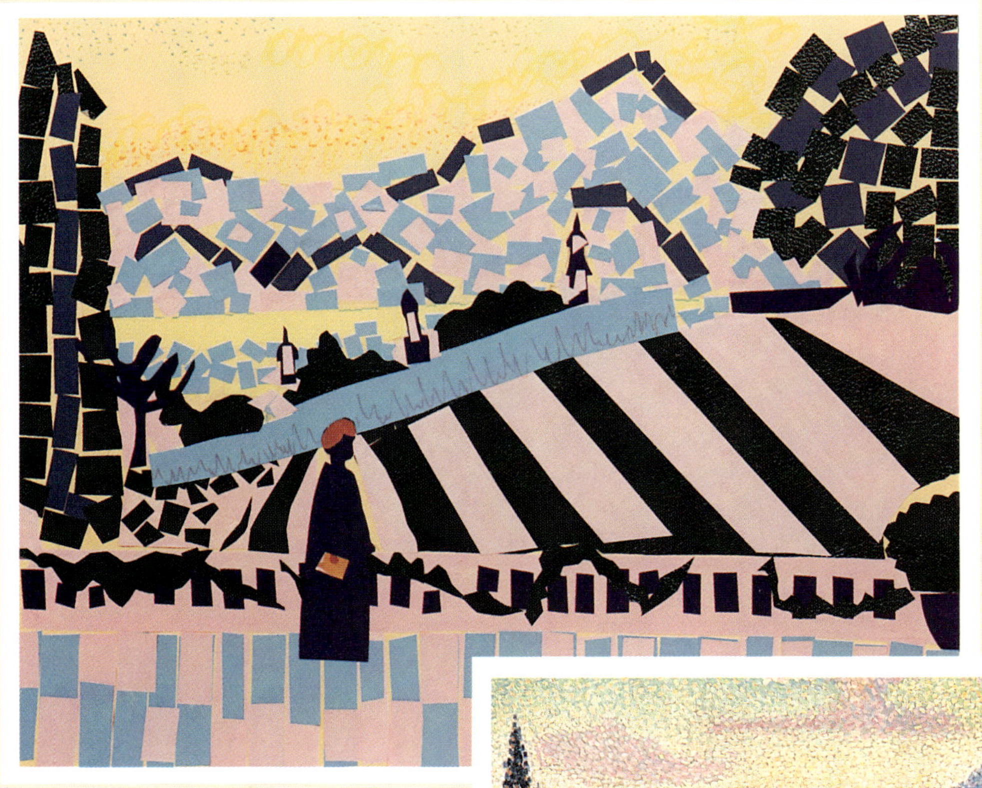

Signac's **Lady on the Terrace** as a dotty mosaic

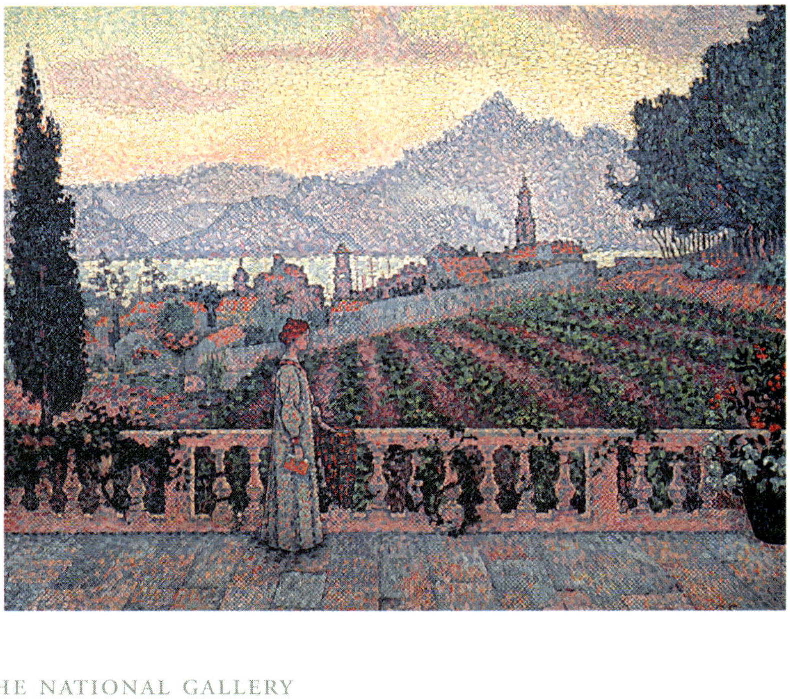

Lady on the Terrace by Paul Signac

2. A 'dotty' mosaic

Show the children the picture *Lady on the Terrace* by Paul Signac. Ask them what they notice and they will probably say that the picture is made up of dots. This provides a good opportunity to explain a little bit about the different ways artists paint pictures. You could use a number of Gallery works to illustrate your point.

For a class project, the children could make a picture either by painting it entirely of dots, or by creating a mosaic. Suggest they copy *Lady on the Terrace* in mosaic. Get a large sheet of paper and organise the children into small groups, with each group allocated one colour, yellow, green, red, blue, purple, etc. Sketch an outline of the picture on the sheet of paper. Using self-adhesive coloured paper, get the children to cut out the pieces and stick them onto the sketched outline. This is a good project for involving all the class, and when it is completed, they can hang it on the wall for everyone to see.

An historic landmark – **Powerscourt Waterfall** by George Barret

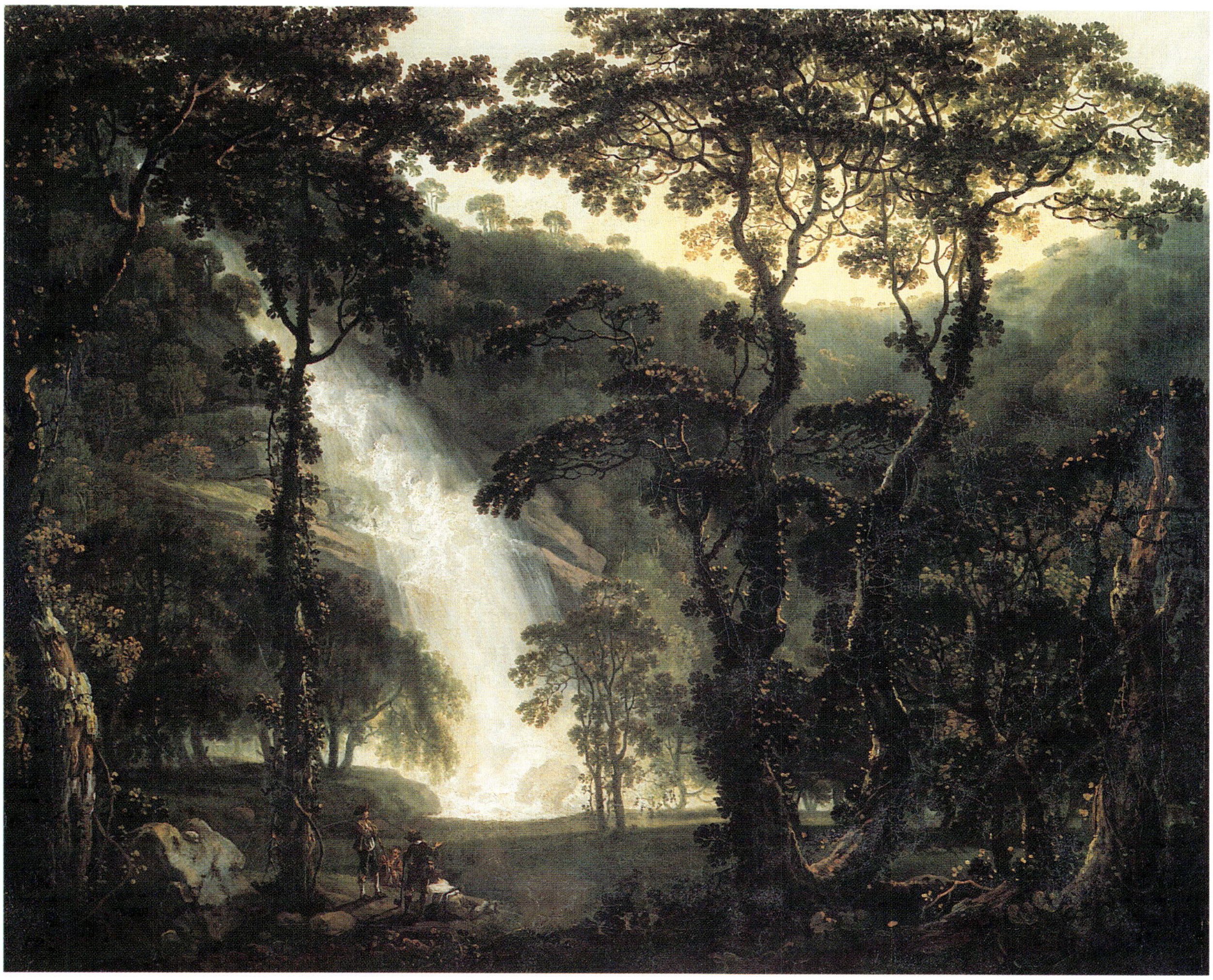

3. Historic landmarks – then and now

This project looks at historic landmarks and allows students to make comparisons between what a site looked like in earlier periods and how it looks now. The students need to select a local historic site or landmark. They will need to research it and see if they can find old prints or pictures illustrating the site.

Our project takes the theme 'Romantic landscapes from County Wicklow' using works by George Barret and James Arthur O'Connor. Different landscapes could be used to focus on other areas of Ireland. Obtain three large sheets of strong paper, and also postcards of the relevant landscapes from the Gallery Shop. Draw identical maps of County Wicklow on two of the large sheets, marking in well-known beauty spots, including Glendalough, Powerscourt, Avoca, The Devil's Glen, etc. Paste postcards of the paintings beside the landmark, including Barret's *Powerscourt Waterfall* and O'Connor's *The Devil's Glen*. Form the students into small groups so that they can research the various landmarks in County Wicklow. Paste the information onto the third (middle) sheet of paper, together with the prints and drawings.

The final part of the project is fieldwork. Assign each student to visit one of the landmarks, such as Barret's *Powerscourt Waterfall*, and suggest they take photographs of the same location as that shown in the painting. When each site has been visited, gather the photographs and paste them onto the third sheet with the map of County Wicklow. The completed project will demonstrate how artists depicted a site in earlier periods and how it has changed with the passage of time. The fact that the students have been involved in research and fieldwork will increase their knowledge and appreciation of the historic site.

4. 'Veduta' – view painting

This is a project in three parts which focuses on view painting in Italy, Northern Europe and Ireland, using examples from the National Gallery.

Discuss view painting with the students. Do they know of any pictures showing famous views? If possible, bring the students on a tour of the National Gallery, asking the guide to focus on pictures that show views. While in the Gallery, purchase some prints for use on the project, including the Venetian pictures *St Mark's Square, Venice* by Antonio Canaletto, *The Doge wedding the Adriatic* by Francesco Guardi and *A View of the Piazza*

A subject for view painting – **Dresden from the right bank of the Elbe above the Augustus Bridge** by Bernardo Bellotto

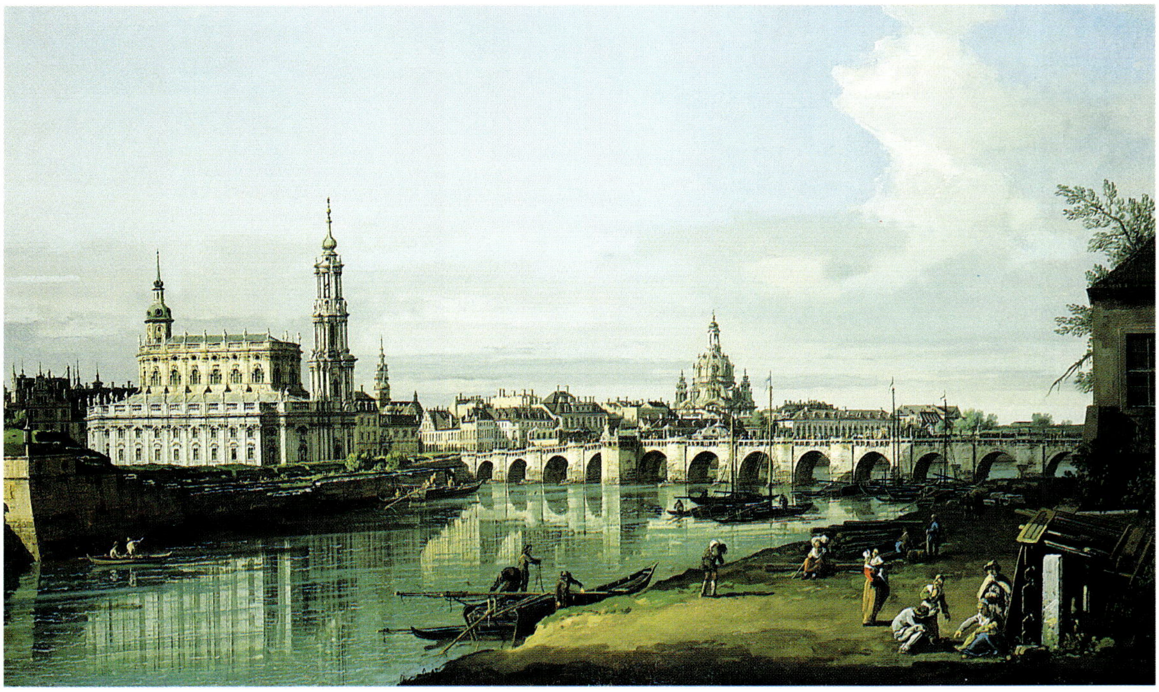

San Marco, Venice by Michele Marieschi, one of the north European paintings by Bernardo Bellotto, *Dresden from the right bank of the Elbe above the Augustus Bridge*, and some prints of Dublin by James Malton.

Talk to the students about how they are going to handle the project. They should form a work-plan with a deadline. Divide into three groups, with each group responsible for one aspect of the project. Assign the students different tasks: to compile and type up research on view painting, to draw maps of the country for each project, to gather information about the geography and history of the country, and to obtain information about the pictures. When all these tasks have been completed, give each group a large sheet of strong paper and suggest they plan the layout and design of the project, using their research, maps and pictures.

Help them to organise the text and illustrations. Title each project 'View painting' in Italy, Northern Europe or Ireland. When the project is completed, the students should have three large panels, with each one demonstrating different aspects of view painting. It is interesting to learn about view painting, particularly when the project relates to their own country.

Write your own activity sheets

Note: This is an exercise for teachers

Worksheets and activity sheets are one of the best ways of happily occupying young people in a museum or gallery. It would be a mistake, however, to view them merely as time fillers because they also perform a useful learning function. By focusing attention on particular works of art, they help young people to appreciate and understand them better. They also encourage students to explore the context in which works of art were created, and often they give them greater confidence in learning new ideas. Teachers feel comfortable with worksheets and themesheets because they enable students rapidly to come to terms with aspects of the collection at a point when they are planning a visit to the Gallery. While the worksheets are normally provided in the Gallery, teachers sometimes distribute them back in the classroom as a way of consolidating information and reinforcing the visit. Parents too find that activity sheets help them to structure a visit to the Gallery. Children tire of looking at pictures, but if they have worksheets to complete and if tiny tots have activity sheets to colour in, they will settle contentedly in one area while the parents look at the pictures nearby. If parents, teachers and young people benefit from and enjoy using worksheets, then it is worth spending the time finding out how to make them practical and effective. These guidelines may help and encourage you to write your own worksheets and activity sheets.

Steps for organising the worksheet/activity sheet

1. Write the worksheet or activity sheet for a specific age-group, e.g. tiny tots (ages 3-5), children (ages 6-12), teenagers (ages 13-18), and adults. Puzzle /clue sheets can be aimed at the 12-15 age-group. Make it effective by gradually progressing from the simple to the complex. Define difficult terms, keep sentences short, words simple and give clear instructions.

2. Vary the questions by first asking ones that require easy answers (yes/no, how many?, what?, which?). Follow this with questions that require some thought (how do X and Y differ?, imagine that you…, Describe…, is X significant?). Progress to questions that need a view or an opinion (do you agree?, what do you think?, How could X be important?).

3. Design attractive and well-laid-out worksheets and activity sheets. Divide the sheet into different areas, e.g. questions, information, drawings and projects. It helps to vary the size of the typeface – use bold lettering, italics and capitals. Label clearly, and use small boxes for 'either/or' questions. Provide variety through exercises, e.g. word searches, crosswords, treasure trails, spotting similarities, joining matching pairs, quizzes, etc.

4. Relate the worksheet to the curriculum. If you want students to use worksheets, then spend time doing research, asking the advice of teachers and relating the worksheets to their work study programme. The curriculum positively encourages the use of this type of resource and museums and galleries provide many opportunities to develop them further.

5. Good illustrations are essential. Illustrations must be of the highest standard possible. Good worksheets and activity sheets vary the nature of the illustrations, employing photographs, maps, line drawings, painted images and cartoons. Use your computer to create the artwork and print the worksheet.

Making worksheets and activity sheets look easy

Before you begin to write a worksheet, develop a themesheet or design an activity sheet, make sure you have your research information and illustrations to hand. For children with different learning disabilities or special needs, the worksheet or activity sheet should be short, well designed, with simple vocabulary, and adaptable to include structured activities. A different approach is to write a worksheet based on themes, including portraits, landscapes, narratives, religious painting or still life, all of which are described in this book. A new series of theme-based worksheets and activity sheets for primary and post-primary students is available free of charge by writing to the Gallery's Education Department. Themes covered include the following:

- Every picture tells a story
- Faces and fashion
- History: real and imagined
- Land and sea
- Music and games
- Scenes from the Life of Christ
- Signs and symbols
- The meal
- Town and country
- Wildlife

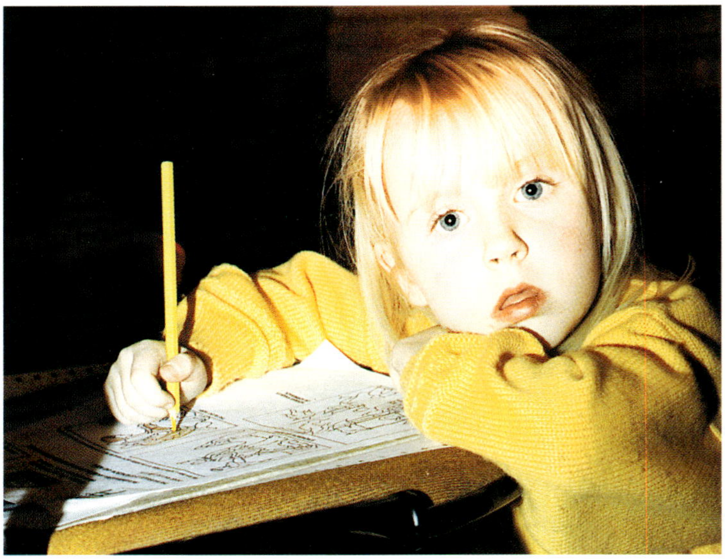

A child using the Tiny Tots EyeSpy activity sheet

Puzzle activity sheets, which contain hints and clues, cartoons and half-completed drawings, poems and funny questions, are popular because they are unpredictable and require that the student approach the works of art in a different way. They can be fun and frustrating for the student who, nonetheless, feels a great sense of victory when the puzzles have been solved.

Another idea is to provide your students with an unusual situation, for example, suggest that they are film producers looking for a location to shoot a murder scene. They decide to investigate the National Gallery as a possible venue. Instruct them to sketch the layout of the rooms, noting the position of the pictures, sculpture and furniture, identifying the windows, doors and stairs, taking into account lighting and sound requirements. Plan the film sets taking note of the equipment and costumes required. The students should finalise the project by presenting a film schedule in the form of a proposal. The type of situation where students can project themselves into the role of someone like a film producer, newspaper reporter or TV presenter is ideal, because it allows them the opportunity to use their imaginations and give free expression to their ideas. It also requires that they view the works of art and Gallery rooms from a different perspective. This can produce some very interesting results, plus a feeling of great satisfaction when the project is completed.

These suggestions represent a number of different approaches to worksheets, themesheets and activity sheets. When your first worksheet/activity sheet has been drafted, test it out on a number of different adults and children. Use a simple method to evaluate it – either it is effective or it isn't! Don't be too discouraged if it was not a great success; just review the design, clarify the questions, reduce the text, and try it out again. Comfort yourself in the knowledge that the perfect worksheet or activity sheet has not yet been written!

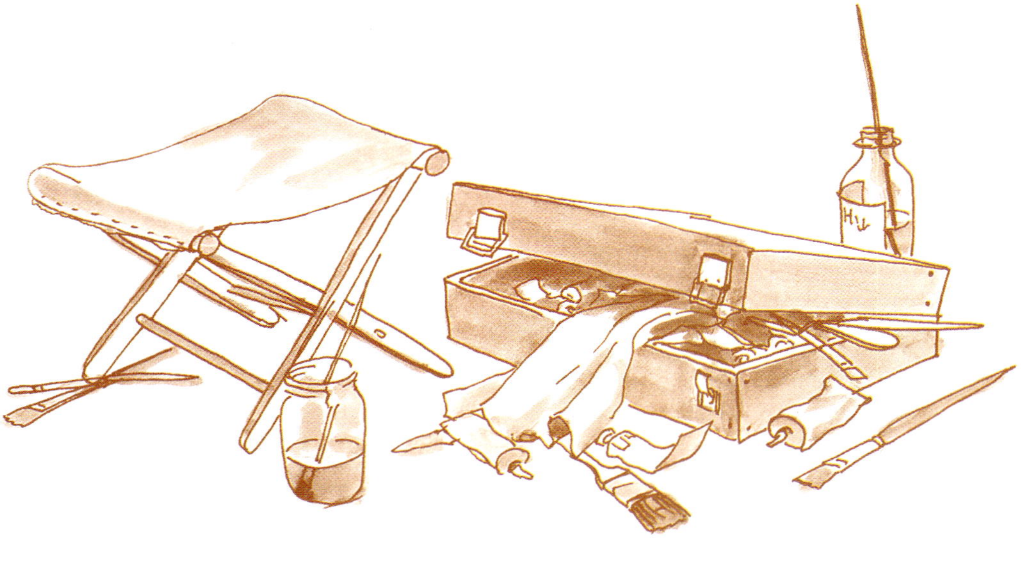

4

'Looking' at Paintings

There is more to paintings than meets the eye. We need to know how to look at paintings and how to learn from what we see. There is a big difference, for example, between casually looking at something, and visually studying it. In the second instance, not only are the eyes focused but the brain is also active in registering and assessing what is seen. Think how often we 'see' without registering what we are looking at.

Examining the details

One of the benefits of examining a painting closely is that it makes us look at familiar works with a new eye. Interesting details can catch our attention, such as the cat under the stool in *The Holy Family* by Murillo (1618-82), or live insects crawling over a still life

The Peasant Wedding by Pieter Brueghel the Younger – note the table

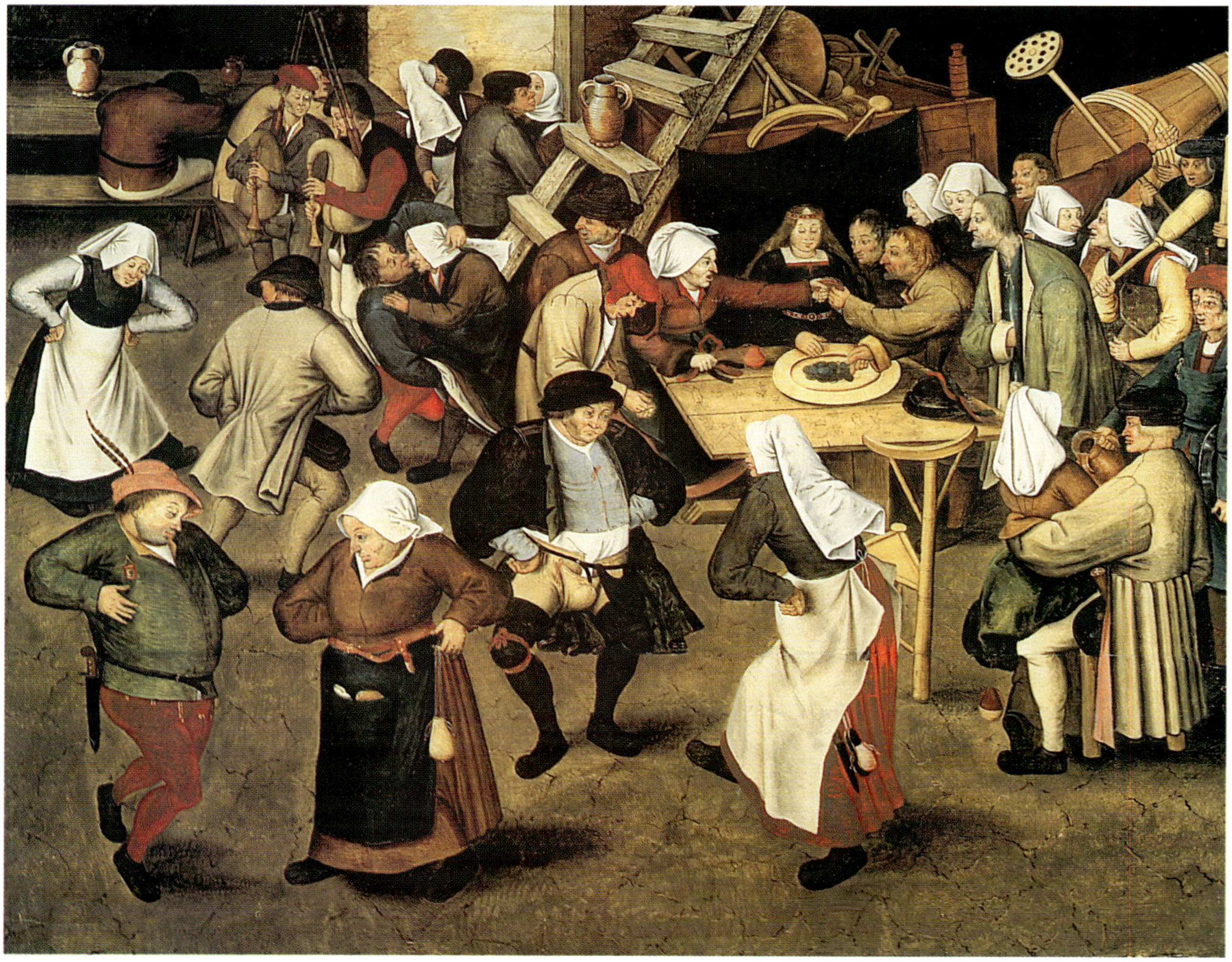

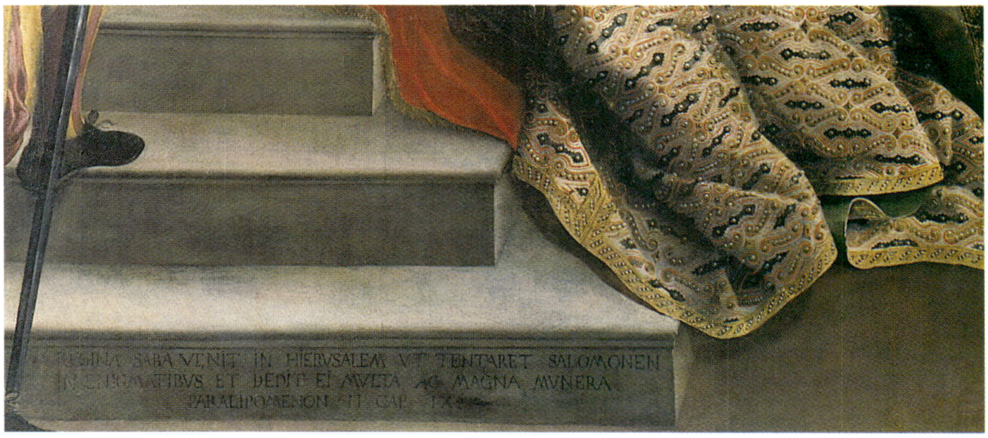

A detail of **The Visit of the Queen of Sheba to Solomon** by Lavinia Fontana, showing the inscription

in the case of *A Vanitas Fruit Piece* by de Heem (1606-83/4), or where an artist includes his own portrait among a group of bystanders, as Jack B. Yeats (1871-1957) does in *The Liffey Swim*. In *The Peasant Wedding*, executed in 1620 by the Flemish artist Pieter Brueghel the Younger (*c*1564-*c*1637), the painting reveals the scene of a lively country wedding dance, with the bride seated at a table gathering her dowry. The table at which the bride sits is covered in crude carvings that look remarkably like twentieth-century graffiti. Art historians speculate whether the carvings are significant or symbolic.

Other noteworthy details in paintings are items such as inscriptions, the identity of portrait subjects, views and buildings. The composition of *The Visit of the Queen of Sheba to Solomon*, painted about 1600 by the Bolognese painter Lavinia Fontana (1552-1614), is based on an episode from the Old Testament. But it would appear that the picture is also a portrait of Vincenzo I Gonzaga, Duke of Mantua, and his wife Elenora de' Medici. A colourful, stately work, the picture represents a rich tapestry of seventeenth-century Italian court life. On the steps of Solomon's throne, an inscription can be seen which translates: 'Queen Sheba came to Jerusalem to test Solomon with hard questions and she gave him many great gifts, Chronicles, II Chapter 9'. In all probability, the Duke of Mantua chose the biblical theme because his family considered it had some ancient links with Sheba.

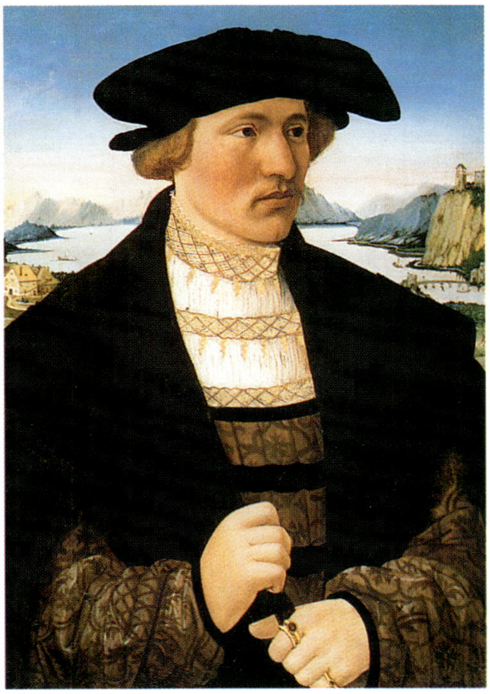

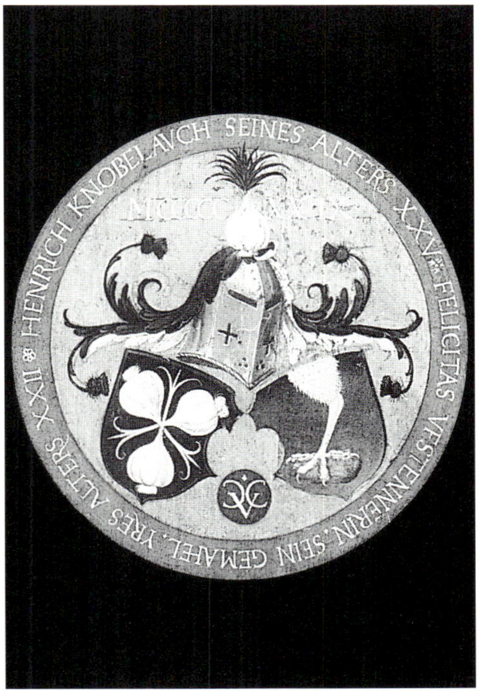

(Left) **Portrait of Heinrich Knoblauch**

(Right) The reverse of **Heinrich Knoblauch** showing the coat of arms

A number of paintings in the collection contain fascinating signatures, seals and coats of arms. There are, for example, approximately forty known portraits attributed to the German painter Conrad Faber (*c*1324-1552). Fourteen of these contain his monogram 'CVC' (Conrad van Creuznach), including *The Portrait of Heinrich Knoblauch*, painted on panel by Faber in 1529. On the reverse side of the painting, included in the roundel containing the coat of arms, is Faber's monogram. 'Knoblauch' is the German word for garlic, which explains the liberal use of cloves of garlic in the family coat of arms. The inscription translates: 'Heinrich Knoblauch his age 25; Felicitas Ufstenner his wife age 22'.

Unveiling the secrets

When we begin to look at works of art carefully, we open the door to a fascinating world. Behind the scenes in the conservator's studio, with scientific techniques, we are able to explore the layers beneath the picture surface without disturbing them. With such aids we can see how great painters achieved their effects. Our understanding of the creative process behind a work of art is enriched by a knowledge of how it was produced. This knowledge enhances our admiration for Old Master paintings.

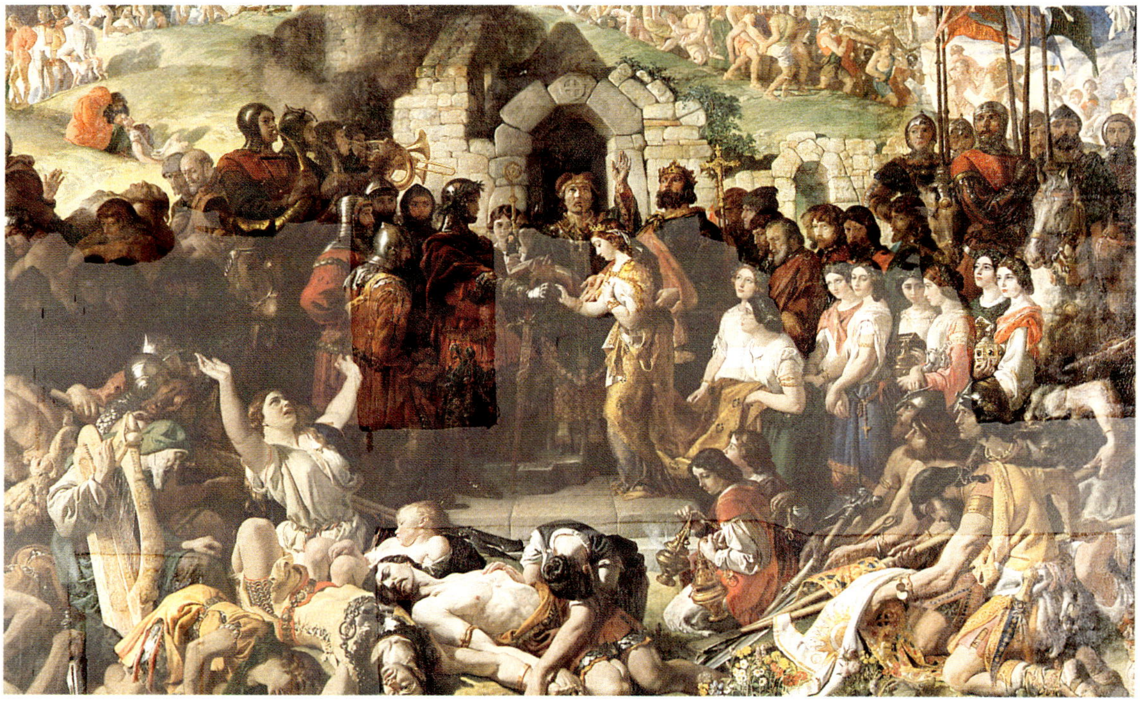

A section of the nineteenth-century painting **The Marriage of Strongbow and Aoife** during restoration

A detail of the restoration

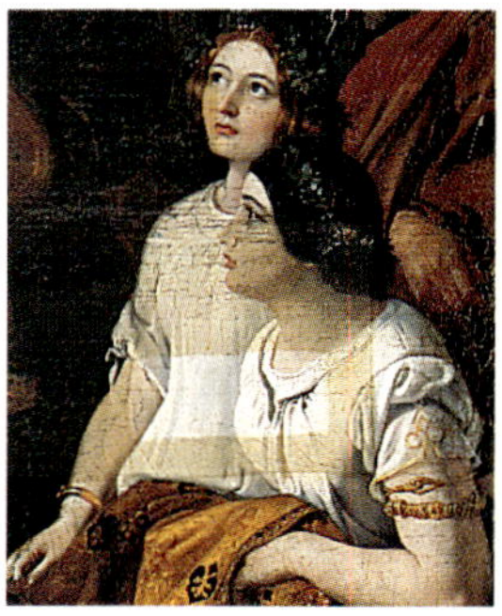

Over the years paintings become dark as a result of changes in the pigment. They also become discoloured by layers of dirt and old varnish that has gradually turned brown. In order to rectify this, the paintings must be cleaned, and it is often during the cleaning process that many secrets are laid bare. Conservators use tiny pieces of cotton wool dipped in solvents (liquids that dissolve other substances) to clean the discoloured surface. The solvent is applied gradually so that the old varnish dissolves and is then mopped up by the cotton wool. The work has to be done slowly and carefully, inch by inch, so as not to remove any of the original paint. Cleaning old paintings is only one of many interesting tasks that conservators perform. For instance, if a panel painting has warped, they can insert wooden cradling at the back to prevent it from splitting. In extreme circumstances, conservators can take a painting off an old cracked wooden panel and re-line it by placing it on canvas, where it will be safe. They can remove mural paintings from walls, repair the wall, and put the painting back.

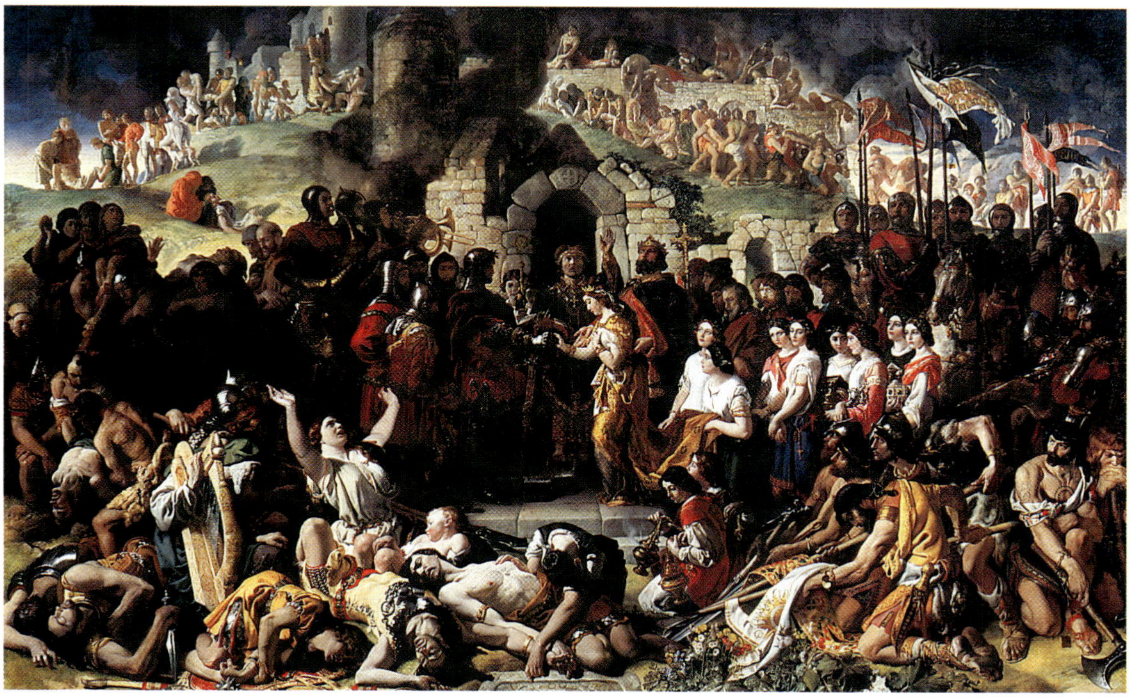

The Marriage of Strongbow and Aoife by Daniel Maclise after restoration

Sometimes the process of cleaning a picture can reveal the outline of a different composition underneath the original. After buying a picture, an owner might change his mind and ask another artist to paint over an area of the picture he disliked. Could this be what happened in the case of one of the most appealing early Italian Renaissance pictures in the collection, the *Madonna and Child* by Paolo Uccello (1397-1475)? In this picture, Uccello has combined his understanding of the shape and form of the human figure with the mathematical precision and perspective of the early Renaissance. The

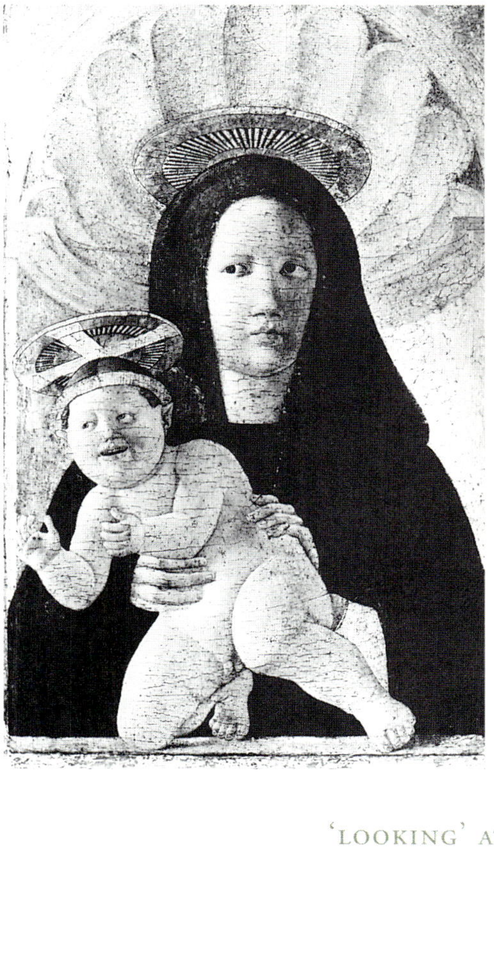

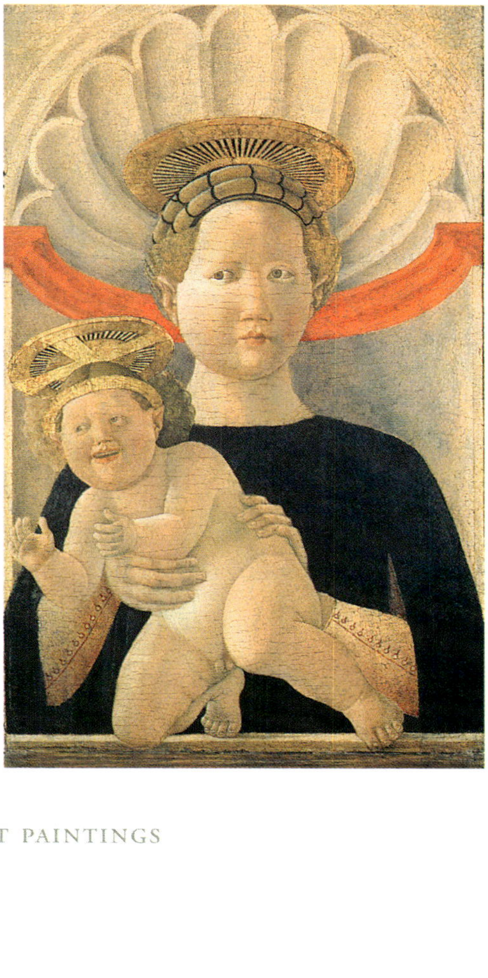

(Left) The **Madonna and Child** prior to restoration

(Right) The **Madonna and Child** by Paolo Uccello as it was originally intended

Madonna and Child are set against a simple backdrop, with the infant playfully crossing the picture into the viewer's space. At some later stage the Madonna was given a dark veil headdress that altered the picture's appearance. Why was this done? It could have been due to changes in fashion or perhaps to make the appearance of the Madonna more dignified. In any case, when the overpainting was removed during restoration in the 1960s, the picture was returned to its original fresh appearance as intended by Uccello.

While working on a picture, artists often change their minds, sometimes more than once. The artist may plan the picture, paint the composition, and then find he or she is not happy with some aspect, and will paint that detail again. Art historians have a special term for alterations like this, an Italian word *pentimento* (meaning to repent – a term used to indicate repainting or overpainting by the artist). There are several pictures in the collection that contain a *pentimento*, one of the best known being the *Ecce Homo*, painted in the late 1550s by the Venetian artist, Titian (1488 /90-1576). It shows an image of the tortured Christ, beaten, wrists tied with a rope, holding a reed in his hands, and crowned with thorns. During the cleaning of the picture in 1954 conservators removed all of the overpainting and revealed alterations in the area of the reed and the rope around Christ's wrists. While the evidence of these changes demonstrates Titian's concern to have the details accurate, for the modern viewer it enhances our understanding of what is one of the most moving and deeply spiritual pictures in the National Gallery of Ireland.

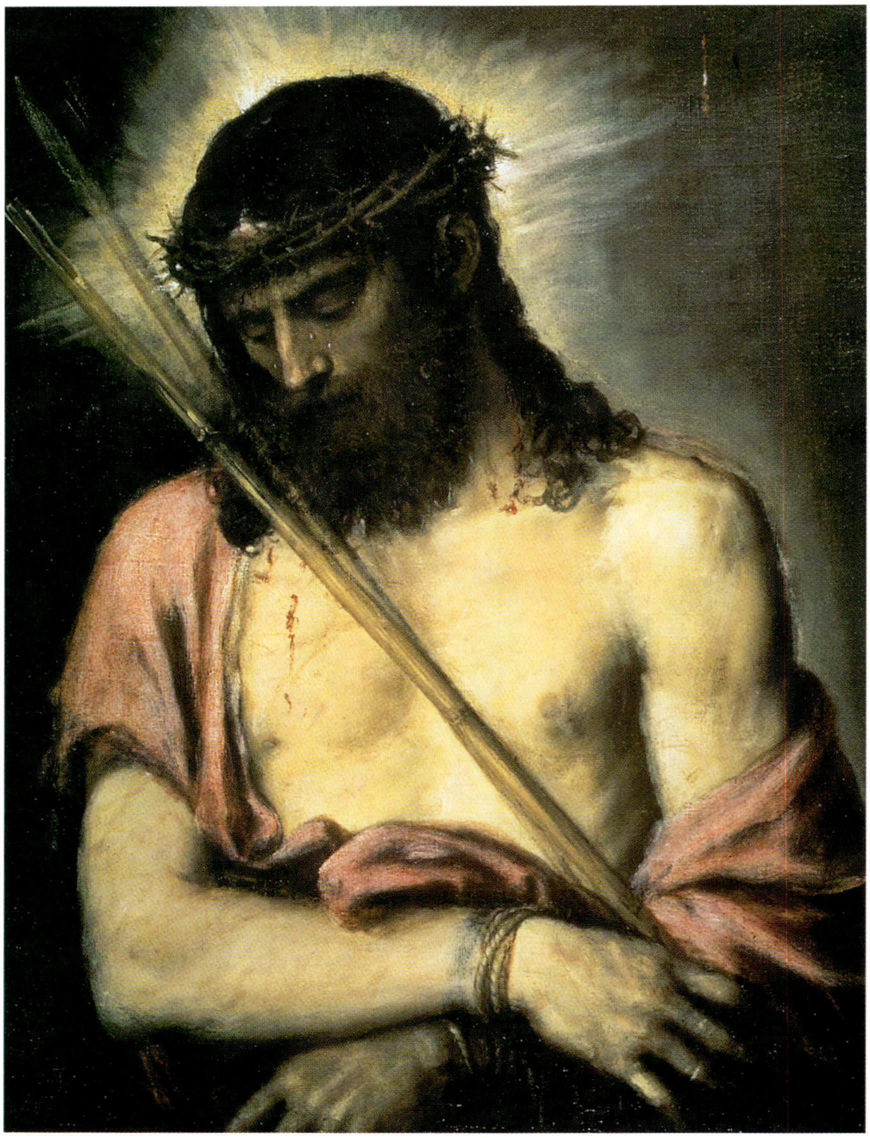

Ecce Homo by Titian – see the alterations to the reed and the rope around Christ's wrists

In the case of *The Lute Player* painted in the studio of Frans Hals (1582/83-1666), a different situation arose. One of the most striking features of *The Lute Player* is the quality of the strong, fresh brushwork, which gives the figure of the musician an extraordinary vitality. The alterations or *pentimenti* in this painting are in the area of the head and hat, which reveal the Dutch artist's change of mind about its shape and position. Oil paint can become more and more transparent with age, which is one of the reasons why the changes can be seen as they gradually become visible again.

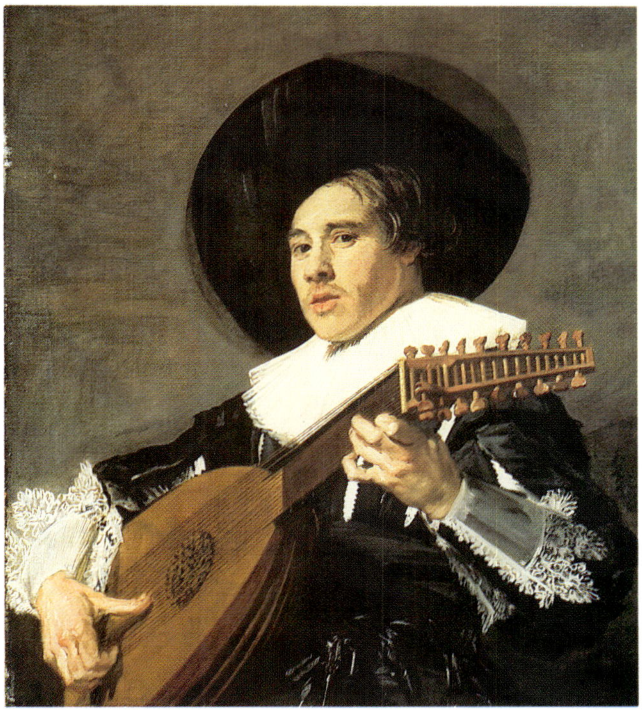

Note changes in the area of the head and hat in **The Lute Player**, studio of Frans Hals

Over the past fifty years the techniques of x-ray and infra-red photography have been applied to paintings, as have new methods of distinguishing paint layers and analysing colour pigments. Some paint contains lead, which does not allow x-rays to pass through. So areas with lead paint on them show up white on the x-ray image. It is a bit like looking at the skeleton of a painting. As a result, it is now possible to know more about how many Old Master paintings were created. *Players at Tric-Trac* was executed by the Dutch artist Pieter de Hooch (1629-81) in the mid 1650s. It is an amusing scene showing several figures gambling while playing tric-trac or backgammon. An x-ray photograph of the painting shows that the woman was originally painted facing to the left, whereas in the final composition she is facing towards the right.

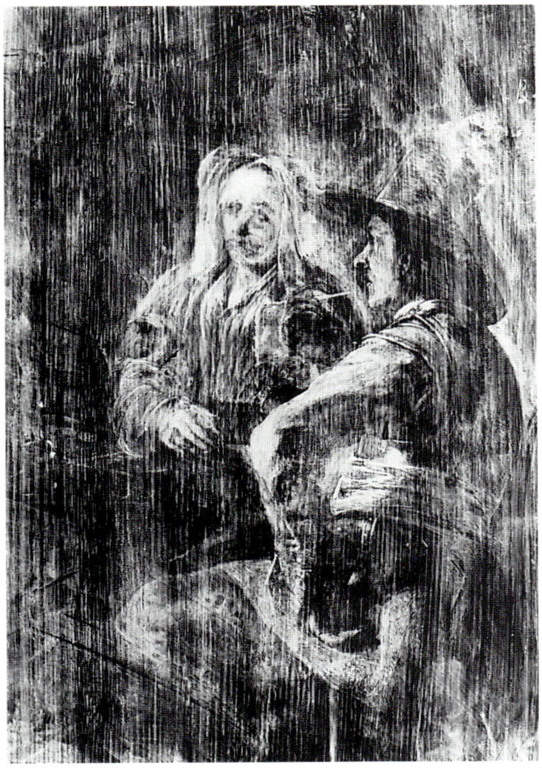

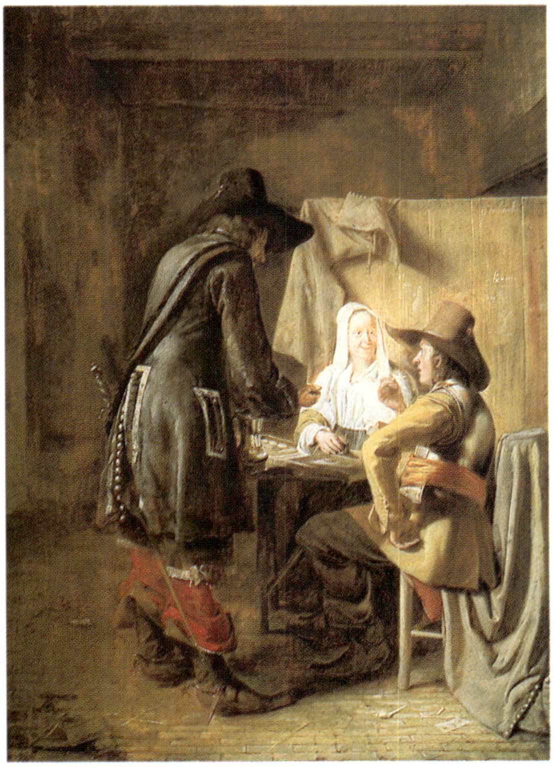

(Left) An x-ray of **Players at Tric-Trac** by Pieter de Hooch

(Right) **Players at Tric-Trac**

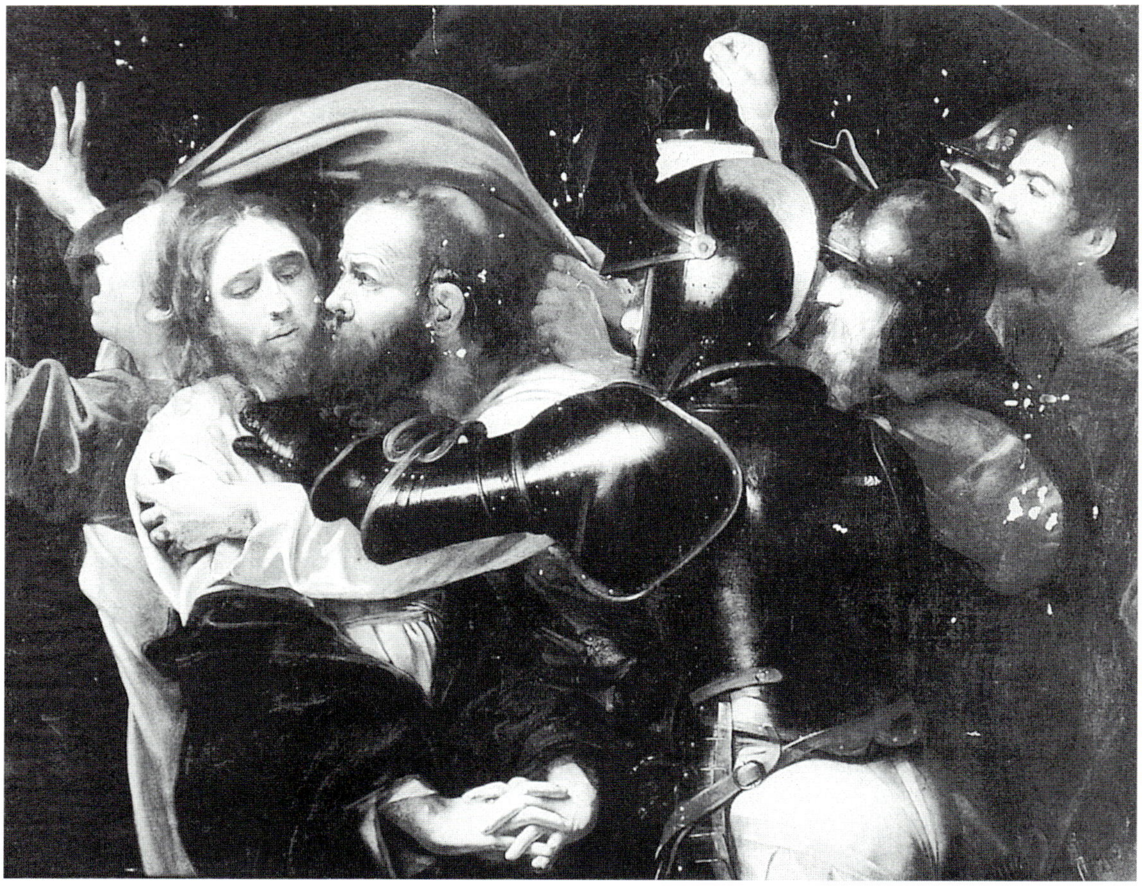

An infra-red photograph of Caravaggio's **The Taking of Christ**

Infra-red photography can penetrate the paint layers and reveal earlier drawings (if they are drawn with something made of carbon, such as charcoal), and thus show an artist's progress at different stages of the painting process. Following the cleaning of the recently discovered masterpiece *The Taking of Christ* by Caravaggio (1571-1610), now on indefinite loan to the National Gallery from the Irish Jesuit Fathers, several *pentimenti* made by the artist came to light, including minor adjustments to the profile of Judas's face.

Identifying the author of a painting is a combination of instinct, based on long experience and knowledge of works of art, and research. Sometimes labels or inscriptions on the back of the stretcher can give clues to a picture's history. One of the most fascinating aspects of the discovery of *The Taking of Christ* was the misleading label on the painting identifying the author as Gherardo della Notte (see illustration). The painting, which was originally commissioned by Ciriaco Mattei and paid for in 1603, hung in the

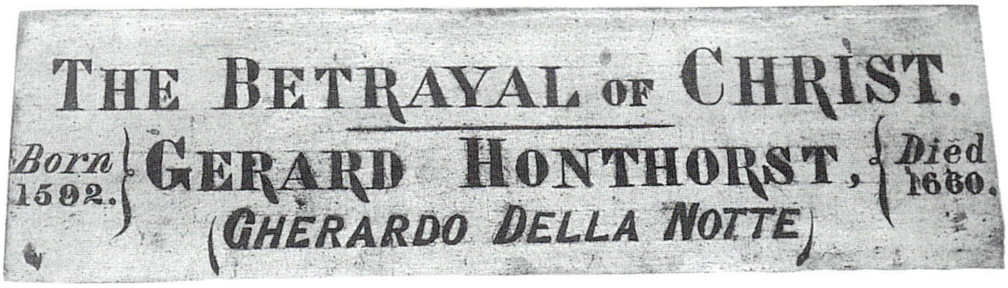

The label from **The Taking of Christ**

Mattei Palace in Rome. Sometime during the eighteenth century, a number of works in the Mattei collection were reattributed. Among these, *The Taking of Christ* by Caravaggio was mistakenly attributed to his Dutch follower Gerrit van Honthorst, known to Italians as Gherardo delle Notti. It was recorded incorrectly in Italian as 'Gherardo della Notte' instead of Notti, a mistake that was repeated in every successive document and transaction.

The incorrect attribution was continued when, in 1802, the painting travelled to Biel House in Scotland, having been purchased by William Hamilton Nisbet from the Mattei family in Rome. Around 1921 it was sold privately in Edinburgh and came into the possession of Dr Marie Lea-Wilson in Dublin. At the beginning of the 1930s she presented it to the Irish Jesuit Fathers, bearing the incorrect label with Gerrit van Honthorst's name. It remained in the care of the Jesuit Fathers until 1990, when it was recognised as the work of Caravaggio and restored by Sergio Benedetti of the National Gallery of Ireland.

Preliminary drawings

Preliminary drawings are a further element in the secret life of paintings. These can be sketches, studies or designs executed on paper, canvas or panel. Sketches and drawings have a number of uses. They can be studies for individual details, such as the sky, trees, buildings or figures. The artist may wish to refer to such sketches when planning a composition. Study drawings can also be useful for investigating particular effects, such as folds of draperies, the ripples on water or the shine of dew on grass. The French artist Thomas Couture (1815-79) prepared a preliminary drawing for *La Peinture Realiste*, one of the painter's best known and most controversial paintings. The picture was a clever attack on the artist Courbet's realist approach to painting and showed a young student sitting on an antique head of Jupiter, ignoring its classic beauty, while copying the crude head of a wild boar. The painting is signed and dated 'TC 1865'. The preliminary drawing for the painting, which is executed in black chalk on grey paper, provides an interesting insight into Couture's mind as he was working towards the final composition.

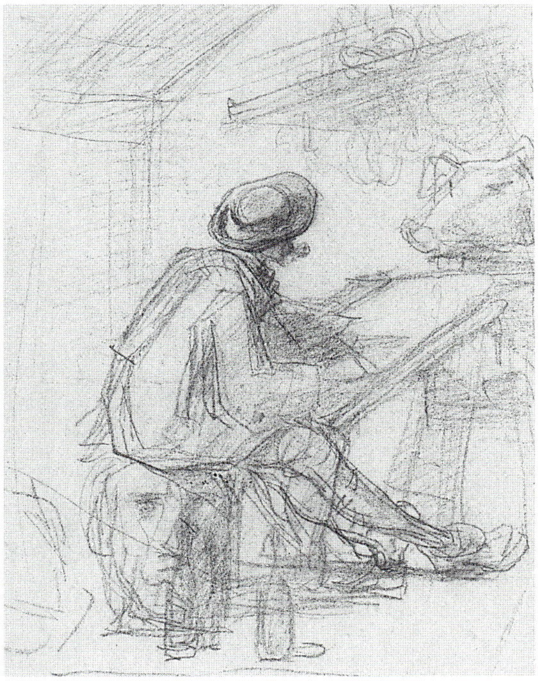

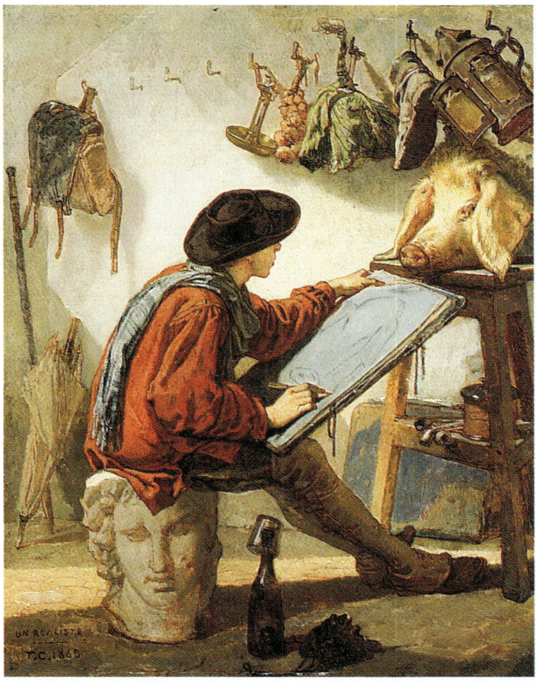

(Left) A study for **La Peinture Realiste**

(Right) **La Peinture Realiste** by Thomas Couture

Note: Visitors might like to consult the Gallery's fine collection of drawings, which provide a fascinating insight into how artists use the process of sketching and drawing to develop ideas for their paintings.

5

Exploring Art through Themes

Paintings and sculpture tell us about different countries and their cultures over the centuries – their people, landscapes, animals, customs and history. The way they have been created tell us about the artists too. The works of art presented on these pages were created between one and five hundred years ago. The artists who created them often worked in studios using the same basic tools: an easel, a brush and a palette to hold paint, or a hammer and chisel to sculpt stone. The selected works include oil paintings, watercolours, panel paintings and drawings, chosen to show the enormous variety of techniques artists have employed to represent their world.

For this exercise, five themes have been selected in order to introduce you to a particular way of looking at works of art. The history and development of each theme is explored by examining a number of carefully chosen works from the National Gallery's collection. There are suggestions for practical projects accompanying each theme, ranging from the simple to the complex, aimed at both primary and post-primary students.

New discoveries are constantly being made about the paintings, revealing details of their original surroundings, such as churches, palaces or major public buildings where the public viewed them by flickering candlelight. Some were created privately by artists who wanted to experiment with new ideas, but such works often did not sell. Most of the works were painted not by the artist's free choice, but by commission for a client or a patron. The artist was required to paint what the patron, who might have been a pope, a duchess or a merchant prince, commissioned and paid for.

Note: As you read through this chapter, you may occasionally come upon art terms, or references to artistic techniques, or styles and periods, which you are unfamiliar with. These are explained in the following chapters, but they may be looked up immediately by using the index.

Theme 1: Portraits and faces

Why paint a person's portrait? Possibly because you want to try and understand the person, not just the physical appearance of the face, be it plain, beautiful or ugly, but also to discover what lies underneath – is it a happy, sad or moody personality? All these elements combine to reveal the personality and character of the subject. Portraits usually do more than just show what a person looks like. A good portrait captures some individual feature or identifying expression which renders the image memorable – and paintings live longer than people.

The concept of portraying a physical likeness in painting and sculpture goes back to the Egyptians, who for their royalty and gods chose an idealised impression, such as the gold burial mask of the boy-king Tutankhamun, whereas a naturalistic image was deemed more suitable for mere mortals. The Greeks adopted an heroic and idealised portrait, as seen in many of the sculptures on the Parthenon in Athens, but avoided naturalism until Hellenistic times. The Romans sometimes chose realistic images, but bearing in mind their stature as an empire, frequently chose the heroic idealised image, as in case of the emperor, Augustus of Prima Porta. In the Renaissance period, both idealised and naturalistic approaches were adopted, in painting and sculpture, inspired by examples from antiquity. Antiquity also influenced the design of Renaissance coins and medals. For instance, the Gallery owns a *Portrait of Count Baldassare Castiglione* by Titian, which shows a renowned sixteenth-century writer on courtly matters, whose book *Il Cortegiano* was considered one of the masterpieces of Renaissance literature. As an important Renaissance figure, Castiglione's image was also portrayed in the form of a bronze medal. In Western art, there is also the tradition of artists trying to present a likeness of Christ and the apostles by creating stylised images, due to the fact that there was no available physical likeness. The Middle Ages passed on stylised portraits of such holy figures to the Renaissance. At the same time, important people such as saints, bishops, kings and abbots were characterised through their attributes: a wheel for St Catherine, keys for St Peter and a lion symbolising St Mark. Following the Renaissance emphasis on the individual, portrait painting and sculpture became and still remains one of the major features of European art, providing a useful source of income for many artists.

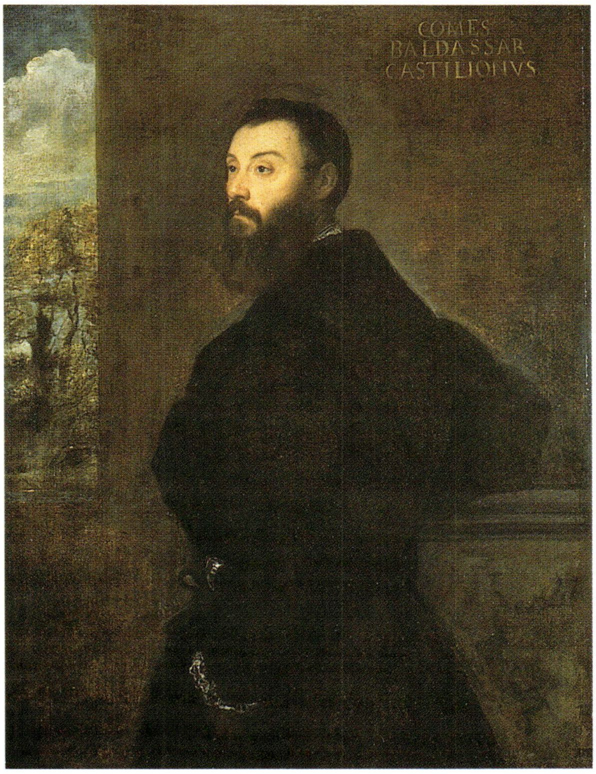

Count Baldassare Castiglione
by Titian

The person who commissions a portrait is called the patron, and the subject of the portrait is called the sitter – frequently they are one and the same. When an artist paints a picture of her or himself, it is called a self-portrait. A picture of two or more people is called a group portrait. *The Earl of Bellamont* (p36) is a magnificent, dramatic formal picture, whereas *Stella* (p37) is a provocative and informal portrait. Some portraits focus on the sitter's features in an attempt to capture the essential likeness of the person. Others include possessions, fashionable poses and background details to give a fuller picture of the person's character and lifestyle. The sitter may want to be flattered and shown as beautiful or important. Costume is a particularly interesting aspect of portraiture, as it conveys so much information about the sitter: where ragged and patched clothes may indicate poverty, black cloaks, gowns and robes indicate a religious figure, a legal person or a scholar, and richly embroidered fabrics, made into decorative and ornate garments, indicate a wealthy person, an aristocrat or perhaps a princess.

Most portraits are commissioned to be a lasting reminder of someone special. Others have been painted by an artist who simply wants to capture on canvas a fascinating, unusual and exotic face. The portraits we are going to look at have been chosen because the sitters reflect a wide range of human experience, from different ranks of society.

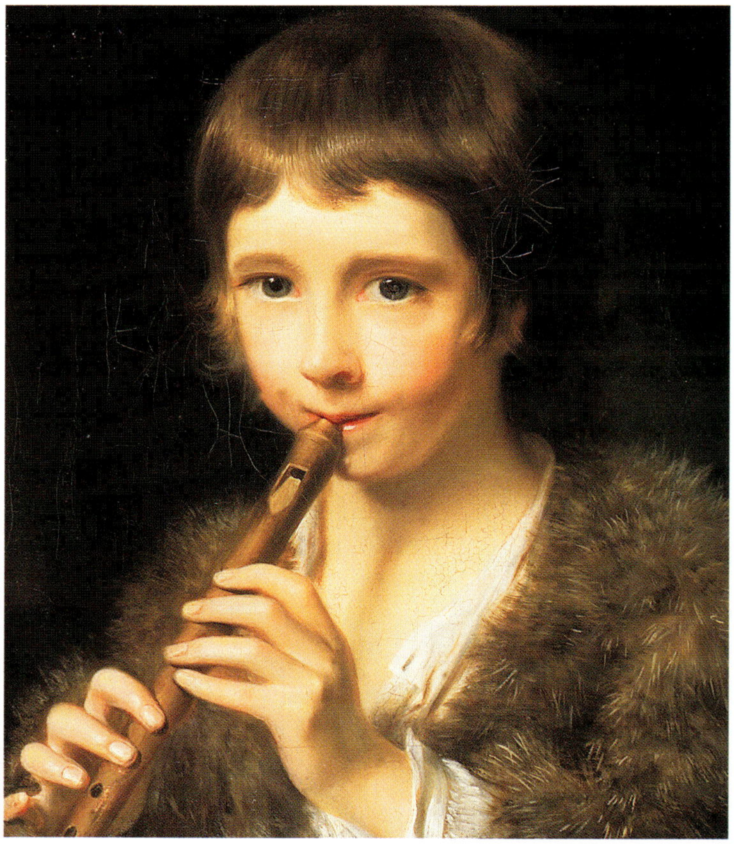

The Piping Boy, 1769
Nathaniel Hone the Elder,
Irish School
1718 Dublin – 1784 London

This is a portrait of a child. The concept of childhood as a distinct and precious state, and the child as innocent rather than merely ignorant, took conscious shape in the eighteenth century. It became almost universal under the impact of Rousseau and the romantic poets. Paintings such as *The Piping Boy* reflect traditional parental tenderness for children, in this instance the artist's own son.

Victorian sensibility combined this new sense of the sacredness of childhood with an acute awareness of the vulnerability of children themselves. While underprivileged children traditionally contributed to the family economy by their own labour, in the nineteenth century many were freed from work and given a measure of education. What were you doing at the age of ten? A boy in the early nineteenth century might have been playing the harpsichord, horse riding or learning how to fence; he might equally have been cleaning chimneys in great houses, or standing in front of a regiment of infantry as a drummer, waiting to receive a volley of shot from the enemy.

At the age of ten, John Camillus, one of several children of the artist Nathaniel Hone, was having his portrait painted playing a wooden recorder. The artist executed a number of pictures of his children, and this appealing, fresh and immediate portrait is a typical example of Hone's style, with the wooden recorder adding an informal note.

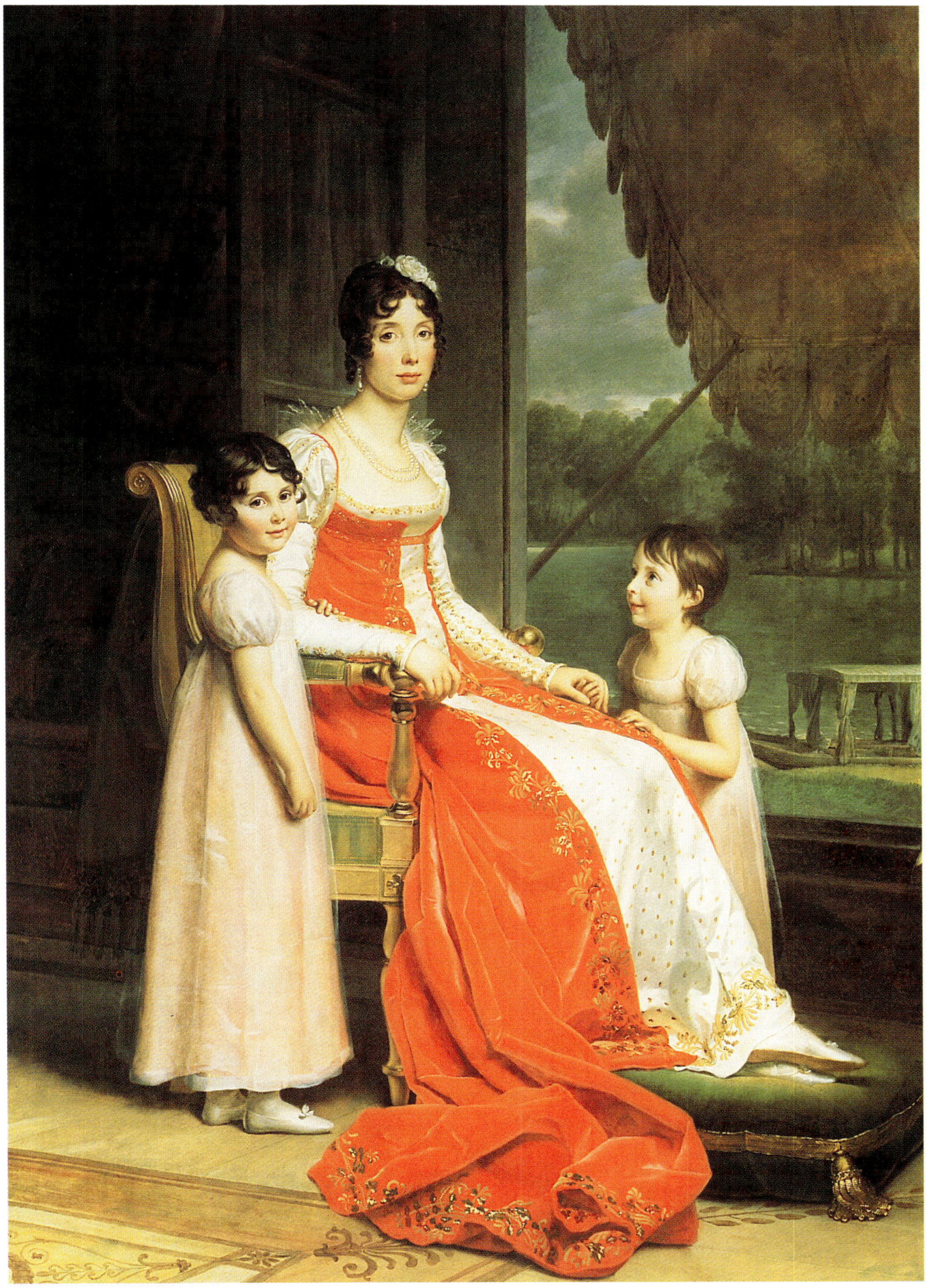

Marie-Julie Bonaparte, Queen of Spain, with her daughters Zenaïde and Charlotte, 1808-9
Baron François Gérard,
French School
1770 Rome — 1837 Paris

This family portrait depicts Marie-Julie Clary and her two daughters. Marie-Julie, who came from a wealthy Marseilles family, reputedly of Irish descent, married Napoleon's brother, Joseph Bonaparte. In 1806 Joseph became King of Naples, and in the year this portrait was painted he was named King of Spain. The portrait was commissioned for Napoleon's Salon de Famille of the Palace de Saint-Cloud.

The artist has portrayed Marie-Julie as the Queen of Spain, seated by the window in a gilt empire chair. The setting is thought to be the Chateau of Mortefontaine, Joseph's residence outside Paris. Zenaïde on her right would have been about eight years old and Charlotte about six. The picture beautifully recreates the neo-classical furniture, fashion and design of the period. The superb detail of the costumes has been built up in fine, meticulous brushstrokes; Marie-Julie wears an exquisite gown of white satin with red velvet overcape decorated in gold lamé (a fabric in which metal threads are interwoven), while the girls wear sheer muslin and voile (thin, semi-transparent material) dresses. While essentially a formal family portrait, it is relieved by the tender expression of affection between the mother and her two daughters.

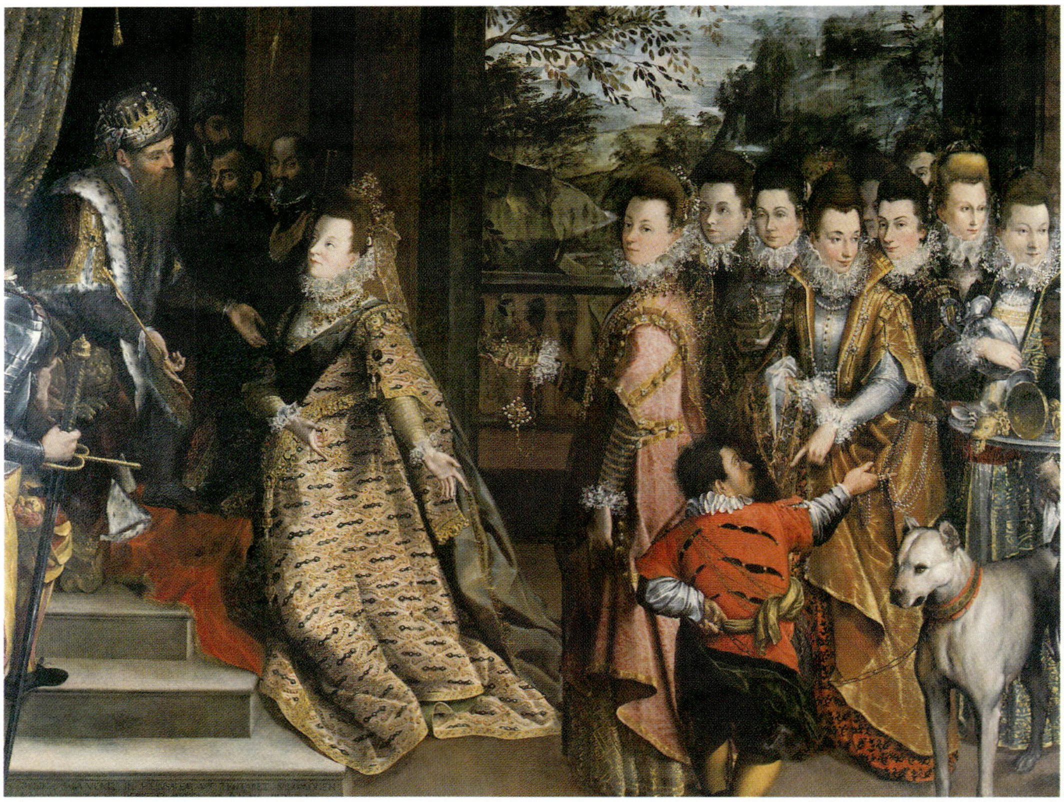

The Visit of the Queen of Sheba to Solomon, *c*1600
Lavinia Fontana,
Italian School
1552 Bologna – 1614 Rome

A notable feature of this religious scene is the elaborate portrayal of known sitters – the Gonzaga Family of Mantua. The biblical subject of the picture, based on an episode from the Old Testament, was chosen because the Gonzaga family had claimed ancient connections with Sheba. The picture depicts, in all probability, a portrait of the Duke of Mantua, Vincenzo I Gonzaga, with his wife Eleonora de' Medici. In 1600 they went to Florence for the wedding of Marie de' Medici, and it is likely that they passed through Bologna on that occasion, and took time to sit for their portraits. The artist, chosen for her sophisticated portrait style, suitably demonstrates the power and wealth of the Gonzaga family.

Lavinia Fontana was an important and very successful female painter. The daughter and pupil of Prospero Fontana, she began her career in Bologna painting portraits and religious pictures. She settled in Rome where her talents as a portrait painter became much sought after among the leading families. This picture is one of the most ambitious of Fontana's great portraits; the Duke and Duchess of Mantua together with their courtiers combine to convey all the pomp and ceremony of contemporary court life.

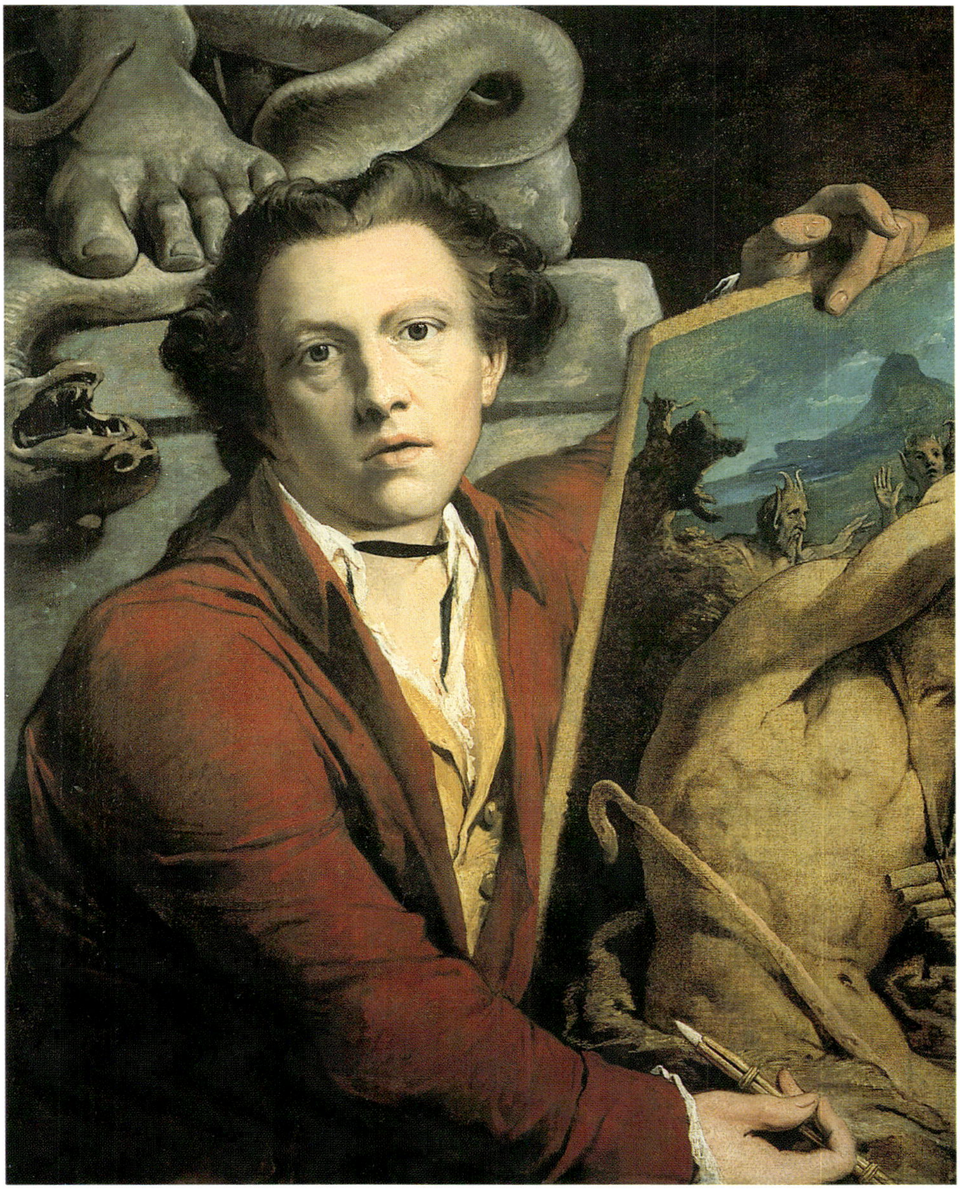

Self-Portrait as Timanthes, completed 1803
James Barry, Irish School
1741 Cork – 1806 London

Self-portrayal is a complex act. The private nature of the task, and the intensity of self-scrutiny that it entails, has challenged artists through the ages. It's not just a question of self-examination, but a process of recording a likeness, the depiction of a psychological state, or social status, or the representation of abstract ideas. Self-portraits by artists as gifted as Dürer, Rembrandt and Van Gogh not only confirm their skill and inventiveness, but also reveal much more about the subject, their character and personality.

Barry's masterpiece, his arresting self-portrait in which he takes the pose of the Greek artist Timanthes, was begun about 1780 and completed in 1803. In his hands he holds his recreation of one of the artist's lost paintings *The Cyclops and the Satyrs*, showing satyrs cautiously approaching a sleeping cyclops. Above his head the artist has depicted the base of the statue of Hercules trampling on the serpent of Envy. It is a striking portrayal displaying the features of a rugged, austere and passionate man. Barry identified with the notion of the artist as an isolated and accursed figure. He deliberately attempted in this portrait to present a dramatic and complex official image of himself as the heroic artist. Despite being a highly successful history painter, Barry had a difficult and troubled life, and died impoverished in London.

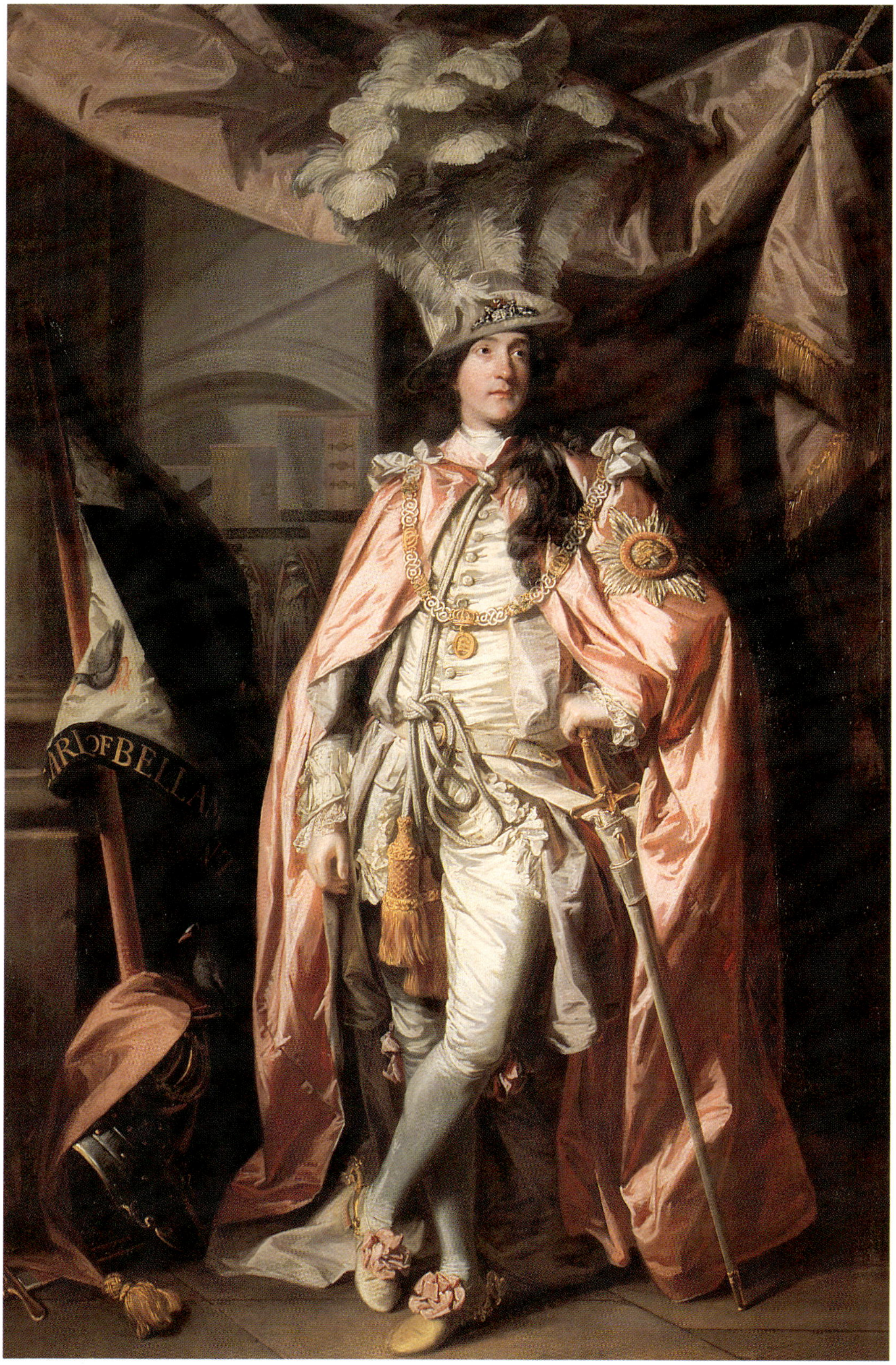

Charles Coote, First Earl of Bellamont (1738–1800) in robes of the Order of the Bath, *c* 1774
Sir Joshua Reynolds, English School
1723 Plympton – 1792 London

This magnificent formal portrait shows Charles Coote, First Earl of Bellamont, portrayed wearing his ceremonial robes as a Knight of the Bath – an order founded in 1725 to reward political and military service. Coote was MP for County Cavan from 1761 to 1766, and was installed at Dublin Castle as a Knight of the Bath in 1764. His ornate costume includes an exotic ostrich-plumed hat and a luxurious satin cloak. Even his shoes are extravagantly decorated with pink-coloured rosettes and metal spurs. The earl was renowned, not only as a witty and fashionable man, but also as a man whose 'ruling passion was vanity'. It was appropriate, therefore, that for his portrait he chose the celebrated British portrait painter Sir Joshua Reynolds. While the artist successfully portrayed the earl's flamboyant style, he nonetheless managed to imbue his subject with an air of nobility. Reynolds, however, introduced a humorous note into the full-length portrait by including a live coot bird perched beneath the embroidered banner, in reference to his patron's name.

The Countess of Bellamont also sat for a full-length portrait by Reynolds, completed in 1778, and both were probably hung in the saloon at the earl's County Cavan home, Bellamont Forest. Reynolds, the most renowned portrait painter of his generation, was the first president of the Royal Academy and a founder member of the Academy schools.

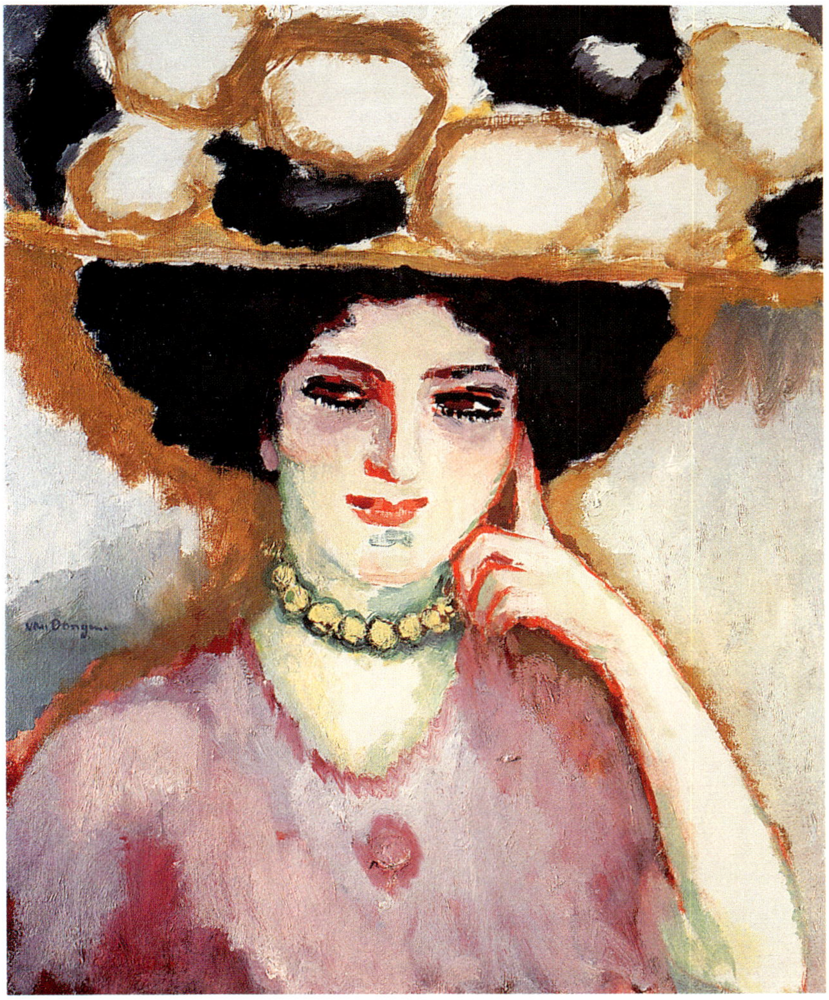

Stella in a Flowered Hat, 1908
Kees van Dongen,
French School
1877 Delfshaven – 1968
Monaco

While commissioned portraits form the basis of most artists' incomes, some are painted purely because the artist is drawn by an attractive and individual face. This informal portrait was painted, in all probability, because the artist Kees van Dongen was attracted by Stella's unusual and beautiful face.

Van Dongen spent most of his life in France. He was a friend and follower of Matisse and the group of painters known as Les Fauves. *Fauve*, meaning wild beast, was a term of abuse coined by a newspaper critic to describe the brilliantly coloured and patterned pictures created by this group of artists. In this half-length portrait, Van Dongen has sought to make a direct statement about the sitter. Using large areas of thick, flat paint and strong, vibrant colours, the subject is presented as a bold and colourful woman. Stella rests her chin on her hand, and glances sideways with a somewhat amused and enigmatic air. The artist's daughter, Dolly, has dated this picture to 1908.

Further interesting themes for practical art and design work: shoes, hats, puppets, jewellery, masks, hair, skin, models, royalty, images, friendship, bonds, silhouette, communication, reflections, the family, conversation-piece, weddings, ritual, my other self, brotherhood, humankind.

Practical projects

1. Draw your own caricature

Choose someone who has a sense of fun. What is special about this person? Is he/she tall and skinny? Does his/her ears stick out? Does your friend smile or scowl a lot? Is their hairstyle funny – long straight hair or short tight curls? Does this person wear glasses or earrings? What hobby do you associate with this individual – reading, music, dancing, sports?

Decide which face and body features you plan to exaggerate and what symbol to identify with them. Do some trial drawings to practise particular effects, such as eyes, hair or skin texture. First draw your caricature in pencil, and when you feel you are happy with it, try drawing it in ink. The best caricatures are drawn with a few clear lines, without too much detail. Is the final picture funny? Does it make your friend laugh? The ability to draw caricatures and cartoons is a rare skill – you might want to pursue a career in this area.

2. A portrait in miniature

The Piping Boy is a record of John Camillus by his father, the artist Nathaniel Hone the Elder. Another of his sons, Horace Hone, became a painter of portrait miniatures. During earlier centuries, many people carried around these small miniatures portraying images of the person they loved. Today we carry photographs, but wouldn't it be wonderful to paint a miniature of someone special to you?

In preparation, students might do preliminary sketches in line, tone and shading. A class could be devoted to life studies, with students taking turns to model in a variety of different poses. Draw attention to the expressions on the face and where the light and shadows fall. Conclude the class by doing a life-size portrait. These preparatory exercises will help prepare students for the miniature portrait.

Obtain a photograph of your friend or the person you wish to paint, or ask them if they are prepared to pose for you. Cut out a small circle of paper, making sure it is the right size and shape to fit into a locket. Copy the photograph by sketching the outline of the person's face in pencil. Paint the face in watercolour, acrylics or oil paints using very fine brushes. When the picture is dry, paste it onto a small piece of cardboard, and varnish it with clear varnish to protect it. Fit the small portrait into the locket. You now have a precious memento of your friend.

Most of the beliefs and teachings of the religions of the world are based on collections of sacred writings or stories. All these stories are told in holy books, ranging from the Koran (Islamic) and the Mahabharata (Hindu) to the Old Testament of the Jewish Bible and the Old and New Testament of the Christian Bible. In the Christian religion, for instance, the Gospels have been a major source of inspiration for artists right down to the present day.

In religious art, the artist attempts to make specific and visible something that is by its very nature spiritual, providing images of the religious figures and events that make up the essential beliefs and traditions of a faith. Christian art has been a major focus for artistic and architectural patronage in the West from the third century AD until well into the nineteenth and, to a lesser extent, twentieth centuries. Artists have provided images of Christ, the Virgin Mary, the saints and other figures, which have given the faithful clear images to focus on, thus making religion less abstract. Religious pictures were particularly important in the past, as they taught people about their faith long before they learned how to read, and they were an important reminder of the Bible stories they heard from the pulpit. While the fundamental doctrine of the Christian faith conveyed that Christ, after his death and burial, rose on the third day, the essential message communicated was to lead a good and decent life.

Images of Christ could be seen in public places in sculpture, mosaics, murals, as icons, or as altarpieces in candle-lit churches, made up from a single panel, a diptych or a triptych (an altarpiece in two or three parts). In order to make it easy for people to understand the Church's teachings, the paintings had to be simple and the stories told clearly. In many ways, pictures turned out to be a particularly good way of telling religious stories.

Traditionally, there were rules to be followed when painting religious pictures. During the Middle Ages, for instance, artists could not show Christ looking too much like an ordinary person, as the Church felt that he should look like a god, otherwise people would not believe in him. In a similar fashion, the Virgin Mary, the saints and the Holy Family were depicted with haloes around their heads so that people could identify who they were. In the early days of the Christian Church, statues were frowned upon because they reminded people of pagan idols, which are condemned in the Bible.

When artists first began to apply their immense skills to the depiction of holy figures, they employed highly stylised forms, as in Byzantine art, and later illuminated manuscripts such as the Book of Kells. With time, a gradual change came about to a more realistic and human portrayal, as seen in the work of the fourteenth-century Italian painters. Later, fifteenth- and sixteenth-century Italian, Spanish and North European painting brought this portrayal to a higher level of refinement. In the seventeenth century, in paintings by Caravaggio and Georges de la Tour, a highly naturalistic approach was taken, with Jesus being depicted as a normal man and many of his disciples and people in his company being shown to be poor, with bare feet; this realistic portrayal would have been inconceivable in an earlier age. Nowadays artists continue to try and interpret religious themes, but are often doing so in new and original ways.

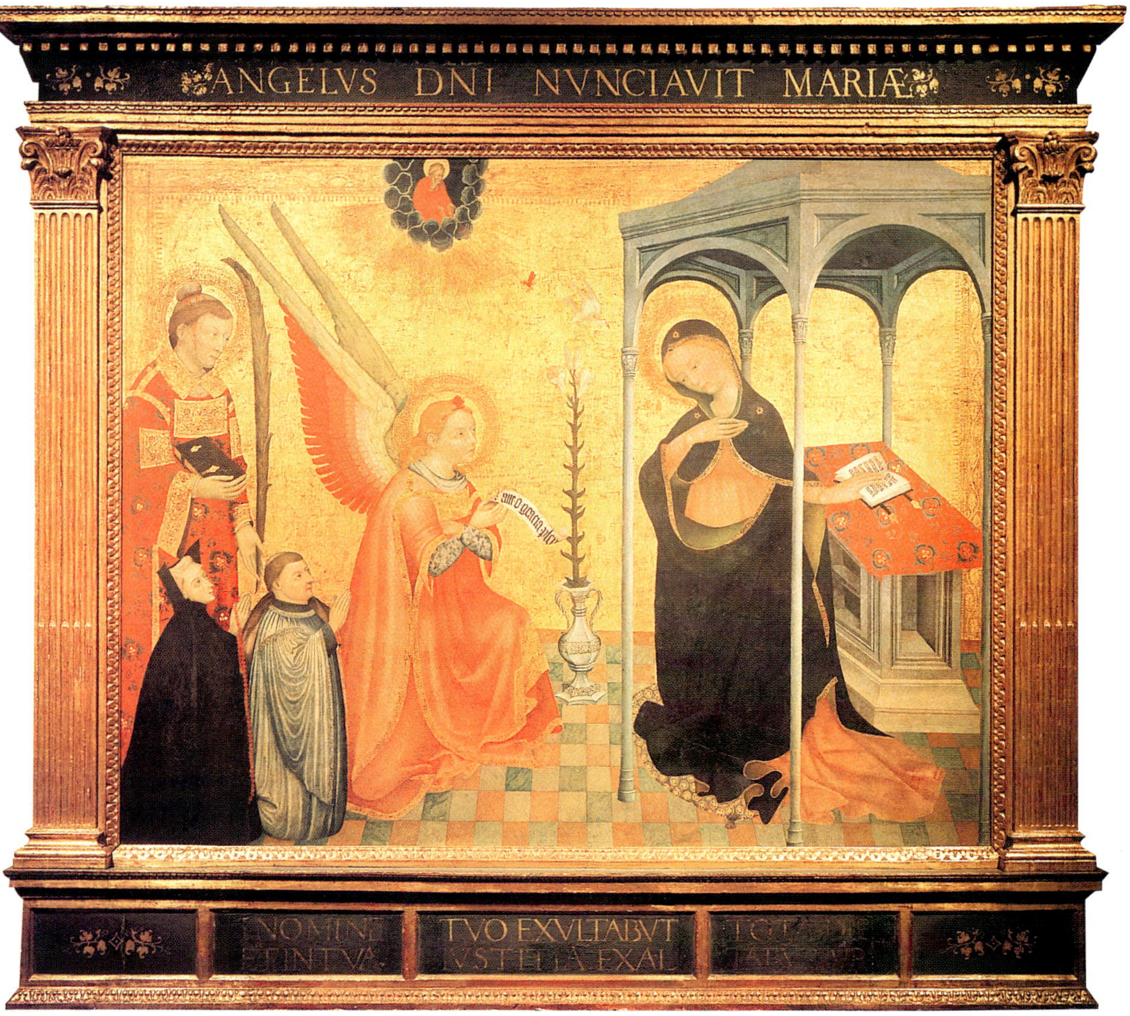

The Annunciation
Jacques Yverni,
French School
1410 active in Avignon – 1438

St Luke's Gospel describes the Annunciation as the occasion when the Angel Gabriel told the Virgin Mary that she had been chosen to be the mother of Christ. From the twelfth century onwards artists have had a particular fondness for this event, depicting it in a variety of different ways.

In this rare fifteenth-century panel painting, the Angel Gabriel is shown announcing to the Virgin that she is going to conceive and bear a son, while above the angel's head, God can be seen directing a tiny baby with the Holy Spirit towards the Virgin. The Virgin's purity is indicated by the inclusion of a slender white lily. To the left of the panel, St Stephen, an early Christian martyr who was stoned to death, points towards the donor of the painting and her chaplain, who due to their humble role are depicted as smaller figures. The palm leaf that St Stephen is holding is a symbol of martyrdom.

This is a votive painting, a work demonstrating devotion to God. During the Middle Ages, wealthy people sometimes made a gift of land to the Church as well as building chapels, dedicating altars, and donating paintings, silver and manuscripts, so that their eternal souls might be prayed for in perpetuity. While the donors are often included, as in the case of this painting, their role is minor in comparison to the religious scene, which is the main focus of attention.

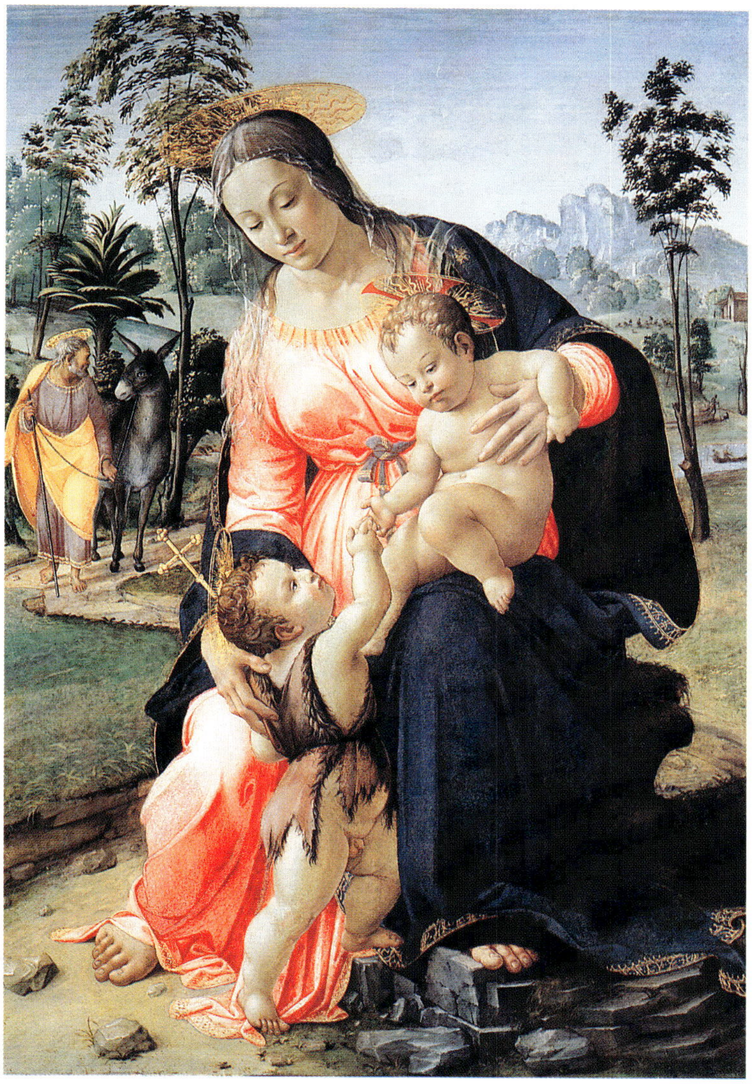

The Holy Family with St John in a Landscape
Francesco Granacci,
Italian School
1477 Florence – 1543 Florence

This picture shows the Virgin with the holy infants seated on a rock in front of a landscape setting. The infant Jesus, seated on her left knee, looks down towards St John the Baptist, who reaches upwards while also holding a cross in his left hand. The painting depicts the scene of the Holy Family resting during the flight into Egypt, with St Joseph, visible in the distance, leading the donkey towards his holy charges. This episode from the life of Christ illustrates the Christian doctrine of the Incarnation, which affirmed that Jesus, the Son of God, took human flesh from his human mother, and, as a result, Christ is both fully God and fully man. While sixteenth-century audiences would recognise the doctrine of the Incarnation being conveyed, nowadays the picture is more frequently viewed as reflecting the loving atmosphere in which the child Jesus was raised.

Granacci thought hard about how to arrange or compose his painting, and he used lines, shapes, colour and patterns to organise the composition. He probably devised a master outline, executing numerous preliminary drawings, before he began painting. This way of dividing up the space was especially popular in the fifteenth century and was used to give perfect proportions which were pleasing to the eye. An excellent picture to demonstrate the balance and harmony of Renaissance painting, it is attributed to Francesco Granacci, a Florentine master, who like Michelangelo studied under Ghirlandaio.

Christ in the House of Martha and Mary illustrates a scene from the life of Christ taken from the Gospel of St Luke. The two sisters of Lazarus reacted in different ways when Christ visited them in their home. Mary sat down and listened attentively to Christ's words, while Martha got on with household chores. After a time Martha, wishing the work-load to be shared, asked for Christ to intervene, only to be told that 'Mary hath chosen that good part which shall not be taken from her'.

Martha is traditionally portrayed as the busy housekeeper, an active person, in contrast to her contemplative sister, Mary of Bethany. The theme of contrasting the active and material life with the contemplative and spiritual life became popular in the seventeenth century, partly because it allowed artists to paint a religious subject in a domestic setting. While great care has been taken by Brueghel in painting the details of the domestic scene, including the birds, animals, fruit and flowers, it is Rubens who conveys the message taking place through the eye contact and gestures of the key figures.

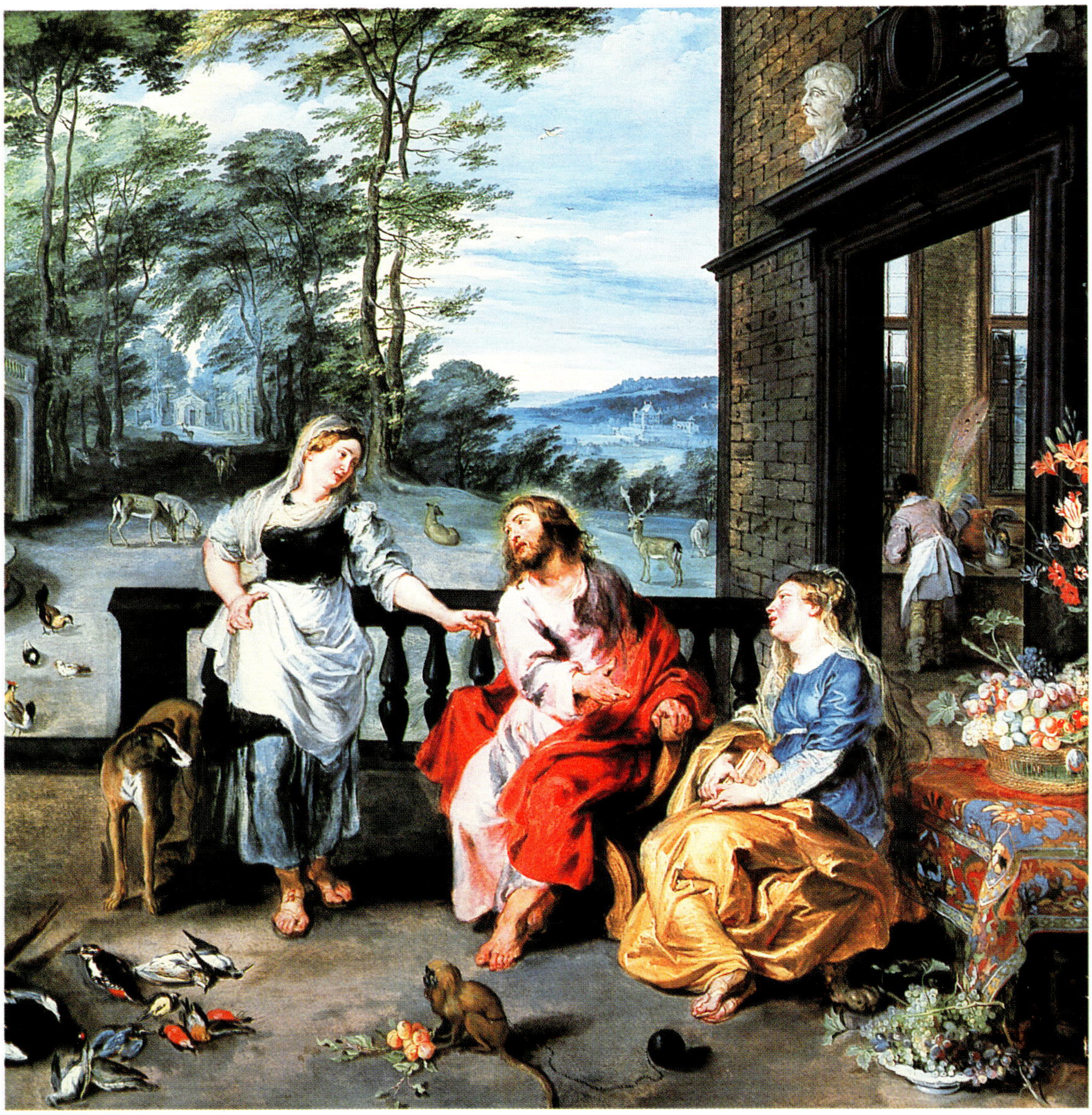

Christ in the House of Martha and Mary
Jan Brueghel,
Flemish School
1601 Antwerp – 1678
Antwerp, and
Peter Paul Rubens,
Flemish School
1577 Siegen – 1640 Antwerp

The story of the Passion has exercised the minds and talents of artists down through the centuries. The arrest of Christ is a particularly poignant moment in the story, one that is conveyed with extraordinary originality in Caravaggio's outstanding canvas, *The Taking of Christ*. The picture shows Judas arriving with the soldiers, about to identify Christ and so betray him with a kiss. Following the betrayal, Christ stands composed, waiting to be arrested. The features of the lantern bearer in the background are those of Caravaggio himself.

This picture was painted in 1602, during a prolific period of the artist's career while he was living in Rome, where he had a circle of ready buyers among cardinals and noblemen. Caravaggio's dramatic lighting illuminates the tragic event being depicted. The scene of drama is further underlined by his skilful use of gesture, together with the striking realism of the figures. All these elements combine in *The Taking of Christ* to create a powerful emotional effect on the viewer.

The Taking of Christ, 1602
Caravaggio, Italian School
1571 near Milan – 1610 Porto Ercole

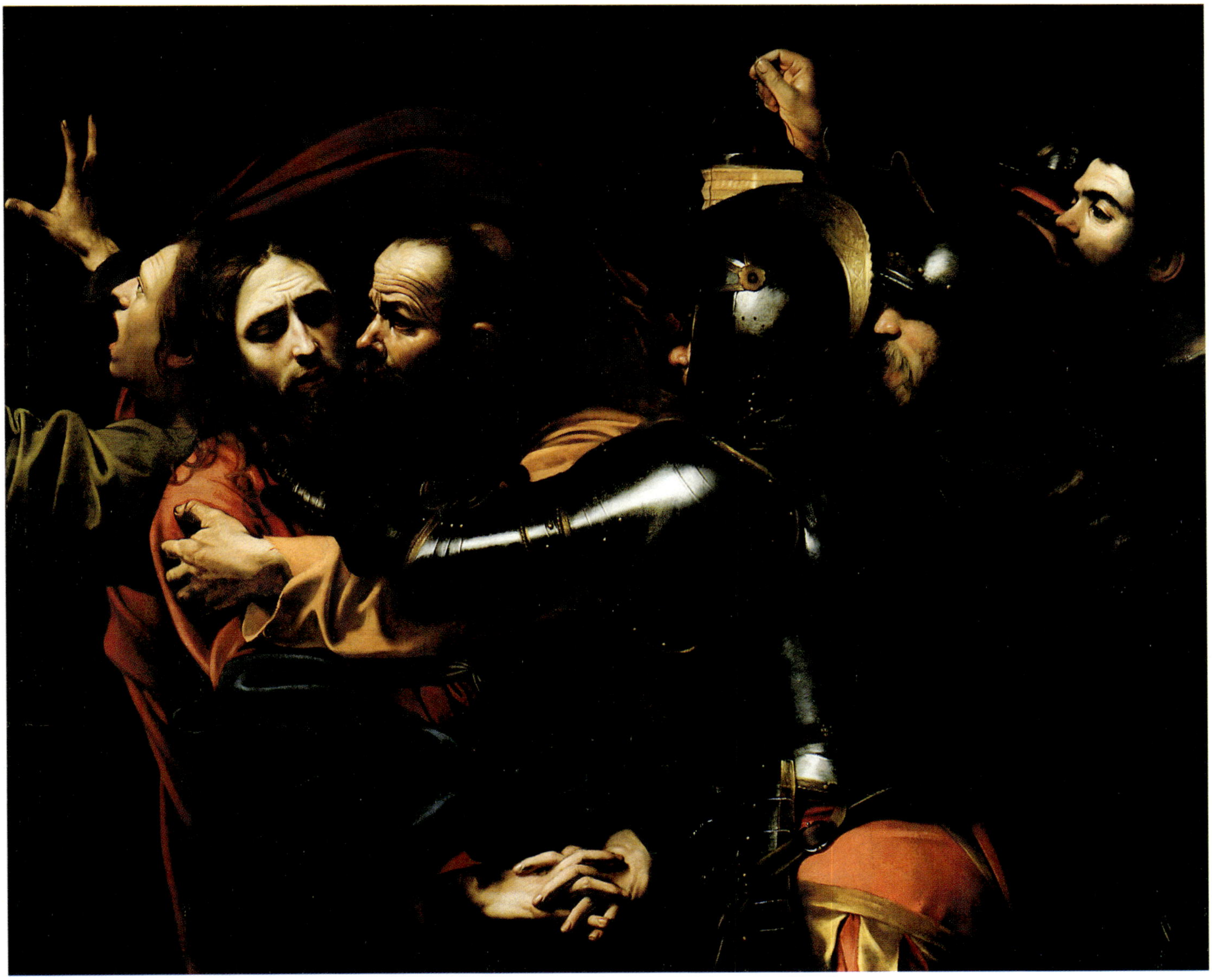

The Crucifixion, the most moving episode of the Passion, is illustrated here in stark realism, with the emaciated figure of Christ nailed to the cross. Having first been tortured, Christ was then crucified alongside robbers on a hill at Golgotha. Just before dying he cried out in anguish: 'My God, My God, why have you forsaken me' *(St Mark 15:22:37).*

This version of the Crucifixion was originally painted for a Sienese church, where it would have hung at the entrance to the choir. The cruciform shape of the panel helps to emphasise the raw intensity of the scene taking place. Barely visible in the background are several angels engraved into the gold panel. Giovanni di Paolo spares no feeling in conveying the horror and pain of the Crucifixion, despite which the finely painted body manages to convey a strange beauty.

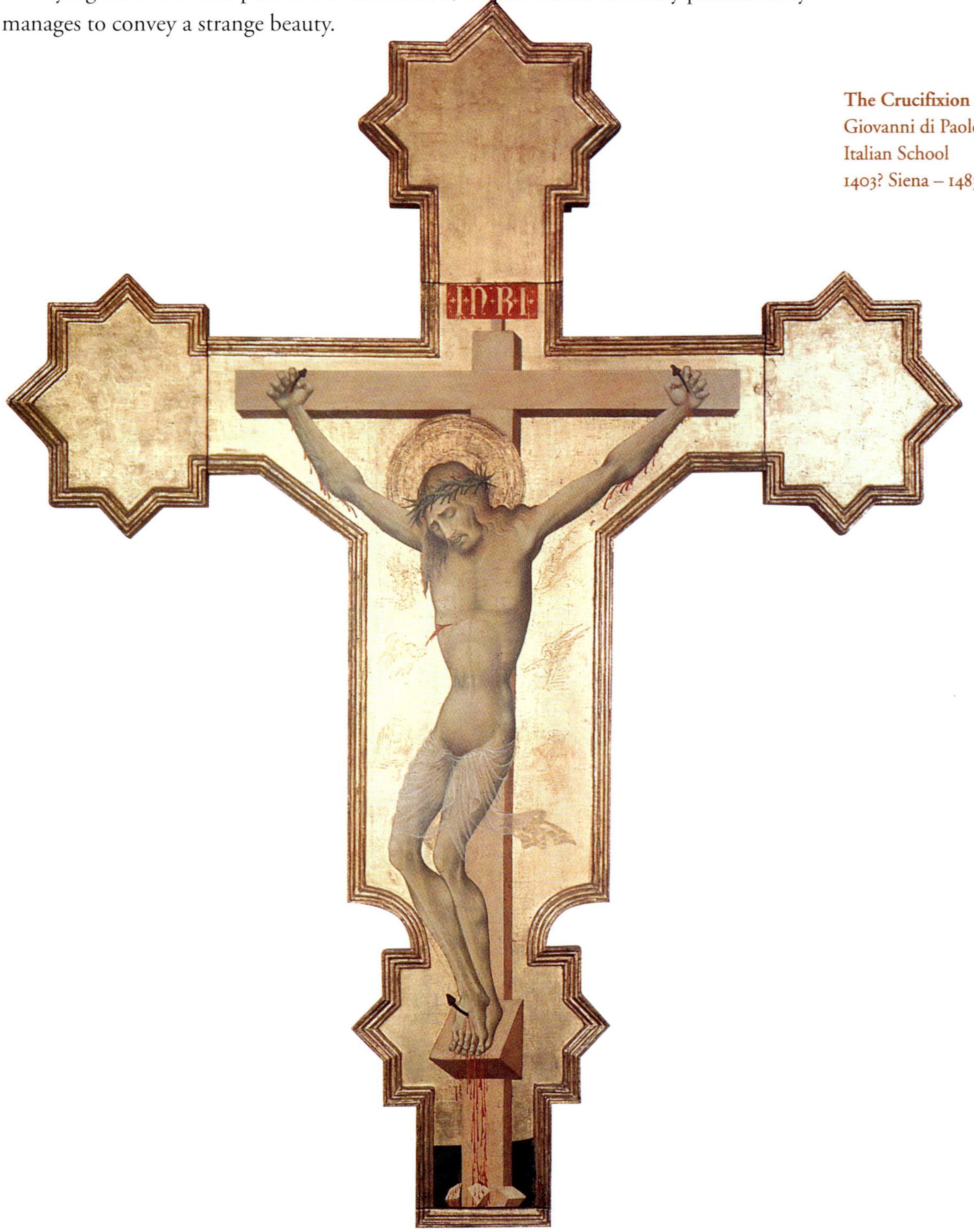

The Crucifixion
Giovanni di Paolo,
Italian School
1403? Siena – 1483 Siena

In the evening following the Crucifixion, Joseph of Arimathea went to Pilate and asked him for permission to remove the body of Christ from the cross. Taking down the body, he 'wrapped it in a clean linen sheet' and laid it in front of the sepulchre.

This moving painting depicts the moment when the Virgin and the disciples grieve and mourn over the dead body of Christ. St John raises Christ's head onto his lap, Mary Magdalen kisses his hand, and behind her the other Mary looks on in distress. The intense feeling of sorrow is concentrated on the upright figure of the Virgin, who holds her blue cloak in order to wipe the tears from her face. Her stark expression of grief reflects her acceptance that the sacrifice of her son was necessary for the salvation of humankind. Behind her, a tree bearing new shoots alludes to the regrowth that will follow the Resurrection.

Poussin is acknowledged as the finest history painter of the seventeenth century. This painting is the work of the artist in his sixties, whose close friend Cassiano dal Pozzo had recently died. The ageing artist was suffering increasingly from ill health and consequently painting more slowly. This picture forms part of his late, highly personal output, in which the compositions aim for perfect clarity, leaving out anything incidental. Perhaps the hallmark of this period is the severe restraint, simplicity and understatement of his pictures. His interpretation of the lamentation is therefore seen as a meditation on death, and in so doing he has created one of his most memorable images.

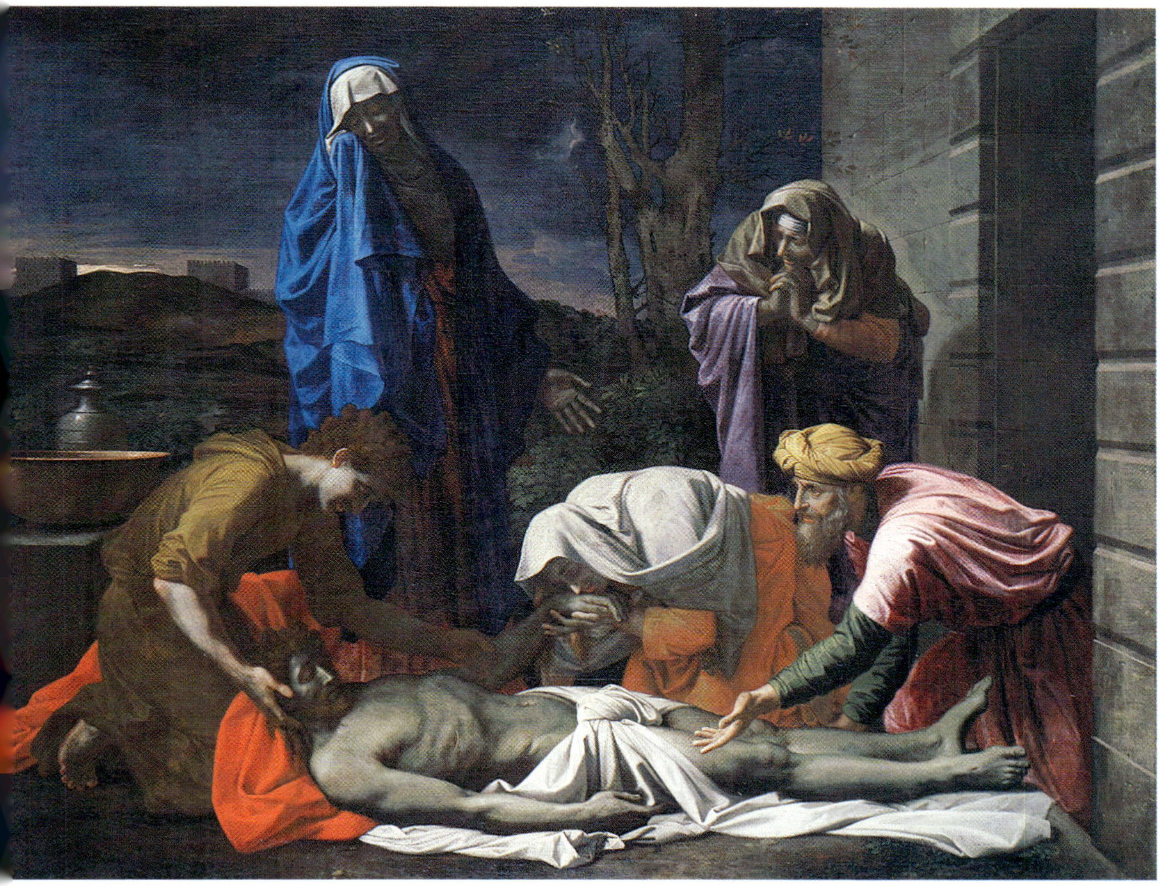

Lamentation over the body of Christ, 1657/60
Nicolas Poussin,
French School
1594 Les Andeleys – 1665 Rome

Further interesting themes for practical art and design work: discovery, alienation, harmony, grief, wonder, peace, love, mystery, the desert, birth, death, memorabilia, magical forces, amazing places, star quality, haloes, strange events, another life.

1. An illuminated manuscript

Reflect over the past months and note any major events that have occurred, including birthdays, a meal in a restaurant, holidays, a pop concert, a great film, winning a sports event or taking part in the school play. To do this project you need a scrapbook, glue, pen and paints.

Use the scrapbook for a variety of different purposes: to jot down your thoughts, write out any ideas or projects, tease words into sentences or a poem, or to paste in sketches and drawings. Paintings should be included, in addition to favourite photographs and pictures. Concert, film or football tickets would be worth collecting, together with train, aeroplane and ferry tickets. Gather anything that you can use to record a special event and carefully glue them onto the pages.

Years ago scribes used to make books and manuscripts beautiful by decorating each of the pages. Perhaps the best-known example is the Book of Kells. You could decorate the margins of your scrapbook with colourful drawings and designs. The first letter of each page could be enlarged and painted carefully. The cover of the scrapbook would look impressive if you painted a pattern and included your name on it, just as the monks illuminated their manuscripts.

2. Design a poster, record sleeve or book jacket

If you did not know the story of the Annunciation, you might guess that the painting of the *The Annunciation* by Jacques Yverni had to do with the subject of birth, if only because of the image of the tiny baby represented above the Virgin's head.

This exercise involves doing a series of drawings on the theme of 'birth' or 'childhood' as a design for a poster, record sleeve or book jacket. The object of the exercise is to make a completed design in black and white, and later a version in colour. Think carefully about what birth/childhood represents for you. Collect items of clothing, toys, children's books or keepsakes. Make a series of studies based on these objects and the feelings associated with them. Work out the design carefully on paper, planning the lettering to include the word 'birth' or 'childhood'.

See how the design compares with other books and posters. You may need to sharpen the drawing or improve the lettering. When you have completed the design, store for future use all the preliminary research, notes and sketches. Do an outline drawing of the original design and colour it with pencils, markers, pastels or paint. You might be interested in pursuing a career in graphic art if you find you are particularly good at this type of design work.

Theme 3: Still life, fruit and flowers

The term 'still life' comes from the Dutch phrase *still-leven*, meaning an arrangement of inanimate objects. In still-life paintings or drawings the artist arranges fruit, flowers, game or household objects to be the subject of the painting. In other pictures, still-life objects add interest or give clues to what is going on. For example, in the seventeenth and eighteenth centuries, not alone in Northern Europe, especially in the case of Dutch art, but also in Italy, France and Spain, the still life of food became a subject worthy of attention, an important genre that has survived down to this day.

The genre of still life is mainly associated with the North European schools. While still lifes were painted in Renaissance art, it was mostly as background or in a supporting role to human action. The popularity of still life in seventeenth-century Holland was partly due to the lack of religious patronage and the rise of the merchant class, who appreciated paintings both as aesthetic objects and as commercial items. In the eighteenth century still life found a great exponent in the French academician Chardin, but he remained something of an exception. The nineteenth century saw still life rise to a new level of interest in the innovative works of the impressionists and Van Gogh, but most especially Cézanne, who invested still life with many of the visual complexities once reserved for history painting.

Objects in still-life painting may be selected because the artist finds them visually interesting, for instance, the still life of flowers in a vase is a perennially popular subject. Flowers picked in the garden quickly wither and die, and it may be that Dutch flower paintings were meant to remind people of the shortness of life. Alternatively, the artist may choose objects for their symbolic meaning: books might be included to represent human knowledge; the shell, to represent worldly wealth; musical instruments to suggest the pleasures of the senses; a sword to represent earthly power. In today's world, the clock is just a machine that tells the time, but to someone living in the seventeenth century it may have symbolised time itself. Similarly, an hour-glass, which we use to time a boiling egg, may represent an image not just of time, but of time running out.

When something is included in a picture as a reminder of death it is called a *memento mori*. *Vanitas* is also a type of still life that depicts groups of objects which express the brevity of life and its pleasures, for example, skulls, clocks, scythes and wilting flowers. Similar motifs have made the same point throughout the history of painting by warning the beholder of the folly of taking comfort in life because of its inevitable end. In earlier centuries people were accustomed to death because it was so common and because life expectancy was short. As a result, artists included objects such as skulls and watches as symbols to remind people that no matter how rich, powerful or learned they became, or how much time they devoted to pleasure, one day they would inevitably die and would then have to account for themselves in the next life.

The twentieth century has seen still life continue as a serious form of expression for artists, though they are less occupied with symbolic content and more concerned with innovative avant-garde approaches. If you have ever tried to draw an apple, a plant, a jug or a bottle, you will know just how complicated even a simple-looking object can be.

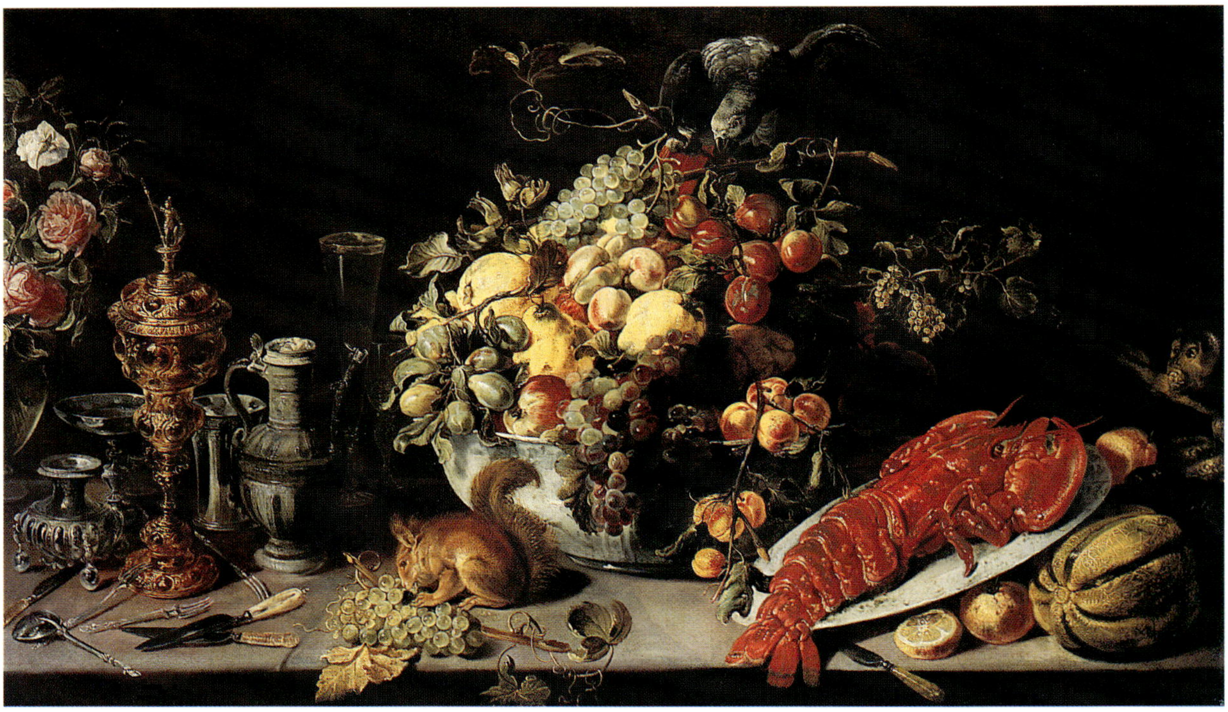

A Banquet-Piece
Frans Snyders,
Flemish School
1579 Antwerp – 1657
Antwerp

A 'banquet-piece' is the name given to a picture showing table settings with a lavish array of food. A wealth of costly and exotic food and objects is spread across this table, including a vase of roses, glasses, precious metal and silver ware, a bright red lobster, oranges, a melon and a large porcelain Chinese bowl containing many kinds of delectable fresh fruits. Animal motifs, such as the squirrel nibbling on grapes, the parrot, and the monkey reaching for a branch of currants, feature in many of Snyders' paintings. The picture's most obvious allusion is to celebrating wealth and abundance for its own sake.

Snyders' outstanding talent as a still-life painter is apparent from the care taken to present a balanced and lively composition, and by the painting of textures, surfaces and colours portrayed in an enticingly realistic manner. This banquet-piece is largely comprised of fruit, which unlike vegetables was considered very much an upper-class food. Antwerp, where the artist lived and worked, was renowned as a market place for exotic fruit and vegetables in the sixteenth and seventeenth centuries. The prices that fruit commanded, especially when out of season, were costly. A variety of techniques was therefore developed to keep fruit fresh as long as possible. The sumptuous fruit and tableware, combined with the large size of the canvas, suggest it was intended to decorate an aristocratic dining-room.

Velázquez was one of the greatest of the Spanish painters. In this early work by the artist, a Moorish kitchen maid is depicted leaning over a table on which kitchen utensils are arranged. She pauses in her work, as though aware of the scene taking place in the background. Seen through a hatch in the background (a picture within a picture) is the Supper at Emmaus. St Luke's Gospel tells us how Christ revealed himself on the day of his Resurrection to two of his disciples at Emmaus. Velázquez's great achievement is seen in the profound feeling for humanity which underlies all his work – the poor and the kitchen maid were of as much interest as a king or a courtier.

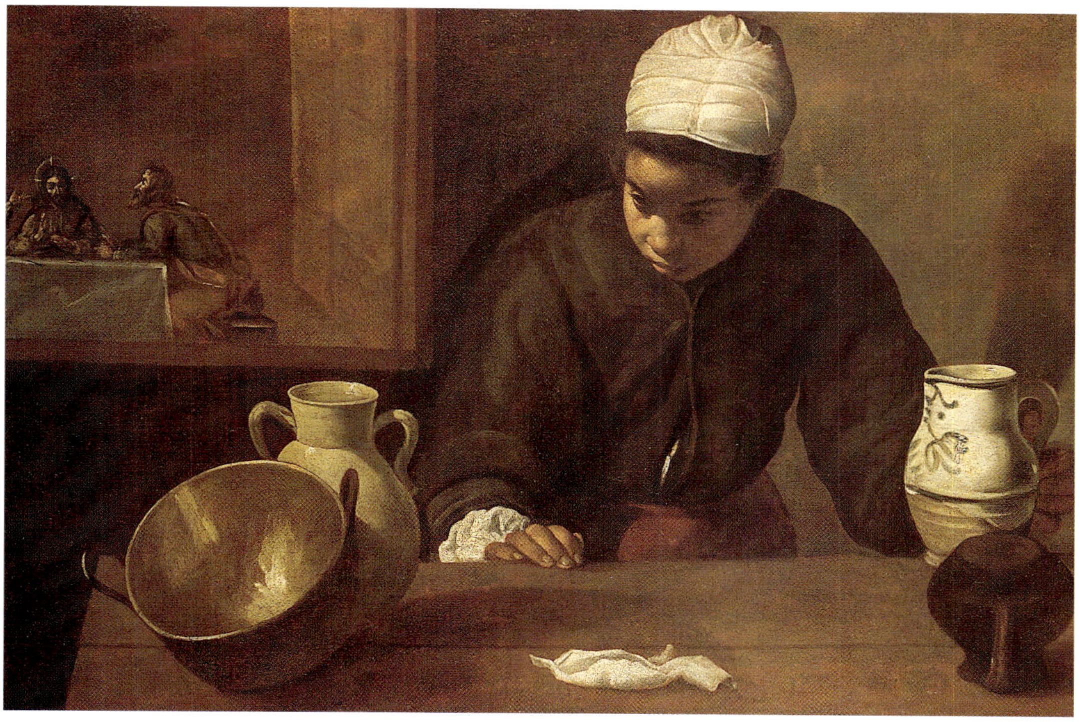

Kitchen Maid with the Supper at Emmaus, *c*1618
Diego Velázquez de Silva,
Spanish School
1599 Seville – 1660 Madrid

In sixteenth- and seventeenth-century Spain, the term *bodegón* was applied to paintings of low-life subjects which combined still life and genre in a kitchen setting. The inclusion of a religious scene would have raised the humble *bodegón* to a higher, spiritual level.

Like Caravaggio, Velázquez uses a dark backdrop with light coming in from the side, so that people and objects are brightly illuminated in places and cast hard shadows. The artist uses a restricted palette of ochres, earth colour and white, features of his early work, to convey the surface texture of the vessels. The burnished and glazed pottery jugs and dishes, the mortar and pestle and the head of garlic are all familiar objects in Velázquez's *bodegónes.*

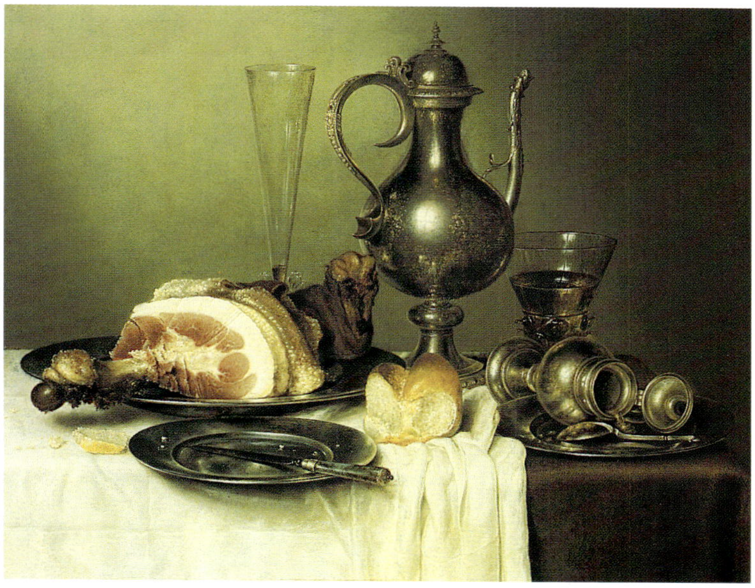

A Banquet-Piece, *c*1635
Willem Claesz. Heda,
Dutch School
1593/4 – 1680/2 Haarlem

In this banquet-piece we can see that the artist has spent a long time arranging the food – a piece of ham and a bread roll – and serving vessels on the table. The white tablecloth has been folded over the left-hand side of the table so that the composition does not appear too symmetrical. All the dishes – plates, flagon, mustard pot – and the spoon are made of pewter, which was common in Northern Europe in the seventeenth century. Whereas for quite some time food was included just for display, this work demonstrates a still life in the aftermath of an opulent meal. The affluent citizens of Haarlem, where the artist worked, were particularly open to the refined taste depicted in such still lifes.

Painting still life can give an artist the opportunity to work in an illusionistic way, reproducing objects in such a convincing manner that they seem real and palpable. Heda has arranged the various components of this still life in order to reflect the light and demonstrate the artist's fine balance of tonal values and illusionistic painting skills. Although there can be no doubt that these banquet-pieces are a display of culinary luxuries, the food was frequently linked to religious ideas that were diametrically opposed to such abundance. The broken bread and wine may allude to the sacrament of the Holy Eucharist, and it is worth noting that it was customary to fast prior to receiving the sacrament.

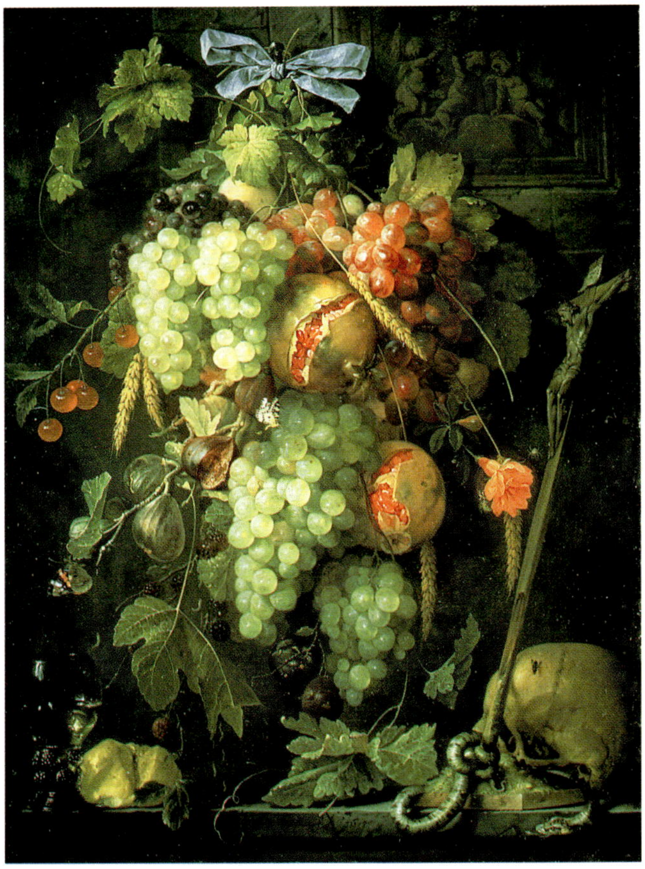

A Vanitas Fruit-Piece, 1653
Jan Davidsz. de Heem,
Dutch School
1601 Utrecht – 1683/4
Antwerp

Sometimes still-life painting holds a deeper meaning, beyond the initial impression. In this picture it is the *memento mori* symbolism, which here is understood to mean that salvation is to be found through the Passion of Christ. The Church, for instance, put forward the argument that the accumulation of wealth through profit was totally meaningless – mere vanity. It therefore became an integral part of many still lifes to include a skull, as a reminder to the viewer of the transience of all things.

The lifecycle is shown by references to the fig (fall from grace), through youth, and adulthood (crucifix) and death (skull). Christ on the crucifix symbolically rises over the devil (snake) and mortality (skull and fly). The Resurrection is symbolised by corn, which is cut, harvested and reborn as communion bread, and the grapes will also become communion wines. The pomegranate represents Christ and the Church, while the plum signifies fidelity. The whole composition, which is a sumptuous display of fruit already on the point of decaying, reminds us that our earthly life passes quickly and that everything decays with death. It also alludes to worldly possessions, which compared to spiritual riches are empty and worthless.

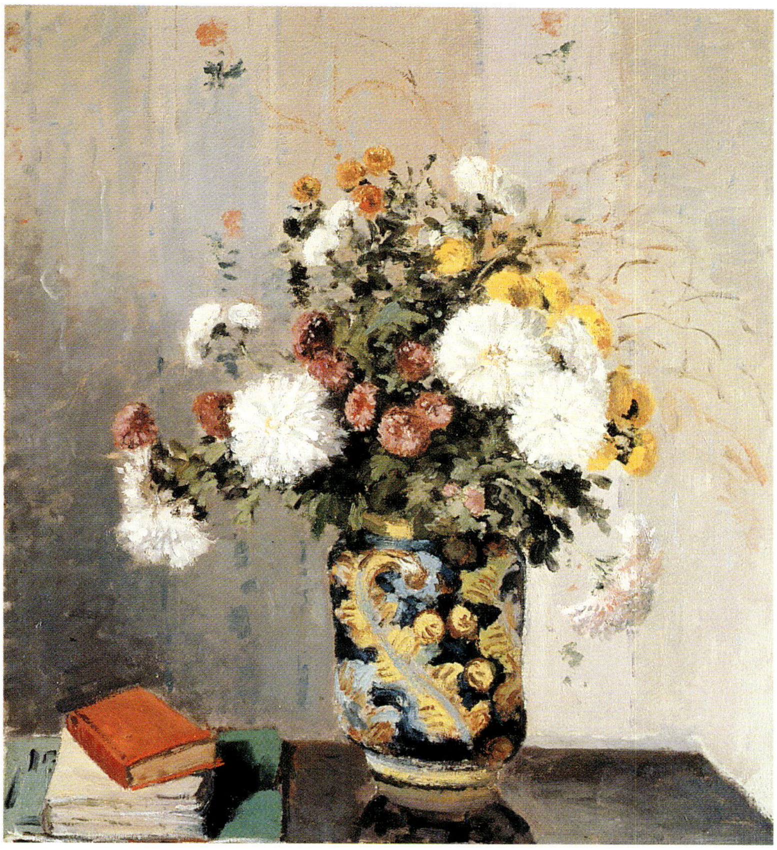

Bouquet of Flowers in a Chinese Vase, *c*1872
Camille Pissarro,
French School
1830 Saint Thomas – 1903
Paris

Pissarro studied under Corot and at the Academie Swisse, where he met Manet, Monet and probably Courbet and Cézanne. It was Corot who advised him to paint small sketches before nature and to study light and tonal values. From the late 1860s he was a major figure in the impressionist circle and he alone exhibited at all eight exhibitions (1874-86), which he largely organised. Pissarro was influential as a teacher to Cézanne and Gauguin, and he was himself open to the changing influences of pointillism. All the impressionist artists painted flowers, partly out of a need to generate income, but also to occupy themselves on rainy days, when working out of doors was impossible. Monet and Renoir were also brilliant exponents of the art of flower painting.

The bouquet of flowers illustrated here consists of a variety of chrysanthemums arranged in a yellow and blue Chinese vase on a small table. The vase of flowers forms the centre of the composition, while the books, table and wallpaper provide depth. Pissarro's interest was to capture the play of light on the scene, making it a spontaneous, fresh work rather than a calculated studio picture. In 1872 the artist was living at Louveciennes and the same wallpaper appears in other works of this date. The flowers are painted in an impressionist technique, using short brushstrokes, with the paint applied both thickly and sparingly, built up in overlapping layers. Pissarro reminds us that a simple subject such as flowers in a vase can become a noble and uplifting work in the hands of a master.

Picasso's *Still Life with a Mandolin* was executed on the Côte d'Azure during the summer of 1924. He has arranged on a bright tablecloth, with lively arabesque border, a pile of textiles, a carafe or bottle and a mandolin – do you agree? The shape of some of the objects show Cubist influence in their simplified forms, and he has taken obvious delight in using Matisse-inspired vivid colours and rhythmic patterns, evocative of the Mediterranean climate. It is as if the artist has drawn parts of the still life from a number of different angles and combined several of these views in one painting.

Picasso felt free not to follow the traditional rules of perspective and proportion. Instead of trying to paint objects realistically, he has deliberately flattened the individual elements, because he is more interested in making decorative patterns on the surface of the picture. He only gives us clues as to what real-life objects these shapes resemble – we have to work this painting out for ourselves. Picasso, Cézanne and Matisse are just a few of the modern artists who have sought to reinterpret still life in a new and intriguing manner.

Still Life with a Mandolin, 1924
Pablo Picasso,
Spanish School
1881 Malaga – 1973 Mougins

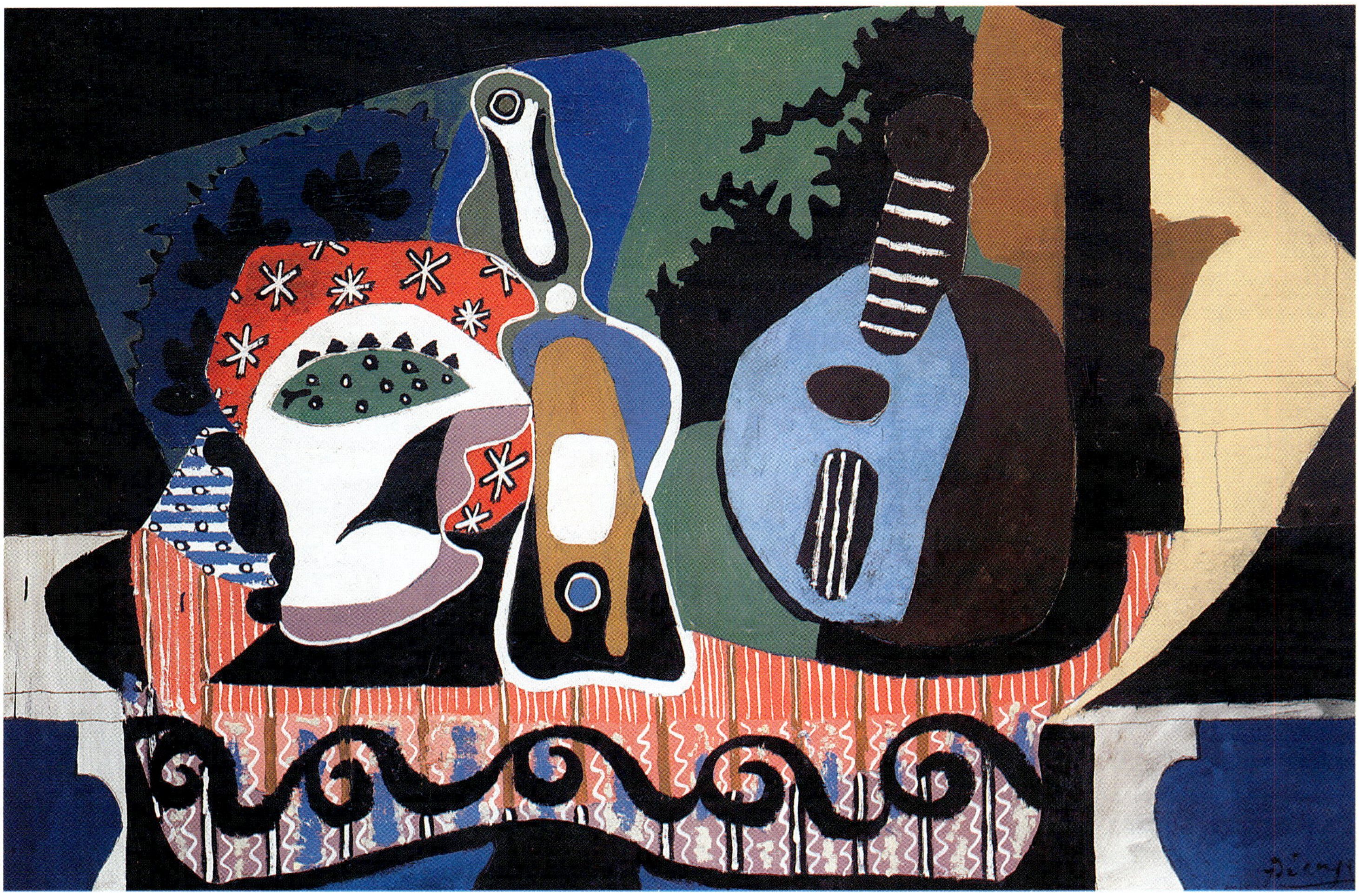

Further interesting themes for practical art and design work: celebration, the meal, the feast, the senses, the table, country produce, touch, fur, textures, skin, decay, solid forms, raw materials, impressions, the shape of the seasons, pattern in the seasons, time, sound, music, instruments.

Practical projects

1. Still life in colour

The practice of sketching still life helps to develop good observational skills and accurate drawing ability. Start by drawing a single object such as a banana. Take time to study its shape, size, colour and texture. Complete the drawing in colour. Then try a selection of objects. Collect a number of items such as a jug, a plate, a knife, a vase of flowers, some fruit and a patterned tablecloth, and arrange them in a pleasing composition. Begin by sketching the composition. If you find any of the objects too difficult, then replace them with something easier – a bottle instead of a jug, for example. Take care over the drawing, observing the light reflections on the glass or china, and the particular texture of the fruit and flowers. Pay attention to the folds of the tablecloth and the shadows they create. Finish the picture using coloured pencils, pastels or paints. Compare the two pictures.

If you found this exercise successful, you might like to try exploring still life in a more modern and abstract way, taking Picasso's *Still Life with a Mandolin* as an example. Don't be too ambitious, start experimenting with a few simple objects and see what patterns and shapes you can make of them. Choose bold colours and use them in a decorative fashion. You might be surprised to find how much you enjoy this style of painting.

2. Object drawing: a study of a piece of fruit or a vegetable

Look closely at the way Snyders and de Heem have handled the painting of fruit in their pictures. Observe their meticulous attention to detail.

For this exercise choose a piece of fruit or a vegetable which you think has an interesting shape and texture. Make a drawing of the object you have chosen, outlining it with a fine black pen. Trace the drawing three times onto three sheets of paper. Use these copies to explore the object in the following ways:

- i) do one detailed painting;
- ii) make a colour study using warm colours, e.g. red/orange/yellow;
- iii) make a colour study using cold colours, e.g. purple/green/blue.

Finally, cut or peel the fruit or vegetable. Make some drawings of its transformed shape. Observe the gradual decay of the object, recording the process in your sketchbook. Keep a record of the various studies and drawings you have made – they may come in useful for a portfolio.

Painters take in the natural world through their eyes, work on it with their imaginations, and draw on what they have seen in other paintings. The landscapes they paint may be 'real' or made-up. As the view turns into paint it becomes a unique combination of what the artist sees, knows and feels.

From an early date artists travelled and, in their sketch-books, kept records of what they saw on their journeys. Many travelled to Italy to see the wonders of ancient Rome and the Renaissance. Albrecht Dürer made an outstanding series of landscape drawings and watercolours of his journeys from Germany, across the Alps, and into Italy. The idea that an artist could paint a stretch of countryside directly from nature, without modifying it or tidying it up in any way, became common in the West only in the last century. Critical reaction was also opposed to this genre until the end of the nineteenth century.

Landscape painting illustrates changing views about nature throughout different periods of history. In this context the term 'nature' is taken to mean birds and flowers, mountains and streams, in other words, the external world. The representation of this beautiful external world is sometimes considered the true aim of the artist. Landscapes are present, often in very idealised forms, in the backgrounds of many paintings of the Renaissance and earlier periods, although in China the genre began much earlier. Landscape was an important aspect of ancient Chinese art even before the Ming Dynasty produced a circle of distinctive and highly esteemed painters. As a genre in its own right, worthy of a painter's attention, pure landscape painting in Europe cannot be traced back much earlier than the sixteenth century. Although landscape was important for pastoral painters such as Giorgione, for the narrative and genre painting of Brueghel and the fête galante reveries of Watteau, none of these may be said to embody the landscape tradition.

The development of landscape painting was essentially a Northern phenomenon, dominated by Germany in the sixteenth century, the Netherlands in the seventeenth century and England in the eighteenth and early nineteenth centuries. The landscapes of Claude in the seventeenth century depicted nature as peaceful and idyllic, where the landscape is invented rather than observed, and bears no relation to the kind of countryside in which it might have been painted. Claude's idealised, poetic landscapes had a huge influence on European painting. While Claude, a French artist, was painting in Italy, Jacob van Ruisdael was painting realistic pictures of the Dutch countryside, in which the sky is often cloudy and the trees are blown about by the wind, showing that his intention was to paint scenes from real life. His realistic landscape was a major influence on later painting in this genre.

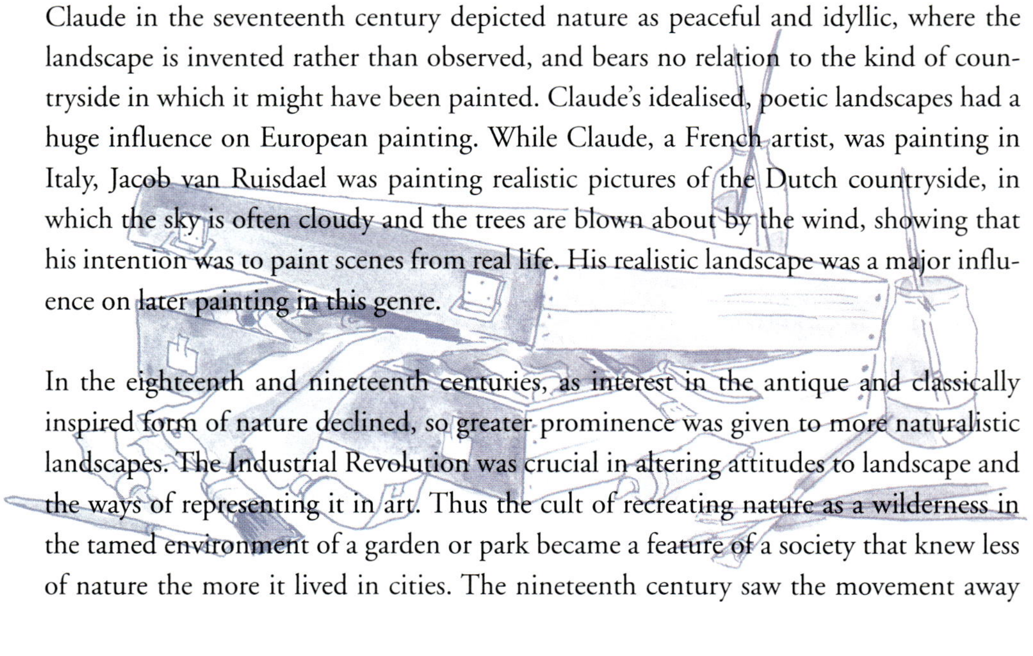

In the eighteenth and nineteenth centuries, as interest in the antique and classically inspired form of nature declined, so greater prominence was given to more naturalistic landscapes. The Industrial Revolution was crucial in altering attitudes to landscape and the ways of representing it in art. Thus the cult of recreating nature as a wilderness in the tamed environment of a garden or park became a feature of a society that knew less of nature the more it lived in cities. The nineteenth century saw the movement away from studio practice to *plein air* painting in the Barbizon School, of which Nathaniel Hone the Younger was an exponent. In the later nineteenth century, after initial adverse criticism, the impressionists finally succeeded in winning acceptance for landscape as a genre worthy of critical attention, and this gave a great sense of freedom to successive generations of artists. Within modernism, landscape has played a significant role in the work of Cézanne and the Fauves, the expressionists and the surrealists. What is important now is what the artist sees and the way he or she feels about the subject, linked together to produce a new view of the natural world.

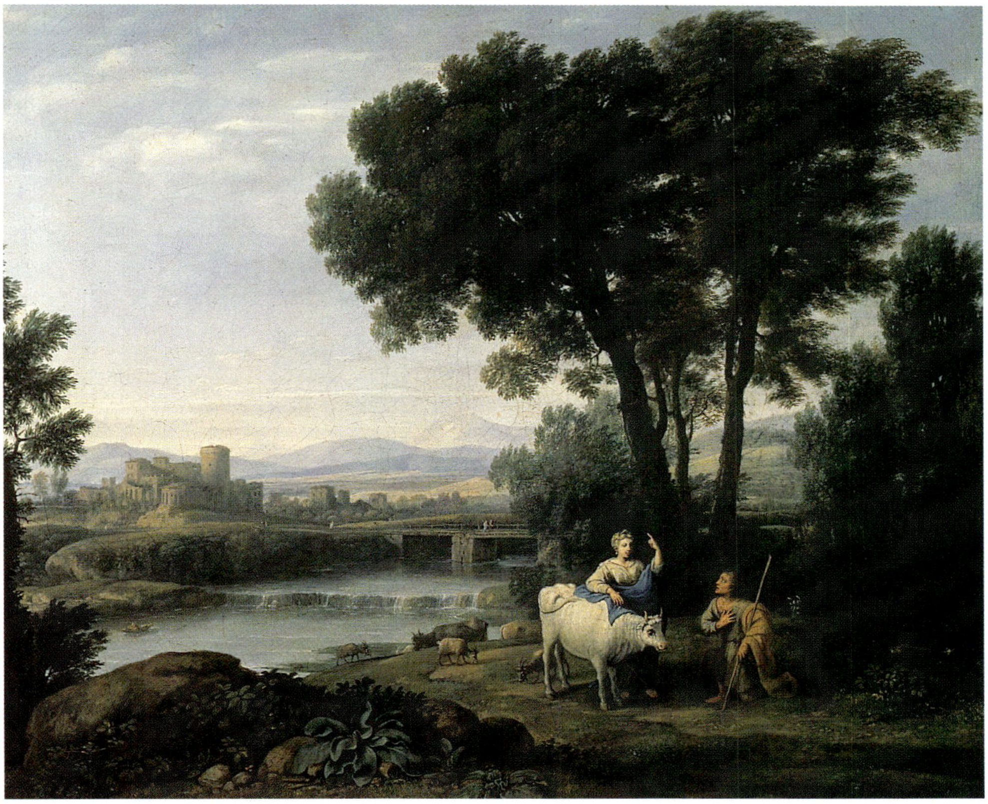

Juno Confiding Io to the Care of Argus, 1660
Claude Lorrain,
French School
1600 Chamagne – 1682 Rome

Claude developed a type of ideal, poetic landscape, which was inspired by classical tradition and antiquity. The story of 'Juno confiding Io' is drawn from classical mythology, as recounted in Ovid's *Metamorphoses.* Ovid describes how Jupiter seduced Io, the beautiful sea nymph, and then transformed her into a white cow to hide her from his wife, Juno. Juno was not fooled and made her husband give her the cow as a present, which she left in the safekeeping of Argus, the hundred-eyed giant. By representing Argus as a young shepherd rather than as a giant, Claude turns the story into a charming pastoral scene.

The artist lived in Rome, where he created his picturesque landscape compositions. The countryside in his paintings is intelligently and sensitively organised, not rough and wild as the real world often is. He was a passionate observer of light and atmospheric changes, which he recorded in numerous line and brush drawings, working out of doors. In order to prevent forgeries, he compiled a book of drawings called the *Liber Veritatis*, which included a drawing of every painting he did. Claude's idealised view of the natural world has had a formative influence on European painting and also on landscape gardening.

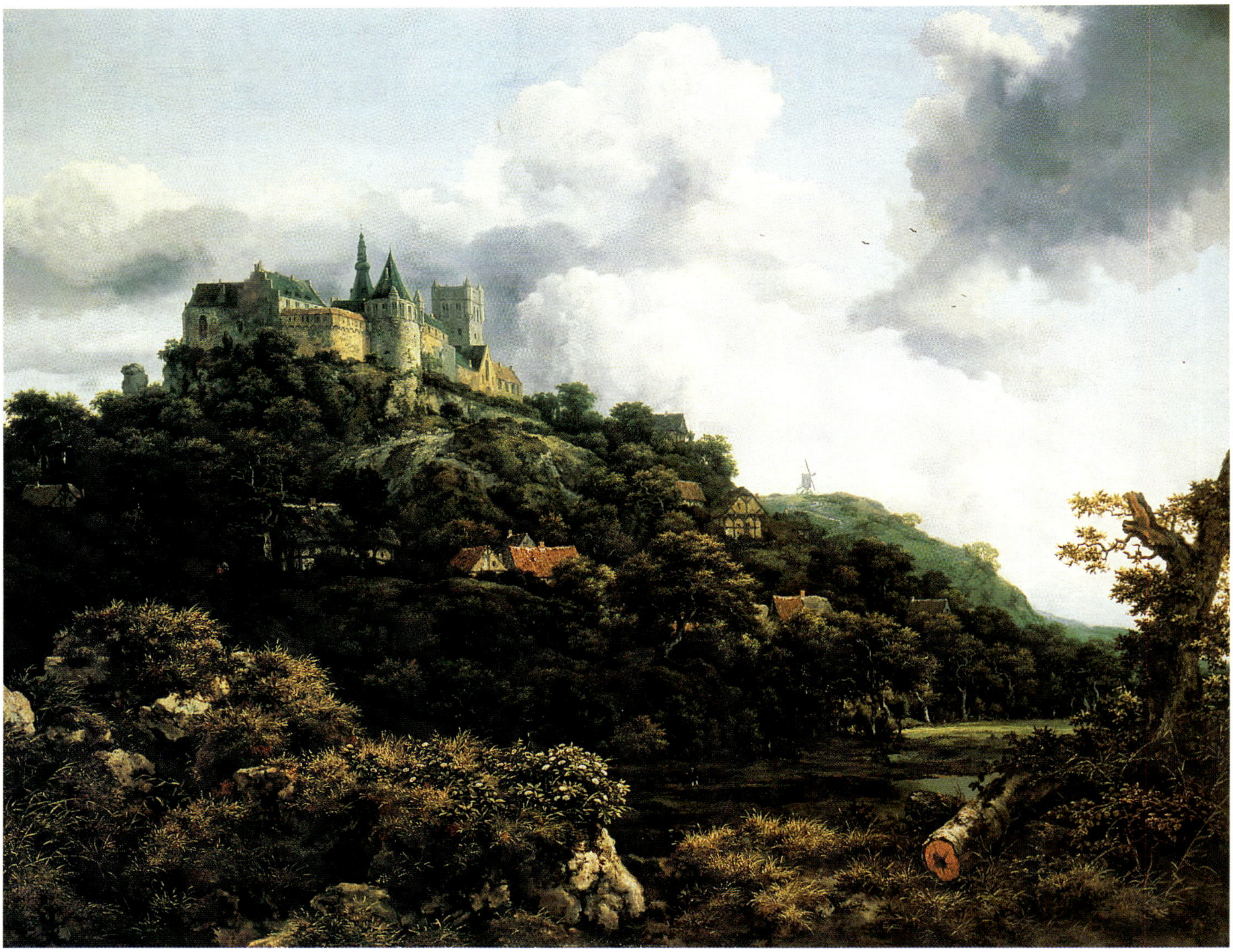

The Castle of Bentheim, 1653
Jacob Isaacksz van Ruisdael, Dutch School
*c*1628/9 Haarlem – 1682 Amsterdam

The seventeenth century is generally regarded as the Golden Age of Dutch Painting, with Jacob van Ruisdael acknowledged as the finest landscape painter of that period.

This dramatic view of Bentheim Castle is an early work, painted when Ruisdael was about twenty-four years old, yet it has always been regarded as one of his masterpieces. It is one of fourteen known views of Bentheim Castle by the artist. The castle, which is shown dramatically positioned on the top of a hill, is situated in a small German town in Westphalia. Placing the castle on a heavily wooded green mountain containing a wealth of detail, the artist achieves an atmospheric effect by painting bright luminous skies and broad sweeping clouds. Ruisdael exaggerates the prominent site of the castle and emphasises the awesome power of nature in order to develop a monumental classical style, which marks this picture as one of the great landscapes of European painting.

The view we see in this picture looks familiar, yet we cannot seem to locate it. The reason is that it is an idealised view of the countryside painted in the manner of Claude, who established a series of rules for painting classical landscapes: the foreground area, painted in dark colours, should recede to the distant horizon using colours that gradually get paler; the feeling of depth is created by placing trees, cliffs, hills or a waterfall on either side of the picture; in order to lead the viewer into the landscape, human figures, animals, ruined buildings (castles, old abbeys), rivers and trees should be placed carefully at intervals in the composition. Roberts seems to have had a particular interest in the ideal or classical landscape which, while depicting nowhere in particular, provides a carefully composed, peaceful and pleasing view of nature.

Thomas Roberts was the most gifted Irish landscape painter of the second half of the eighteenth century. He had superb control over handling paint, combining meticulous attention to detail with a lightness of touch. Unlike many landscape painters, he was skilled at painting both human figures and animals. He was equally competent at painting accurate views of famous houses, such as Lucan House and Carton House.

Ideal Landscape, ***c*1770**
Thomas Roberts,
Irish School
1748 Waterford – 1778 Lisbon

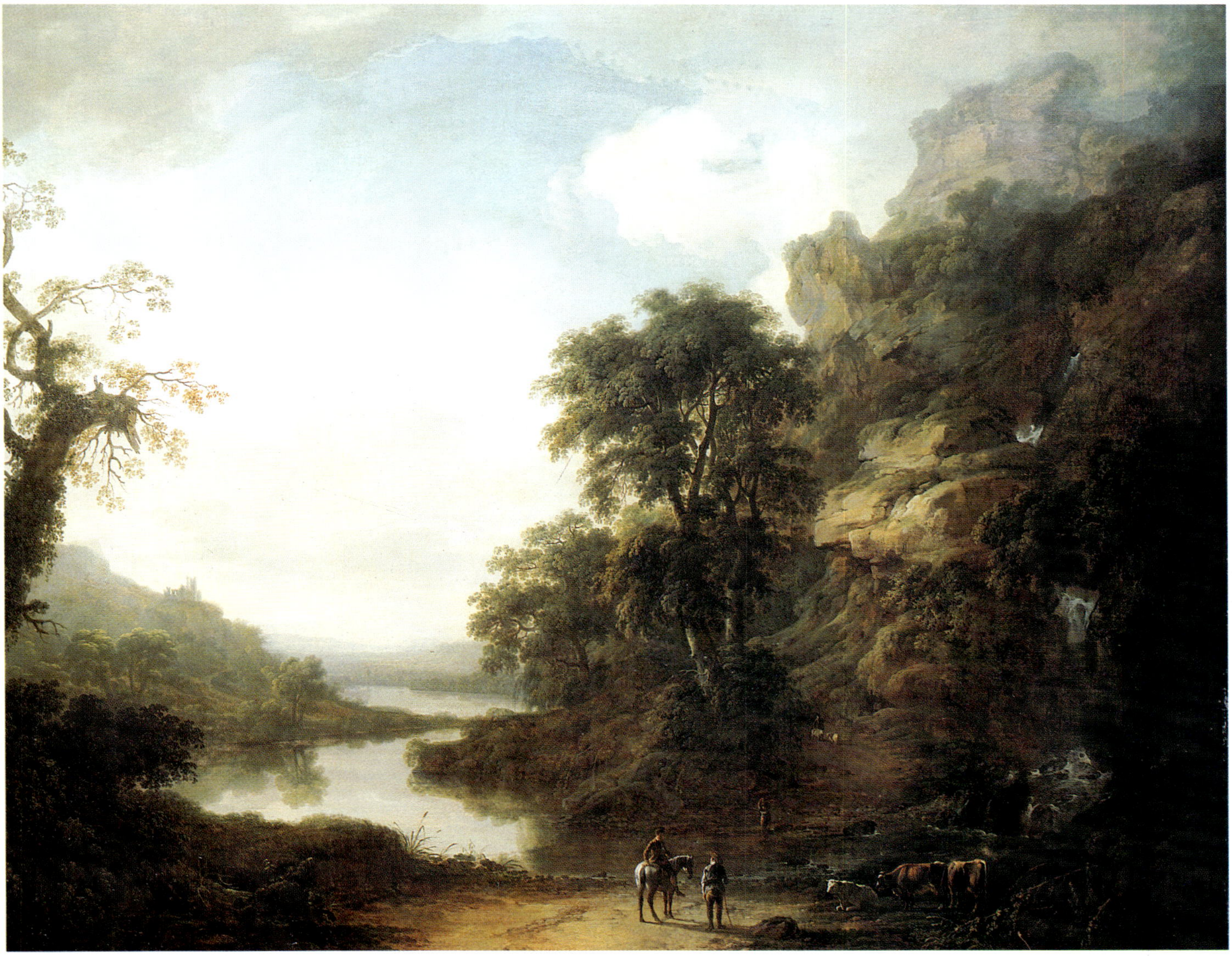

The view depicted in this landscape is Harnham Ridge from Archbishop Fisher's house in Salisbury. Constable did a whole series of painted sketches in Salisbury during the 1820s. The artist made numerous small studies of scenes directly from nature, but the final pictures were carefully executed pieces of studio painting. He loved painting clouds and the way they constantly changed the pattern of light on the ground. This can be seen in *A Landscape near Salisbury*, in which two-thirds of the picture is composed of cloud studies. His aim was to capture a 'brief moment, caught from fleeting time, and make it last for ever'.

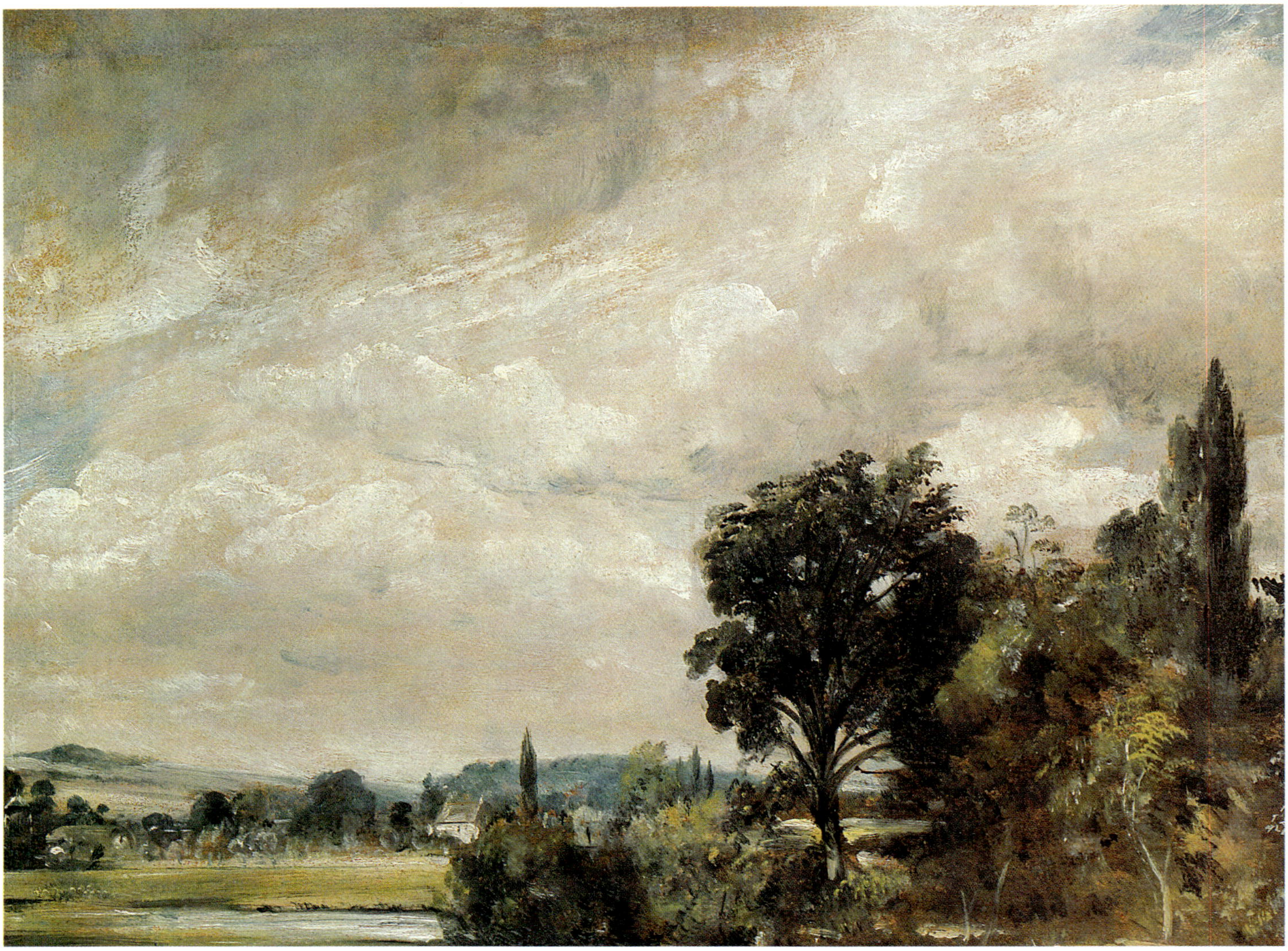

When Constable was painting his much-loved English countryside in the early nineteenth century, he determined not to romanticise it but to paint it for its own sake.The artist greatly admired Claüde's picturesque landscapes, but he wanted to be more true to life. His method was first to make oil sketches out of doors, and then slowly put the painting together in his studio, filling in details from these sketches and from drawings made at different times and in different places. Constable was, with Turner, the major English landscape painter of the nineteenth century.

A Landscape near Salisbury, 1828
John Constable,
English School
1776 – 1837

This is a wonderful picture by Sisley, a landscape painter with an individual talent for capturing in paint the effects of atmosphere and weather on the mood of a scene. First influenced by Corot, the artist met Renoir, Bazille and Monet while a student in the Academy of Charles Gleyre in 1862. They formed a lasting friendship and he became a central figure of the impressionist group, showing at over half of their exhibitions.

He determined to take as his subject matter the landscape around him, using a light and colourful palette to explore the immediate impression of a particular moment, and the effects of different lights upon his subject. His paintings of the Loing and the floods at Marlay are primary examples of impressionism.

Sisley painted the landscape around St Mammès from the early 1880s, but he and his family only moved there in 1883. This period was one of the most difficult of the artist's career; he felt lonely and isolated, and refused to exhibit with the other impressionists during this time. It was at St Mammès, however, that Sisley matured as an artist, and it was here that he became convinced of the importance of series paintings. He painted some sixty pictures of the village, and this was one of the last. He explained his technique: 'You see I am in favour of different techniques within the same picture.... The sunlight, in softening the outlines of one part of the scene, will clarify and illuminate another, and these effects of light which seem real in a landscape, ought to be interpreted in a material way on the canvas'.

Bords du Canal du Loing à St Mammès, 1888
Alfred Sisley,
French School
1839 Paris – 1899 Moret-sur-Loing

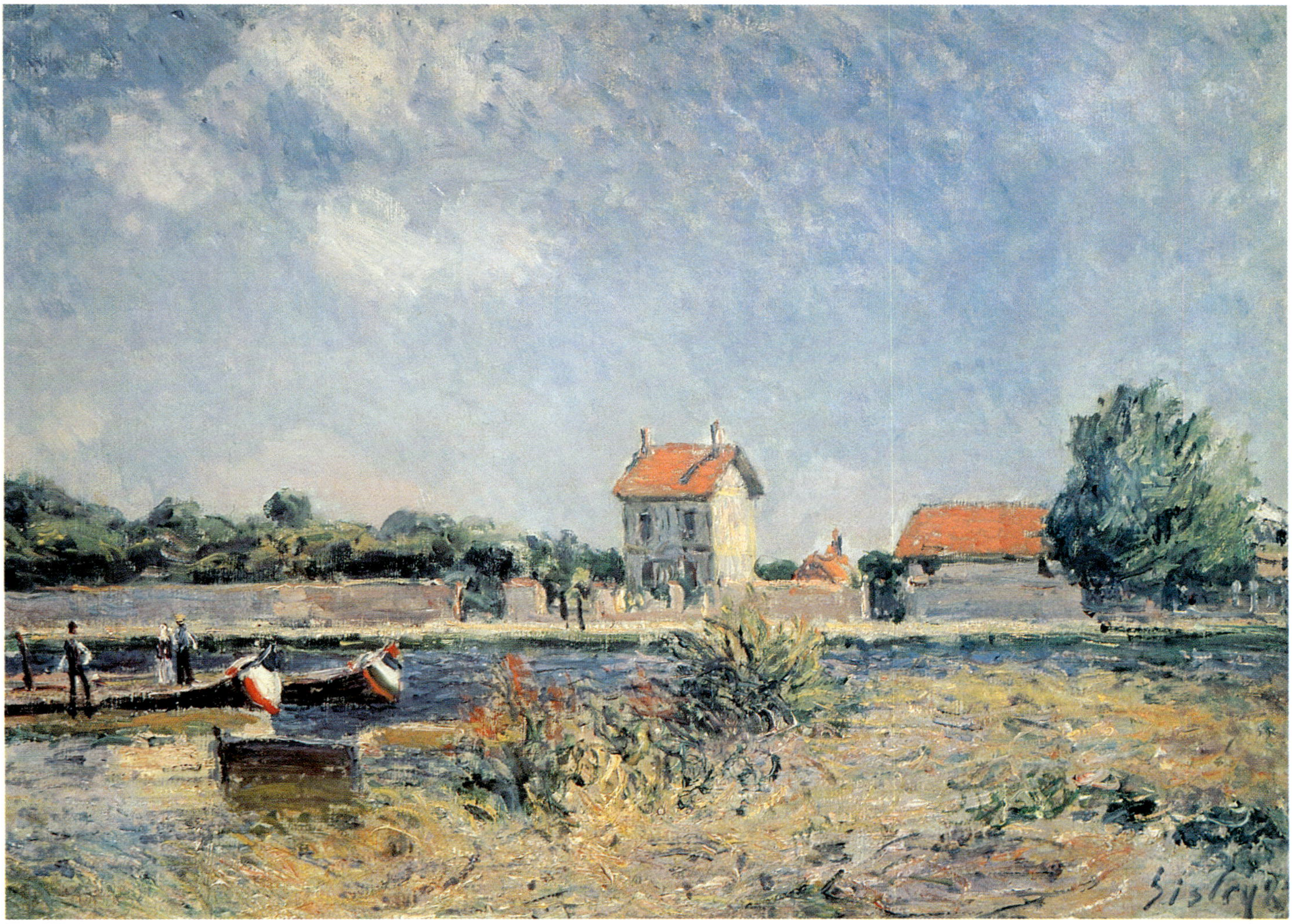

Although often described as Ireland's first modernist painter, O'Conor spent the majority of his life in France. After studying with Richard Moynan at the Antwerp Academy in 1883-4, O'Conor moved to Paris, where he discovered the impressionist painters and Van Gogh's work. Following this, he spent a decade in Brittany, between 1890 and 1904, at Pont Aven, where the stimulus of Gauguin inspired some of his finest pictures.

During his early years in France, O'Conor painted still lifes and landscapes in a bold impressionistic manner reminiscent of Pissarro and Sisley. During the 1890s, he produced a magnificent series of landscapes, including *Farm at Lezaven*, and also portraits of Breton peasants, in which his characteristic use of divisionist striped colour is prominent.

The farm in this picture was a favourite studio for avant-garde artists on the outskirts of Pont Aven. Alternating striped brushwork in pink, maroon and green, with a variety of smaller and thicker brushstrokes in red, yellow and green, enriches and enhances this luscious landscape. While his work of this period is indebted to the post-impressionist painter Paul Gauguin, after his return to Paris it changed under the influence of the Fauve painters.

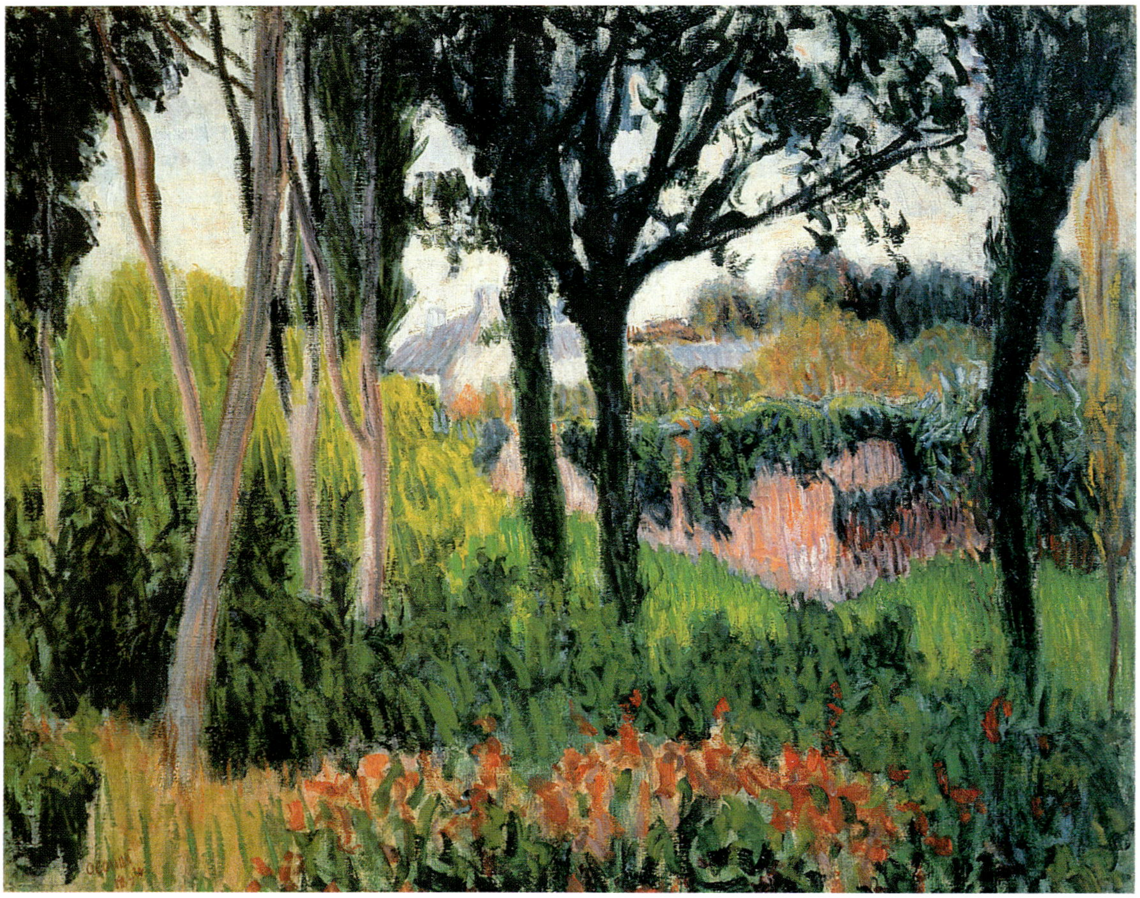

Farm at Lezaven, Finistère, 1894
Roderic O'Conor,
Irish School
1860 Milton, County Roscommon – 1940 Neuil-sur-Layon

Further interesting themes for practical art and design work: leaves, space, colour, light and shadows, nests, growth, pollution, water, rivers, castles, tides, fishing, hay, under the sea, over the rainbow, a place to dream, jungle life, tropical gardens and wildlife, no place like home, smells, farm machinery.

1. An impressionist painting

Collect the following equipment: jar of water, paper and pencil, poster paints and brushes. Decide whether you are going to paint a landscape with hills and trees out of doors, or a still life with flowers. Look to Pissarro's *Bouquet of Flowers in a Chinese Vase* or Sisley's *Canal du Loing à St Mammès* for help. Draw the outline of the subject, e.g. the landscape, on paper. Use small splashes and daubs of paint to fill in the outline, like Monet, Pissarro and Sisley, the impressionist artists. Try not to paint any lines or solid blocks of colour. Don't be tempted to use thick, long brushstrokes. Instead, use the tip of your brush to make small splashes of colour, so that the picture gives the effect of a variety of different colours. If you can, omit black from your palette – use dark purple, brown and green instead. Painting in this way creates a fresh and immediate effect. When the painting is dry, sign it and hang it on the wall.

2. Sea studies

Do you remember a time when you sat beside a calm sea and dreamed of peace and tranquillity? When did you last walk along a pier during a storm, when the sea was rough, the waves were splashing and the sky was dark and heavy? This exercise requires that you look at the sea and think carefully about its different moods.

i) A calm sea: use pencil, paper and watercolour paint, restricting the palette to blue, green and yellow. First sketch the merest outline of the seascape in pencil. Paint the scene, using shades of blue, green and yellow, with a variety of small brushes to convey a quiet, calm sea. If you wish, use overlapping layers of paint to strengthen the quality of the colour.

ii) A stormy sea: use pencil, paper, poster paints/oils and thick brushes. This picture will convey a rough, stormy sea. Sketch the scene in pencil, outlining the wild waves and the coastline. Working with just a few colours, rapidly paint the different areas of the picture. Use thick paint and brushes to convey the rough edges of the waves. Do not define the hills or coastline because the stormy weather will make them indistinct. Use strong shadows to create dark clouds and an angry sky. Keep any written notes, studies or drawings of the sea for reference purposes. Compare the two pictures.

In the National Gallery of Ireland there are over thirty watercolours by the English painter Turner, illustrating landscapes and seascapes in a wide variety of styles, ranging from calm and peaceful to wild and stormy.

A narrative painting is a picture that tells a story. Often narrative pictures focus on a particular moment in a story, so that the viewer can guess what has happened before and what is about to happen next. Storytelling is not simply a matter of describing events. A good storyteller can breathe excitement, drama and atmosphere into the tale, and engage the viewer's fear, amusement and sympathy for the characters in the story. Everyone loves a picture that tells a story!

Genre painting is a form of narrative, a term used for pictures depicting scenes of ordinary daily life, animals or still life. Although these themes have long been represented in art, they were generally incorporated into the major genres, such as religious, history and portrait painting. Genre painting became important in its own right in seventeenth-century Holland, where it met the needs and wishes of the middle class for scenes of everyday life, of people going about their ordinary tasks and activities. A genre painting usually depicts life in a real and unidealised manner. Dutch seventeenth-century painters like de Hooch, Metsu, Vermeer and Steen became specialists in genre painting, with subjects ranging from lively tavern scenes and schoolroom settings to quiet domestic interiors. Many of these genre paintings are important historical records because the artist, in his desire to paint a work that accurately describes a situation, has been careful to include much authentic and anecdotal detail to create interest.

In the eighteenth century, genre painting found a major figure in France in Chardin, whose still lifes and interiors are among the finest of their kind, imbued as they are with a reverent attention to the ordinary that transcends mere representation.

Narrative painting was popular in the nineteenth century. It relied largely on anecdotal subject matter to create interest, and the title often formed an important part of the whole. Many narrative painters approached the picture as if the beholder was seated in a theatre, and as a result the story was conveyed in a fresh and immediate way. The emphasis was placed on the artist's ability to illustrate the story, on the competent handling of paint, with particular attention given to circumstantial detail. Narrative paintings often depict religious stories from the Bible, dramatic tales from history, the lives of saints and scholars, or myths and legends from Ancient Greece and Rome. Periods in history can be brought to life merely by looking at some narrative paintings: *The Marriage of Strongbow and Aoife* by Daniel Maclise (p25) gives some idea of the effect of the twelfth-century Norman invasion of Ireland; *The Peasant Wedding* by Pieter Brueghel the Younger (p22) provides a humorous view of a late-fifteenth-century Flemish wedding party, with an underlying moral reflection on the seven deadly sins; *The Gleaners, Courrières* by Jules Breton illustrates the conditions of the lower social classes and the political changes which affected them. 'The Gleaners' gave Breton the opportunity to combine a scene set in his native Courrières with a new law affecting the rights of gleaners which was passed in 1854. His pictures were, nonetheless, immensely popular because he tempered realism with a touch of romanticism.

Another dimension to narrative painting is when governments or other authorities commission artists to record events of national importance. William Orpen and John

Lavery are two Irish painters who were 'official war artists' commissioned by the British government to make records of aspects of World War I. Seán Keating was commissioned by the Irish government in 1926 to record the development of the hydro-electric scheme at Ardnacrusha on the river Shannon, the largest engineering project undertaken in the early history of the state. Narrative paintings are popular, and will continue to be so as long as they reflect the realm of human experience in a dramatic and entertaining manner.

The Gleaners, Courrières
by Jules Breton

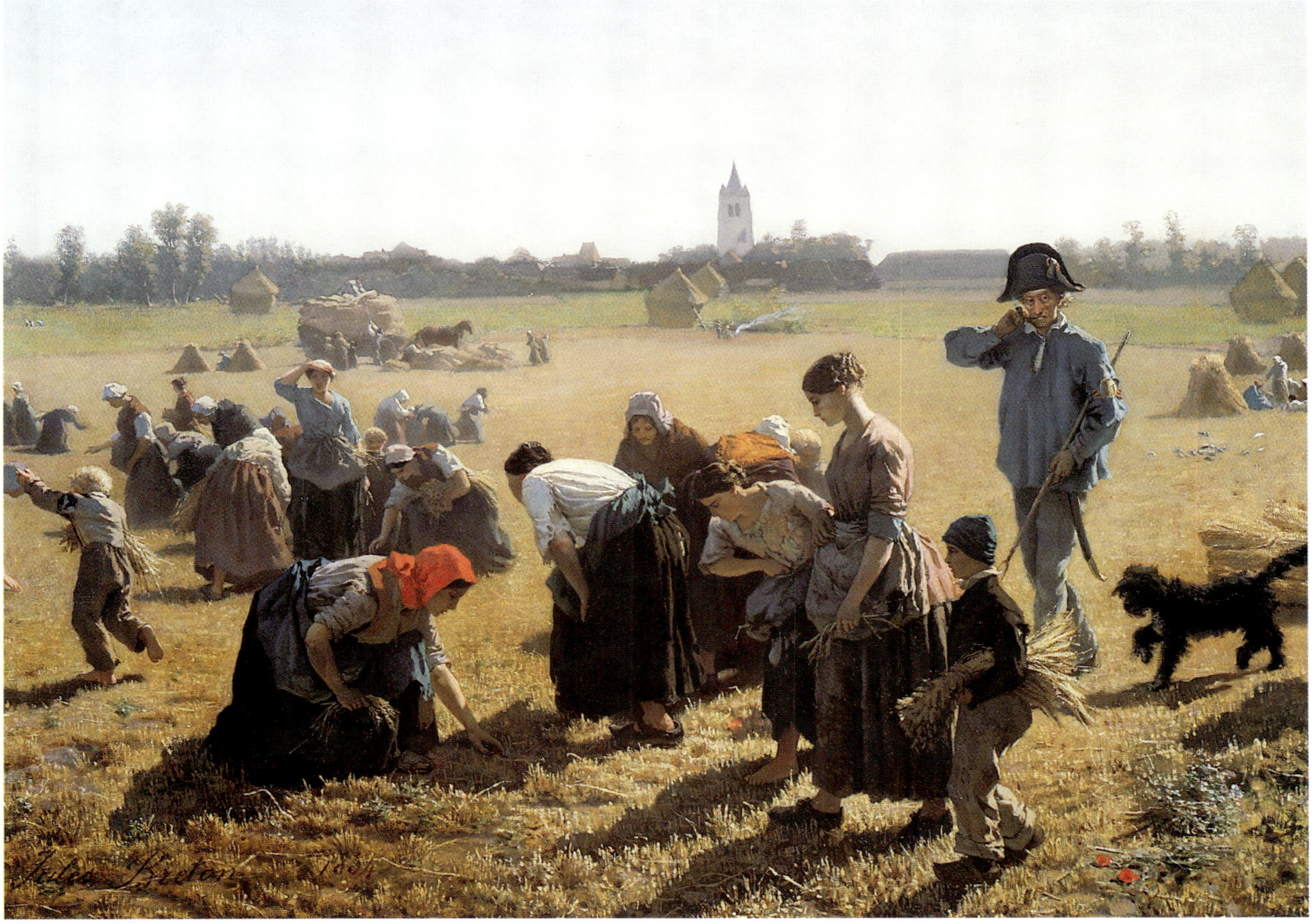

According to one version of the ancient legend of St George and the Dragon, a terrifying dragon, which fed only on human flesh, demanded a regular supply of victims. When it was the turn of the king's daughter to be sacrificed, Saint George came riding to the rescue. There is, however, another dimension to the ancient legend; to the early Christians the dragon symbolised evil, particularly paganism, and the slaying of the dragon represented the victory of the Christian faith over pagan invaders. In this panel the dragon has a pool as his home instead of a cave. The dragon emerges from it to defend himself from the saint, who plunges a spear down its throat. A linear composition, it is defined by clean lines and striking red and white colours.

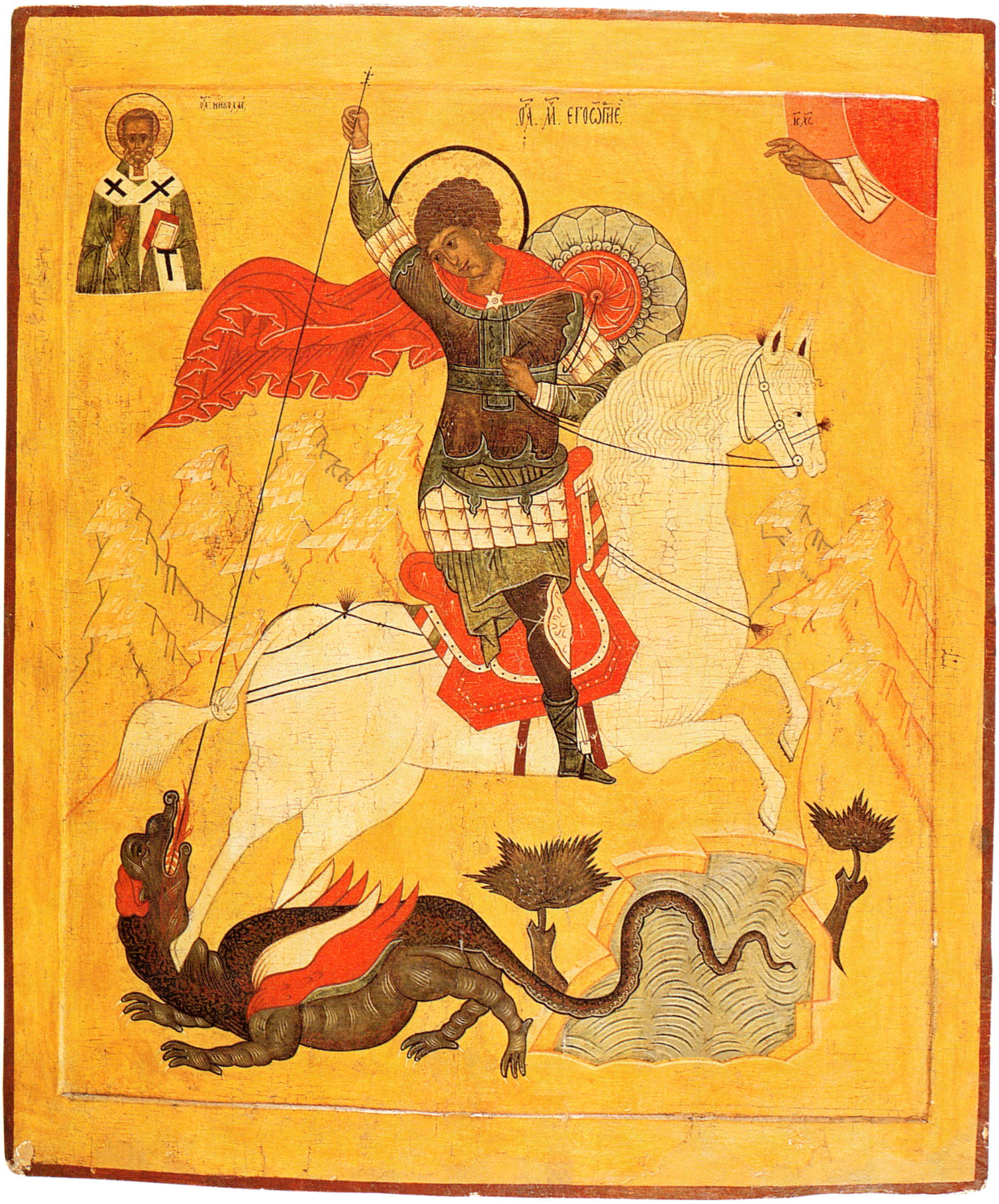

In this icon, the hand of the Saviour blesses Saint George from above (left side), while on the right side Saint Nicholas attends him. Saint George was widely venerated in Northern Russia, and as one of their best loved saints, his image would have hung in churches, chapels and even private houses.

The Miracle of St George and the Dragon
Novgorod School
Early fifteenth century

An icon, which comes from the Greek work *ekion*, meaning 'image', was believed to be sacred in itself. The term icon was used to describe images of Christ, the Virgin and the saints, which were traditionally painted in tempera on wood. Icon artists, who followed strict guidelines in the depiction of religious imagery, treated their subjects with reverence and rarely signed their work.

Fra Angelico was a Dominican monk whose life was devoted to creating holy images. While much of his work refers back to Giotto, his concern for spatial perspective was one of the main preoccupations of contemporary artists in Renaissance Florence. He used the new visual techniques of the Renaissance to serve the devotional purpose of his painting. Cosimo de' Medici commissioned Fra Angelico to paint the story of the legendary Florentine saints Cosmas and Damian, as part of a great altarpiece, to be displayed on the high altar of the church attached to the artist's Dominican convent of San Marco in Florence.

The early Christian martyrs Cosmas and Damian were patron saints of the de' Medici family; the surname Medici means medic or doctor, and Cosmas and Damian, as doctors, were the family saints. The story of the attempted martyrdom of the twin saints Cosmas and Damian and their three brothers was depicted as a series of episodes, painted by the artist as a predella panel forming the lower part of the altarpiece. Each panel is painted in tempera and is linked to the next panel by means of a gold Ionic column. The scene depicted here illustrates the attempted martyrdom by fire. The remaining six dismembered predella panels are distributed among museums in Munich, Paris and Washington.

The attempted martyrdom of Sts Cosmas and Damian with their brothers, 1438-40
Fra Angelico, Italian School
1387 Vicchio di Mugello – 1455 Rome

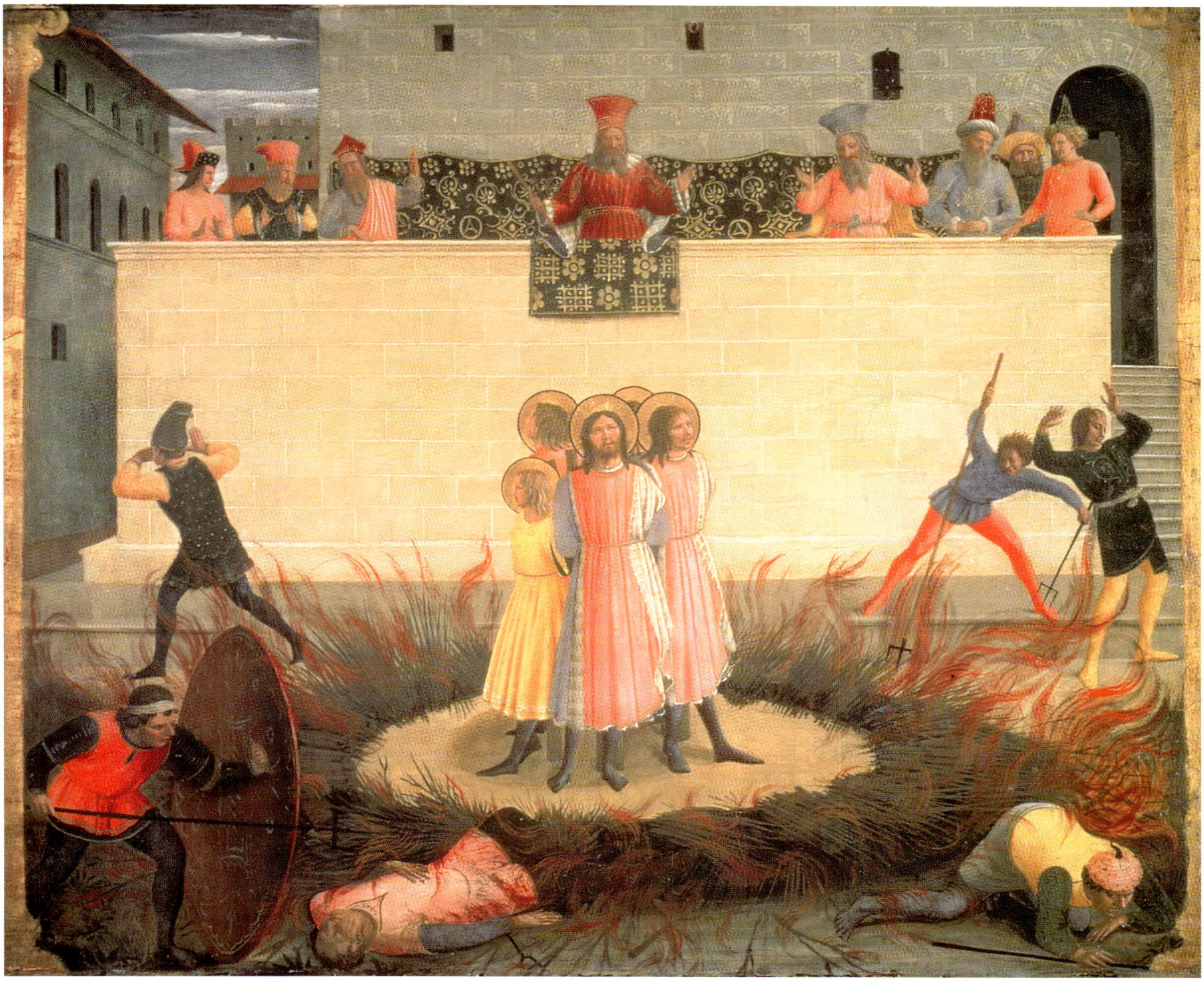

A good artist can breathe atmosphere and an air of mystery into a painting. There is a calm and enigmatic air about this picture, in which a lady busily writes a letter while her maid waits to one side. The scene shows a typical seventeenth-century Dutch interior, with *The Finding of Moses* hanging on the background wall. The Dutch were proud of their homes, their polished furniture, their well-swept tiles and tables covered with oriental rugs. This is described as a letter-writing scene on the theme of love. We can tell by the stillness and tranquillity of the painting that the lady is concentrating hard on her letter, so that not even the presence of her maid, who waits to make the delivery, can disturb the intimate scene.

Vermeer was one of the greatest masters of the Dutch Golden Age. One of only thirty-five existing paintings by the artist, this picture focuses on the subtle effects of light and shade. Building up details in minute meticulous brushstrokes, the artist finely grades the shadows on the wall, lights each fold in the lady's blouse and defines the pleats in the maid's skirt. He paints an everyday scene in a natural light and shows just how interesting and noble a subject it can be.

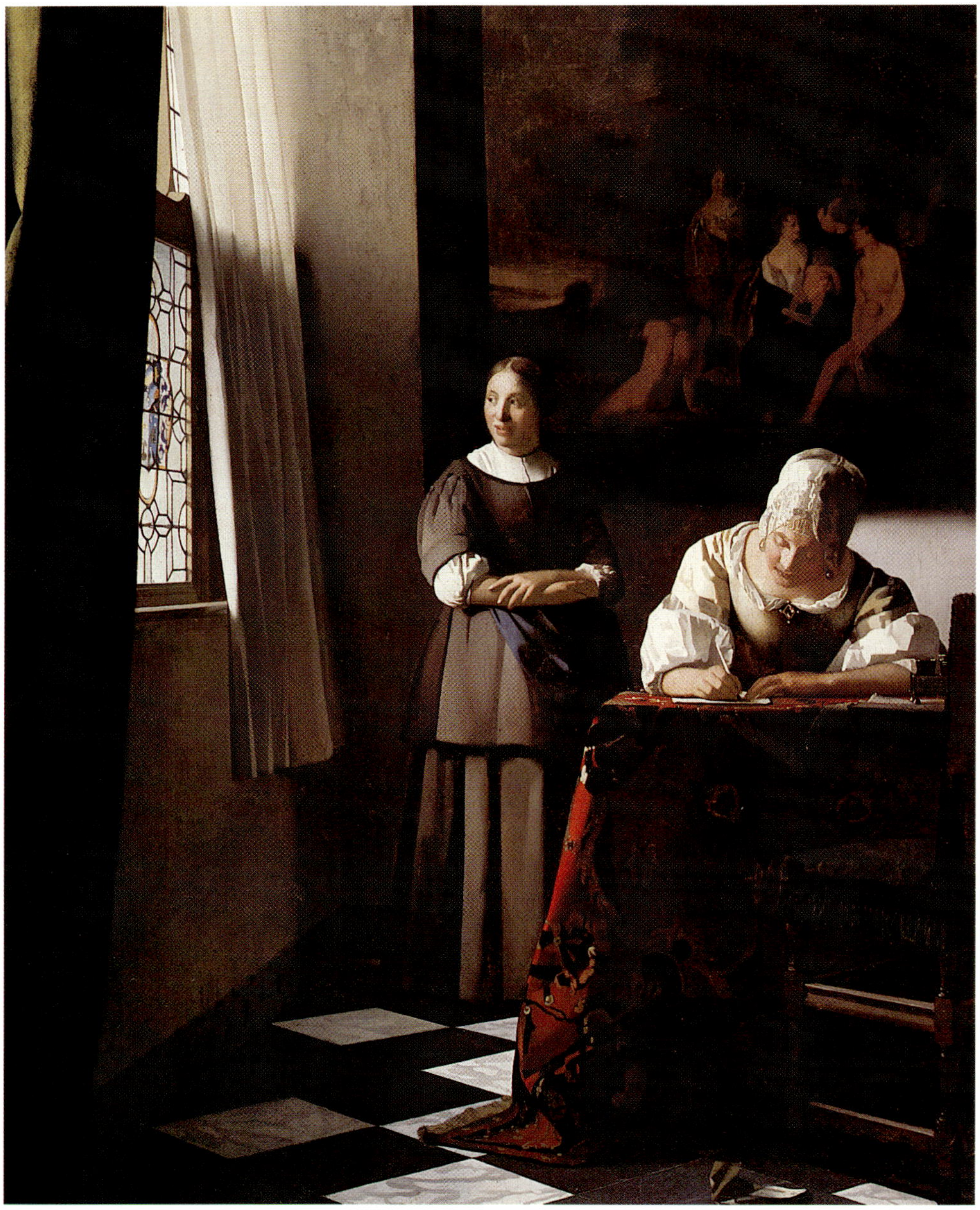

Lady Writing a Letter, with her Maid, *c* 1670
Johannes Vermeer,
Dutch School
1632 Delft – 1675 Delft

Some pictures give the impression that we are witnessing an actual event. This watercolour painting by Frederic Burton tells the story of a most extraordinary episode from a Danish ballad, which was translated and published in 1855. The story describes the ill-fated relationship between Hellelil and her bodyguard Hildebrand, the Prince of Engellend. Hellelil's father disapproved of the union and ordered his sons to kill the unwelcome suitor. Their tragic love results in the slaying of seven of Hellelil's brothers by Hildebrand and his own death at the hand of the youngest. It is a superb example of narrative painting, in which our sympathy lies with the doomed romantic couple.

Burton, a leading nineteenth-century watercolourist, was also an antiquary and art historian. It was his practice to carry out numerous preparatory studies before deciding to paint. In this case he chose the moment of the couple's poignant final meeting on the turret stairs. Regarded as Burton's masterpiece, it was one of the last major works the artist executed, before giving up painting to become director of the National Gallery, London.

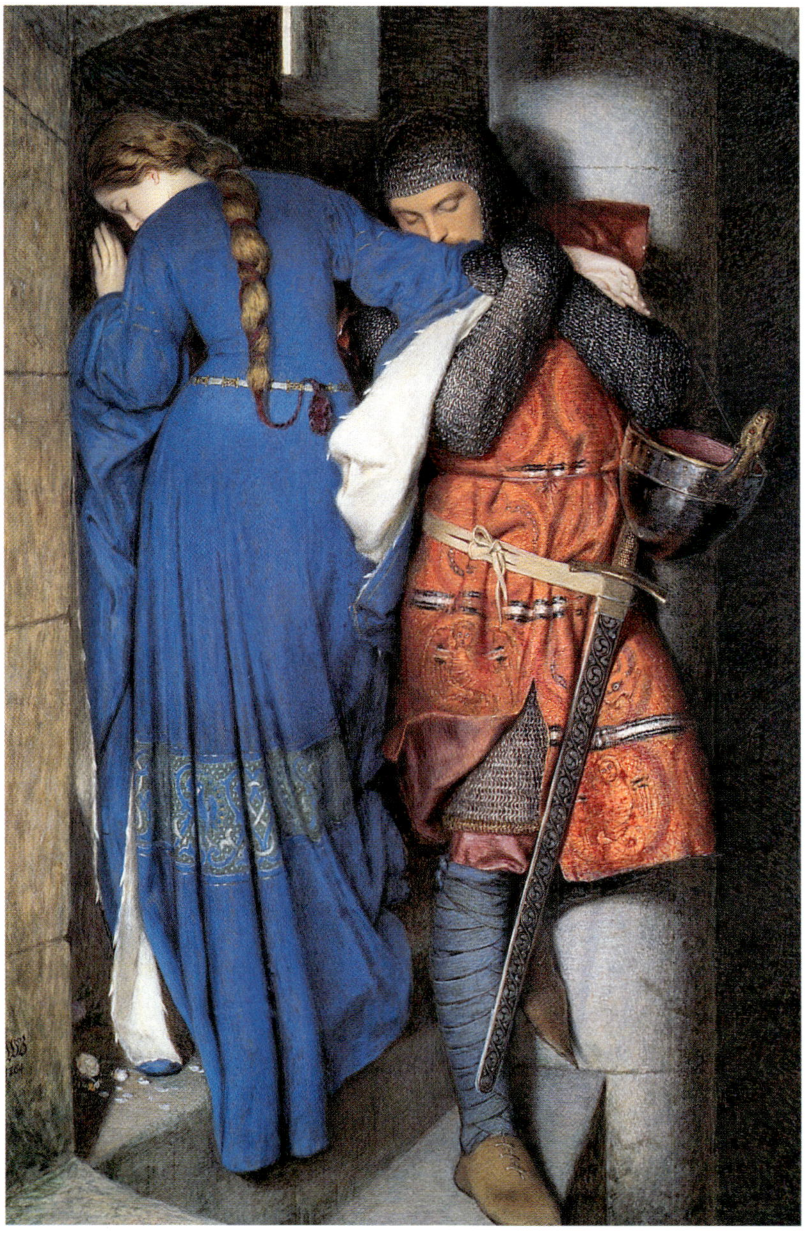

The Meeting on the Turret Stairs, 1864
Frederic William Burton
RHA, Irish School
1816 Corofin – 1900 London

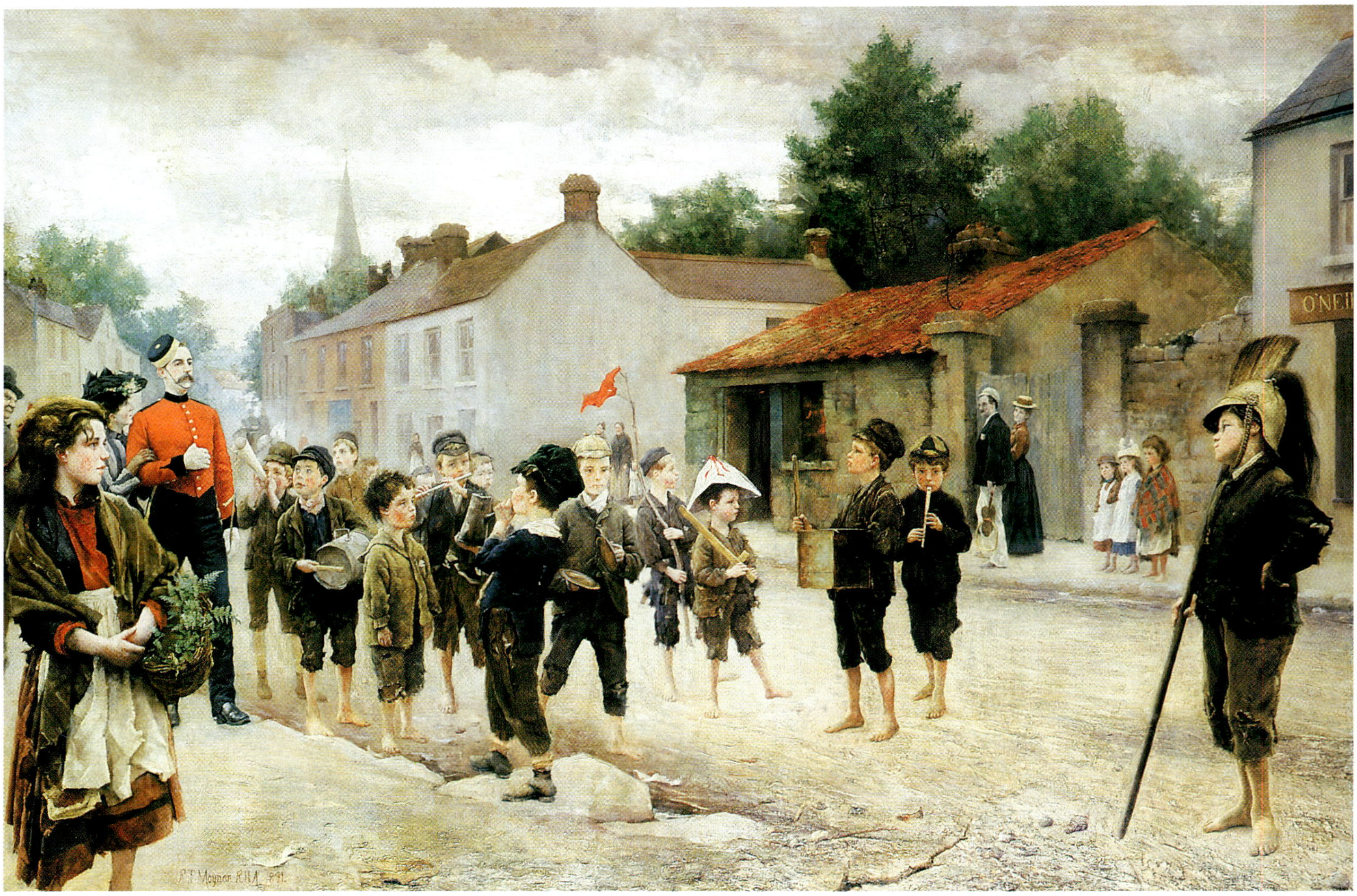

Looking at this picture we feel that we have stepped onto the street to hear the noisy cacophony of music being played. It is a humorous painting, for the manoeuvres referred to are those of the group of children who are pretending to be the regimental band, while a young trooper and his girlfriend walk by. It has all the ingredients of a good story, not simply because it describes events, but because it causes the viewer to try to work out what exactly is taking place.

Military Manoeuvres, 1891
Richard Thomas Moynan,
Irish School
1856 Dublin – 1906 Dublin

The scene takes place in the main street of Leixlip village in County Kildare. The soldier has been identified as a member of the Fourth Royal Irish Dragoon Guards, a regiment which was based in Ireland during the 1880s. He wears the walking-out uniform of the cavalry regiment, and is irritated to see that the leader of the children's group is wearing the regimental band helmet. His fashionably dressed girlfriend tries to make him see the joke. The children provide an extraordinary mixture of shapes and sizes, all dressed in ragged clothes, with only two of them wearing boots. Their musical instruments comprise pots and pans, tin boxes, buckets and saucepan lids. Despite their poverty they are well able to amuse themselves. They tease the soldier, and much to his annoyance, everyone in the town stops to watch. The scene conveys all the excitement and mischief of an entertaining story.

If every picture tells a story, then what is going on in this picture? What colour is grief? Yeats knew what colour it was because he felt it. This was one of Yeats's last pictures, painted when he was in his eighties. He wanted to summarise all his feelings about the tragedy and horror of war in a large emotional canvas, which he called simply *Grief*. By the time he painted the picture in 1951, the artist had lived through two world wars, the Easter Rising, subsequent political turmoil and the emergence of the Irish state. After Cottie, his wife and closest companion, died in 1947, he sank into deep loneliness, and to ease his pain he completed a number of emotive pictures.

In many of his pictures Yeats drew on the memories of his boyhood in Sligo, and also on the mythological land of Tír na nÓg, where people could live together in peace and harmony. This picture is different because the artist only hints at what real-life people and objects the painting contains – we are left to figure it out for ourselves. It appears as though an aggressive leader is leading a troop of soldiers into battle on a beautiful white horse. He is surrounded by crimson red paint, which spills across the soldiers onto the child in the foreground; the blood of war taints everyone. Our attention is drawn to this area of the picture because it is painted in thick brushstrokes of pure colour. To the right of the rider, a fair-haired woman can be seen gazing beyond the soldiers, lost in a world that foresees tragedy and death. Rows of large buildings loom in the background, many on fire and in ruins, revealing a passage of thick black paint interspersed with vibrant yellow, suggesting that out of war comes hope.

Grief, 1951
Jack B. Yeats, Irish School
1871 London – 1957 Dublin

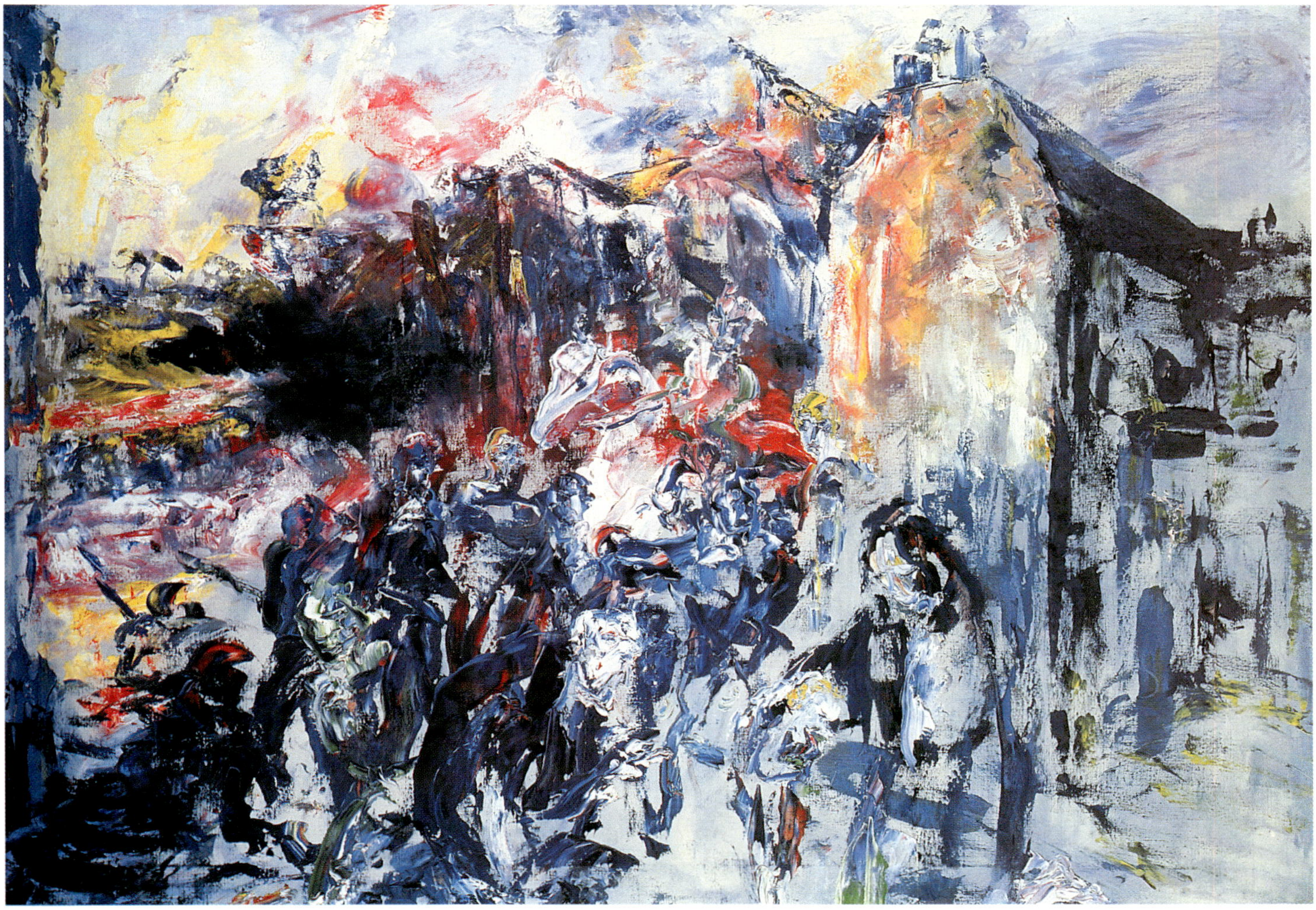

In the centre foreground an old man stoops low, bent with age and weary with pain, resigned to the inevitability of war. Does this figure represent the artist? Is he personifying himself as a lonely traveller in his long dark coat, with his back to the soldiers, turned towards the mother and child, as though pleading to spare the young and innocent?

In his late years the artist took pride in the name Yeats. He continued to be courteous, concerned and interested in life, and his simple, happy humour was everywhere evident. We see him project hope into the figure of the mother, in the foreground, who envelopes a small golden-haired child in a loving, protective gesture. This area of the canvas has been painted sparingly, as though to indicate that the future has yet to be drawn. Yeats's achievement in this picture is to use colour and vivid brushwork successfully to express the deepest feelings aroused by his emotions. So what colour is grief – black, blue, green, red, yellow or white?

Further interesting themes for practical art and design work: entertainment, magic, disaster, war, famine, horror, peace, happiness, memories, camouflage, antiquity, myths, the occult, chaos, festival, fire, outer space, inside the earth, dreams, toys, romance, mischief, dragons, giants, circus, carnival, the moon, the sun and the stars.

Practical Projects

1. Design a stage set based on a picture with a story

In *The Meeting on the Turret Stairs*, Burton captures the drama and suspense of Hellelil's final meeting with Prince Hildebrand. It has all the ingredients of a good story. The challenge you face is to design a number of sets for a play based on the story.

Spend time carefully researching the full story of the painting. Start by outlining the key acts scene by scene. Make notes about each scene, for instance, will a fresh backdrop be required on each occasion or can the same one be used several times? Will lighting effects be restricted to white or several colours? Will the scenery be rolled on and off the stage, or be lifted like a curtain? Will the costumes be designed to integrate with the play?

Draw some sketches of the individual sets, writing clear instructions for the producer in the margin. Complete the project by doing a three-dimensional colour version of all the stage sets using card or even board. You might be able to suggest costumes to complement the stage sets. This is a good project to help you to organise your thoughts about a story sequence. Keep all your notes, research and drawings.

2. Express yourself in paint

In *Grief* by Jack B. Yeats, the artist has used a lot of paint, executed with brushstrokes that seem to be full of feeling. How an artist paints a picture is often as important as what is being painted.

i) Try painting a face or a landscape in an expressive way. Prepare by having a selection of different-sized brushes to hand, and all your paints set out neatly. Use a paintbrush to sketch the outline of the landscape. Is it a scorching hot day or is it snowing and very cold? Are the trees bare as they would be in winter, or can flowers and leaves be seen everywhere? Feel the landscape – it is very hot; sense the vegetation – it is thick and luscious with abundant blossoms and fruit. Now paint how the landscape feels and looks to you, using hot colours, e.g. red, brown, orange and yellow. Have a cool drink when it's finished!

ii) Write down on paper as many different feelings as you can imagine, for instance, happy, sad, calm and angry. Choose a feeling or think of something you feel strongly about. Were you distraught at losing your dog? Was it wonderful to win the race? Were you sad and depressed when your grandmother died? How did it feel when you got the jeans you really wanted? Select colours to suit one of these moods. What colour is 'sad', and what shade is 'contentment'? Imagine how a brushstroke could be 'angry' or 'calm'. Paint a number of sketches or pictures without using pencils, markers or pastels, and without making the figures realistic. Just think about expressing feeling through line, brushstrokes and colour. It is not as easy as it looks. Afterwards compare the pictures.

Some useful reference books on practical approaches to art:

R. Clement, *Art Teachers' Handbook*, Stanley Thomas Publishers, 1993

J. FitzMaurice Mills, *Art for Our Children*, Wolfhound Press, 1991

R. Gilbert, *Living with Art*, McGraw-Hill Inc. New York, 1995

J. Hobbs & R. Duncan, *The Arts In Civilisation*, Bloomsbury Books, London, 1992

C. Holahan and M. Roche, *Art Craft and Design*, Gill and Macmillan Ltd, 1993

S. McArthur, *Journey into Art*, Art Institute of Chicago, 1994

J. Richardson, *Looking At Pictures*, A & C Black Ltd, London, 1997

H. Williams and A. Peppin, *Looking at Art*, Merlion Publishing Ltd, 1992

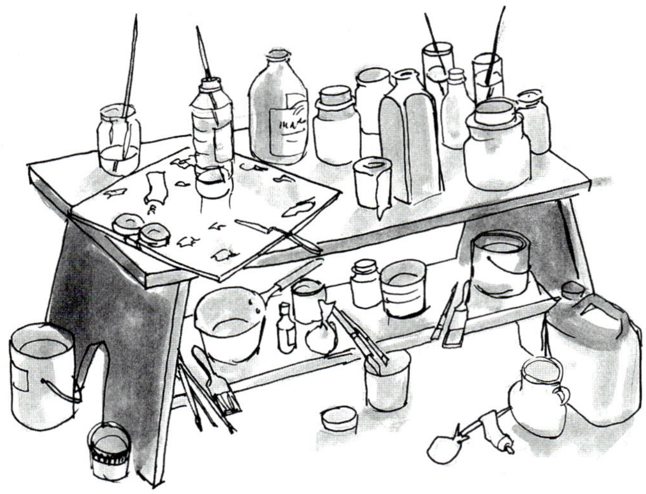

6

Art Styles and Periods

The classical world of Greece and Rome

The classical world of Greece is rooted in the fifth and sixth centuries BC. Under the leadership of the Athenian Pericles (*c*495-429 BC), Greek art, music, literature, architecture and sculpture reached new heights. Typical Greek pottery, which used black figures on terracotta or terracotta against a black background, illustrated myths and legends. Early Greek sculptors included Phidias and Praxiteles, and the painters Polygnotus and Apelles. Roman art borrowed from and was imitative of Greek culture. Under Augustus (27BC-AD14), Roman civilisation reached its peak, producing fresco painting, architecture and sculpture, and famous literary figures including Virgil, Horace, Ovid and Livy, until it ended in the fifth century with the fall of the Roman Empire.

Byzantine art

This style of art had its origins in the fourth and fifth centuries in Byzantium (the capital of the Eastern Roman Empire), and spread to Italy, throughout the Balkans, and to Russia, where it survived for many centuries. Byzantine artists produced wall paintings, illuminated manuscripts, panel paintings and mosaics. Mosaics embody the finest features of Byzantine art, with their gold and brilliant shining colours, while the illuminated manuscripts and panel paintings reflect heavy stylisation, strong linear emphasis and a powerful religious nature. Byzantine art was a very important influence on thirteenth- and fourteenth-century Italian painters.

Romanesque

Western European architecture of the ninth to the twelfth centuries derived from Roman precedents. It was marked by rounded arches, the barrel vault and heavy supporting thick stone walls and columns. Medieval artists worked in a variety of forms, including painting large murals in churches, decorating books, jewellery and metalwork and illuminating manuscripts.

Gothic art

Gothic is a general term used to describe the style in painting, sculpture and architecture that dominated European art from the late twelfth century to the early Renaissance. The great Gothic church façades contained hundreds of beautifully sculpted figures, tracery (ornamental open-work) and profuse ornamentation. The churches made extensive use of stained glass as a decorative feature. Gothic art expressed the world of chivalry and courtly love in panel and wall painting, stained glass and tapestry, miniature book illustration and enamelling.

Renaissance art

The Renaissance is usually described as the revival or rebirth of art and letters under the influence of classical models in the fifteenth and sixteenth centuries. It began in Italy with the rise of a spirit of humanism and a new appreciation of the classical past. In painting and sculpture this led to greater naturalism and interest in anatomy and perspective. The Renaissance was heralded by the work of the early-fourteenth-century painter Giotto in Florence, followed in the fifteenth century by a series of innovative artists: Masaccio in painting, Donatello in sculpture and Brunelleschi in architecture. Renaissance art peaked around 1500 with the careers of Leonardo da Vinci, Raphael, Michelangelo, Giorgione and Titian. In northern Europe the Renaissance spirit was apparent in paintings by the Van Eyck brothers in the early fifteenth century, and later Dürer brought many Renaissance ideals back to Germany from his travels in Italy.

Mannerism

The term comes from the Italian word *maniera*, coined by Vasari and used to describe a style in painting, sculpture and architecture which prevailed between the High Renaissance and the Baroque period. In mannerist painting, while the human figure predominates, it is set in strained, distorted and elongated poses. The compositions are complicated and asymmetrical, with huge differences in scale and colour. The pictures are harsh and vivid, designed to heighten the emotional effect, which can be unsettling. Mannerism is best exemplified in the paintings of Pontormo, Rosso, Bronzino and Parmigianino, as well as the masters Michelangelo, Tintoretto and El Greco, and the sculptor Giambologna.

Baroque

This style, which succeeded mannerism, dominated European art for most of the seventeenth century, and lasted well into the eighteenth century. Baroque art was characterised by extravagant decoration and ornament, asymmetry of design and great expressiveness, which when combined had a dramatic and emotional effect on the viewer. In painting, while Caravaggio was an early leading exponent, the Carracci family produced a more typical vision in great illusionistic ceiling paintings. The style is seen at its purest in the so-called 'High baroque' largely confined to Rome. Its master was Bernini, who pushed to their fullest limits the use of painterly effects in sculpture in order to express profound religious emotion. Poussin and Claude Lorrain, French artists who lived and worked in Rome, developed the classical and intellectual aspects of the baroque. Rubens was the greatest northern baroque exponent.

Rococo

An eighteenth-century European style of art and architecture which tended towards lightness, elegance, delicacy and decorative charm. Rococo, which comes from the French word *rocaille*, meaning shell-work, is mainly a style of interior decoration based on soft colours, delicate 'S' curves and scroll-like forms. The paintings of the period by Watteau, Boucher and Fragonard demonstrate these same qualities. In the second half of the eighteenth century rococo gave way to neo-classicism.

Neo-classicism

A movement in art and architecture in Europe and North America about 1750-1850, which partly arose in reaction to the 'excesses' of the baroque and rococo styles, but also represented a revival of classical art. The excavation of the Roman cities of Pompeii and Herculaneum largely inspired it. For the first time, artists imitated antique art and understood what they were imitating both in style and subject matter. In France, Jacques-Louis David was the great exponent of neo-classicism.

Romanticism

Romanticism in art is a style that emphasises the imagination, emotions and creativity of the individual artist. The term is often used to characterise the culture of nineteenth-century Europe, in contrast with eighteenth-century classicism. The French painters Gericault and Delacroix are often cited as quintessential romantic artists, with Caspar David Friedrich in Germany and J. M. W. Turner in England. The romantic mood ranged from profound despair to dashing bravado.

Realism

A movement in mid-nineteenth-century European art which was a reaction against romantic and neo-classical idealisation, with an insistence on representing ordinary contemporary life as its core subject matter. Naturalism was an extension of the principles of realism. The painters Courbet and Daumier represent nineteenth-century realism in France; both chose to paint scenes from contemporary life while also using their art to expose injustice in society.

Impressionism

A relatively short-lived movement in painting that originated in France in the 1860s and dominated European and North American painting in the late nineteenth century. The impressionists wanted to depict real life, to paint straight from nature, and to capture the changing effects of light. The term was first used derogatively to describe Monet's painting ***Impression, Sunrise***, 1872. The impressionists included Renoir, Sisley, Degas, Pissarro, Manet and others. By the 1880s the movement had dispersed and a number of new styles emerged, called neo- and post-impressionism.

Neo-impressionism

In reality, neo-impressionism has little to do with impressionism. It was a movement in French painting in the 1880s, which was also known as pointillism or divisionism. It developed from contemporary theories of colour. Instead of mixing pigments on the palette, the artist applied pure colours in small dots (hence pointillism) side by side; seen from the right distance, the colour dots would unite and form a clear outline. Primarily associated with Seurat, it was also practised by Signac and Pissarro.

Post-impressionism

The term applies to a movement in painting that followed impressionism in the 1880s and 1890s, incorporating various styles. The English critic Roger Fry first used it in 1910 to describe the works of Cézanne, Van Gogh and Gauguin. Though differing greatly in style and intent, these artists sought to go beyond impressionism's concern with the ever-changing effects of light, and in so doing, return form and structure to painting. Van Gogh moved towards expressionism, Gauguin developed a symbolist use of colour, while Cézanne, perhaps the most radical of them all, sought to make 'something durable like the art of the museums'. These artists linked the nineteenth and twentieth centuries, providing a conduit connecting early modernism, fauvism, cubism and beyond.

Cubism

Cubism, though itself representational, is the early-twentieth-century parent of all abstract movements. Its founders, Georges Braque and Pablo Picasso, were admirers of Cézanne and were inspired by his attempt to create a structure on the surface of the canvas. About 1907-10 in France the cubists began to 'abstract' images from nature, gradually releasing themselves from the slavish imitation of reality. The style began with analytical cubism, an investigation of the components of figure or form, and gradually evolved into synthetic cubism, where the relation of the elements to the resulting composition was more important. While colour was restricted to neutrals in the early stage, it was fully used in the later phase. Cubism proclaimed that a work of art existed in its own right, rather than as a representation of the real world.

Expressionism

A style of painting that expresses and emphasises the artist's emotions. In particular it refers to a movement in early-twentieth-century art in Northern and Central Europe. Expressionists tended to distort or exaggerate natural appearances using strong bold colours in order to create a reflection of an inner world. Leading expressionist artists were Munch, Nolde, Ensor, Kokoschka, Rouault and Soutine. The Brücke and Blaue Reiter groups were associated with this movement, and the expressionist trend in German art continued after World War I.

7

Artistic Techniques

Tempera

Tempera paint, made by mixing natural colour pigments with egg yolk, is usually painted onto wooden panels. Panels were among the earliest type of painting supports and are made from either a single plank or several joined together. Nearly all types of wood have been used at one time or another as painting supports, for example, Italian Renaissance painters liked to use wood from poplar trees, whereas Northern European painters favoured oak. Before painting in tempera, the surface has to be specially prepared. First it is covered with glue, to prevent the paint from soaking into the wood, and then with several layers of liquid white plaster called 'gesso'. This gesso ground is often coated (sized) with a water-based glue called 'size', as a seal to prevent the surface absorbing the moisture out of the paint. If the wooden panels are not carefully prepared, the tempera paint will sink in and crack. Tempera is a fast-drying technique, so artists have to work rapidly. Paintings done in tempera, such as *Judith with the Head of Holofernes* by Andrea Mantegna (*c*1431-1506), retain their light and bright colour for hundreds of years. Like many of his Renaissance contemporaries, Mantegna was fascinated by the heritage of classical Rome and looked to antique sculpture for inspiration. This work is painted in 'grisaille', a technique which uses neutral tones to imitate the effects of stone, giving the impression that the image has been carved in stone similar to a Roman relief. Prior to the 1400s most pictures were painted in tempera, and some painters today still favour this medium, including Hilda van Stockum, a Dutch painter of Irish descent, Carey Clarke, past president of the Royal Hibernian Academy, and the American super-realist painter Andrew Wyeth.

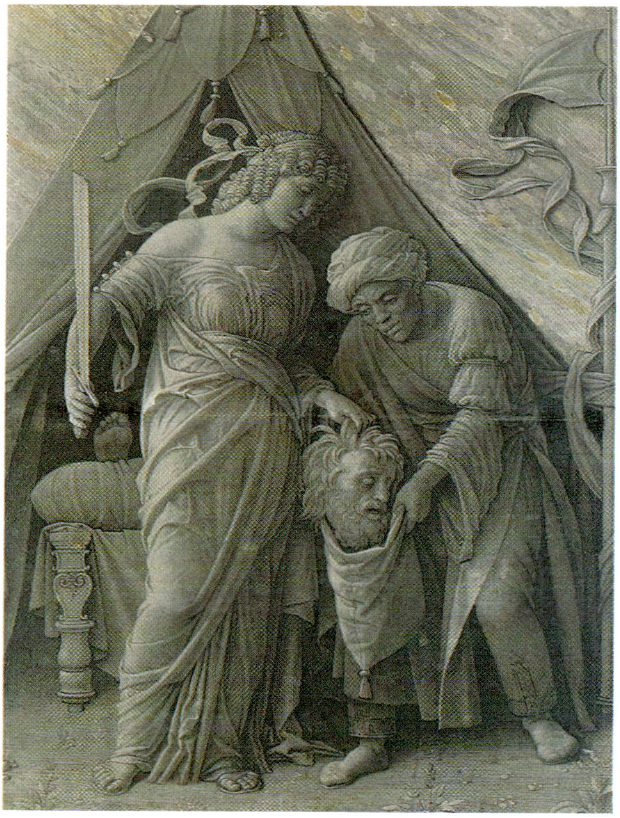

Judith with the Head of Holofernes, a painting in tempera by Andrea Mantegna

Mixing colour pigments with a medium such as linseed oil and turpentine makes oil paint. Linseed oil comes from the crushed seeds of the flax plant, the same plant from which linen cloth is made. Turpentine, used to thin the paint, comes from the sap of a pine tree. For thousands of years colours came from minerals, earths, and dyes made from plants and insects. Some of the pigments were cheap, while others like blue lapis lazuli were rare and expensive. The artist ground the raw material into powder and mixed it with egg yolk or oil to make paint. Since the late nineteenth century the artist's palette has been enhanced by the development of chemically produced pigments in watercolour, acrylics, oil and powder paint. This has made painting outdoors much simpler.

One of the advantages of oil paint is that it does not flake and crack as easily as tempera, and so it can be painted onto a wooden surface and also onto canvas, which is made from fabric. Canvas became a popular support during the fifteenth century because it was lighter than wood and could be rolled up and carried around. In order to make a picture, canvas is fastened over a wooden frame called a 'stretcher', which keeps it flat so that the artist can paint on it. Before the work can begin, the surface is primed with an undercoat of paint.

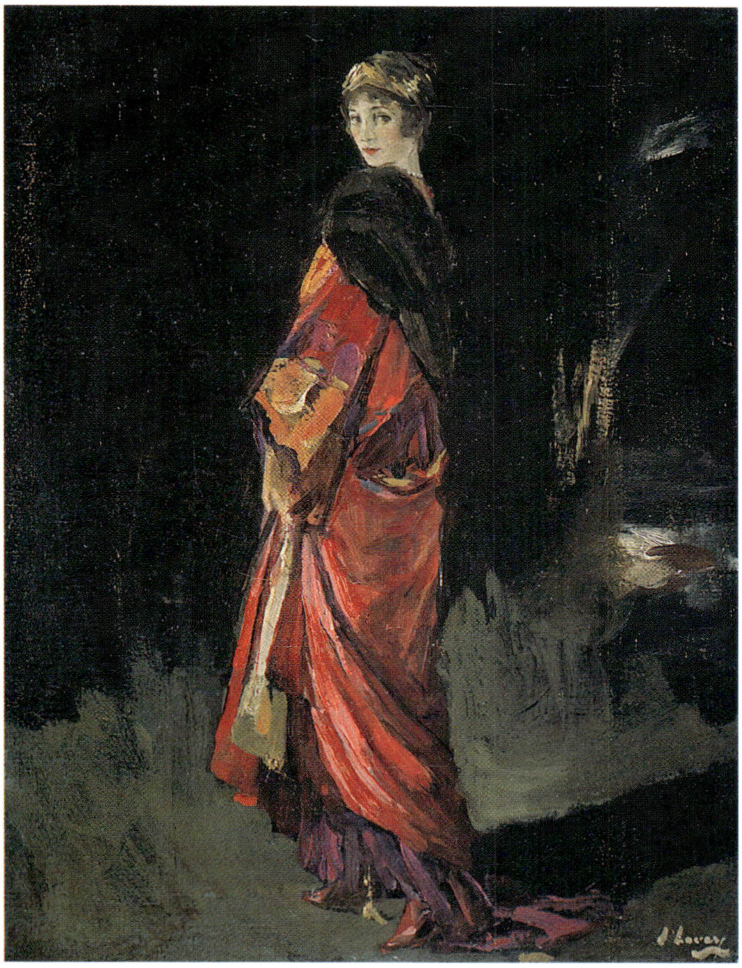

Hazel, Lady Lavery in an Evening Cloak, an oil painting by John Lavery

Hazel, Lady Lavery in an Evening Cloak is a fine example of an oil painting on canvas by the Belfast-born, internationally renowned artist, John Lavery (1856-1941).The subject is Hazel Trudeau, whom Lavery first met in 1904 when she was painting in Brittany. The couple were married in 1910. Hazel, the daughter of a Chicago industrialist, was a fashionable and inspiring woman. Lavery, obsessed by her beauty, painted her many times, most notably as the model for Cathleen Ní Houlihán on the first Irish banknotes, and she survives today as the watermark on Irish paper currency. The richly coloured rose and gold wrap makes a striking colour scheme when combined with purple.

For the Road, an oil painting by Jack B. Yeats

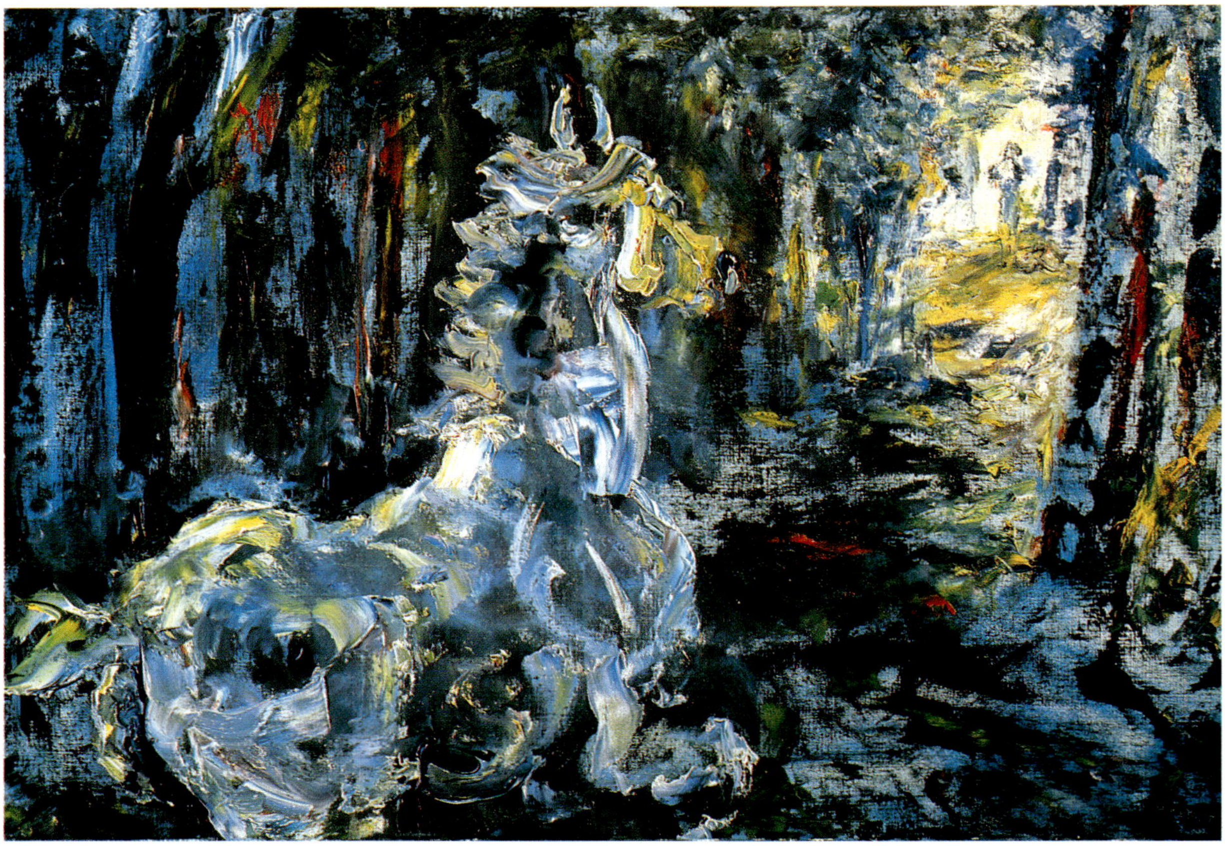

Because oil paint dries slowly, it is a flexible medium, meaning that colours can be carefully blended, layers of paint can be applied on top of other layers, and artists can rework or change areas of the painting many times. Another advantage of oil paint is that it can be applied thickly or as a very thin layer. A picture such as *For the Road*, 1951, by Jack B. Yeats (1871-1957) shows a thick application of paint, referred to as 'impasto'. Yeats included horses in many of his paintings. This late work depicts the understanding and affection that can exist between two living creatures as they set out upon their journey. Oil paint can also be diluted and applied in thin layers called 'glazes'. A masterful example of paint applied in glazes producing a luminous, glowing quality is *Lady Writing a Letter, with her Maid* by Johannes Vermeer (1632-75), (p66).

Although traditionally considered one of the most important methods of painting, it was not until the fifteenth century that the technique of oil painting was developed and refined in Northern Europe, reputedly by the Van Eyck brothers. By the beginning of the sixteenth century, oil painting had become the most widespread medium.

The training of fine artists in Ireland originated with the Dublin Society which was founded in 1731. The Dublin Society School of Landscape and Ornament was founded in 1756, the School of Architecture in 1764 and the School of Modelling in 1811. Teaching was carried out through the copying of plaster casts, original drawings and the best continental engravings available. The Dublin Society Schools were taken over by the Government in 1849 ceding to the Department of Science and Art in 1877, when they were renamed the Metropolitan School of Art, now the National College of Art and Design. The Royal Hibemian Academy (RHA) was founded in 1823, and took responsibility for the training of artists in life drawing, the antique and painting at the Academy schools in Dublin. Teaching at the Academy was very active until it declined towards the end of the last century, aided by the loss by fire of its premises at Lower Abbey Street. The RHA, which held its first exhibition in 1826, became the most important exhibiting venue in Ireland, holding an annual exhibition open to painters, sculptors and architects, which continues right down to this day.

In Belfast, a School of Design was established in 1850 which lasted five years. A new School of Art was opened in 1870, in accordance with the regulations of the Department of Science and Art, which this century became part of the University of Ulster. The first exhibiting society in Belfast was formed in 1879, called the Ramblers Sketching Club, which changed its name in 1890 to the Belfast Art Society. It continued in this form until 1930 when it was renamed the Ulster Academy of the Arts, and in 1951 it became known as the Royal Ulster Academy of the Arts. It holds an annual exhibition open to sculptors, architects and painters. Because of sustained pressure from the Belfast Art Society and the Ulster Art Club, the first public gallery in Belfast was set up in 1890. In 1928 it moved to Botanic Gardens, and with the Museums Act (Northern Ireland) of 1961, the Belfast Museum and Art Gallery was reconstituted as the Ulster Museum.

Portrait painting in miniature

Miniatures are very small paintings that can be held in the hand or worn on a chain as a precious keepsake. They derived from medieval manuscript illustration and Renaissance medals, and survived up to the nineteeth century until the evolution of photography. The main purpose of a portrait miniature, like a photograph, is to create a visual record of someone, usually a family member or a famous person.

The technique of miniature painting was carefully handed down from master to pupil. Miniatures can be painted on vellum (calf skin), on ivory, card and copper, using enamel, pastel, watercolour or oil paints, employing very fine brushes, mostly of squirrel hair. Only impeccable craftsmanship makes these tiny paintings possible. Miniatures painted in watercolour are delicate and can fade, whereas enamel miniatures are fired and are much more robust.

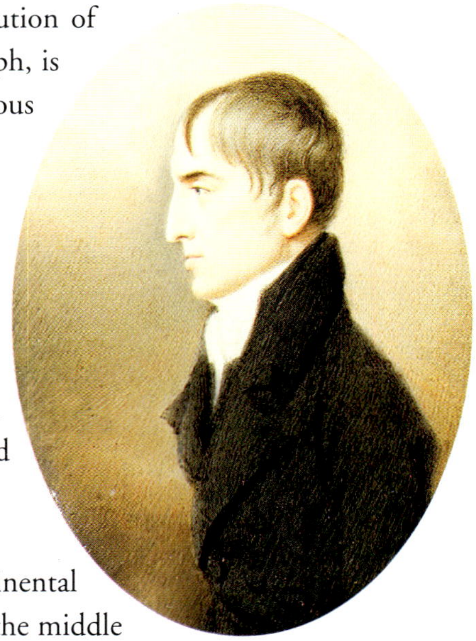

Robert Emmet, a portrait miniature by John Comerford

The National Gallery has an exceptional collection of Irish and continental miniatures. An Irish school of miniature portraiture came into being in the middle of the eighteenth century. The medium flourished in the late nineteenth century and included such notable practitioners as Nathaniel Hone the Elder and his son Horace, Adam and Frederick Buck and Samuel Lover. Traditionally, the primary function of the portrait miniaturist was to record, to give a visual image that could be preserved for historical reference. Were it not for artists like John Comerford (*c*1770-1832), we would have no idea what people from the past, like Robert Emmet (1778-1803), looked like. In 1803 Emmet organised an uprising in Dublin. Comerford portrays Emmet in profile against a plain background, his fine meticulous brushwork trying to capture in miniature form the image of the patriot. Comerford, a Kilkenny-born artist, initially painted portraits in oils before devoting himself to a successful career painting miniatures.

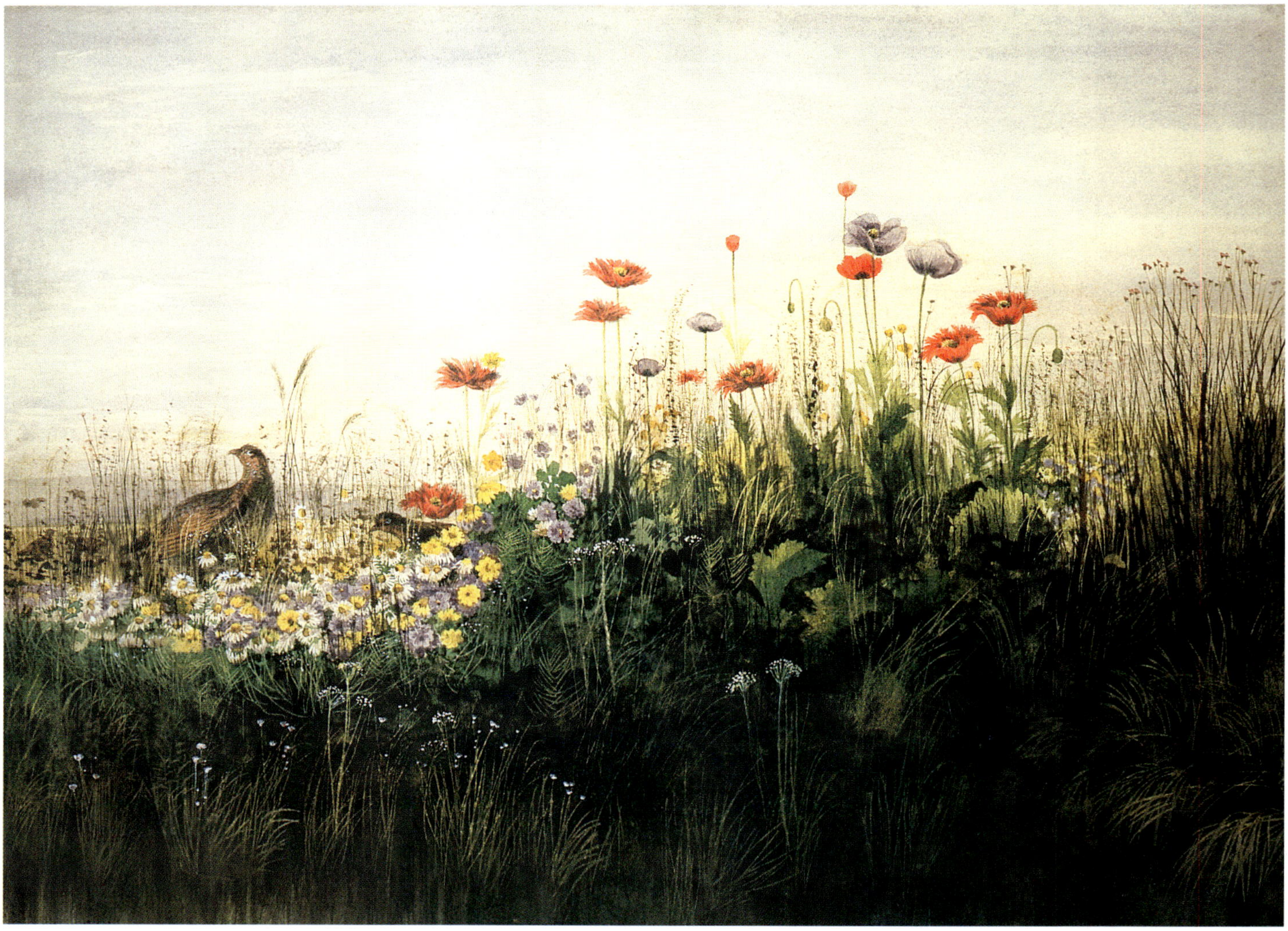

Pheasants in a Bank of Flowers, a watercolour by Andrew Nicholl

WATERCOLOUR

Watercolour is paint made up from coloured pigment suspended in a water-soluble medium such as gum, water being added as a dilutant to spread the colour. It is usually painted onto paper with a granular surface, which lets the colour sink in. Since the layers of colour placed on the surface are thin, this allows light to be reflected from the white paper background through the colour washes, to produce bright, fresh colour with a luminous effect – which is the characteristic feature of watercolour. Watercolour is a flexible medium capable of yielding different effects in the hands of different artists. *Pheasants in a Bank of Flowers* by the Belfast-born artist Andrew Nicholl (1804-86) is an example of a highly finished watercolour with gouache highlights. While Nicholl is best known as a topographical artist, he was also a talented painter of flowers and plants. Here the artist has employed precise, fine brushwork gradually to build up the shape and form of the plants and wild flowers, including daisies, marigolds, poppies and cow-parsley, almost obscuring the two pheasants. Nicholl lived for some time in Dublin, where he conceived many of his most attractive compositions including distant views seen through banks of wild flowers.

By mixing watercolour paint with lead white or Chinese white, the artist produces 'gouache' or 'bodycolour'. *Eucharistic Symbols*, a design for stained glass painted in gouache by Evie Hone (1894-1955), demonstrates how Hone has drawn from the watercolour technique to achieve the type of expression she wanted. The brushwork is loose and free, with details such as the wheat and grapes clearly outlined. Hone's style fully exploits the fluidity of watercolour. The discipline of Hone's early cubist training in Paris combined with the influence of early Italian painters and medieval stained glass, together with her understanding of medieval Irish sculpture, led her to produce some of the finest Irish stained glass in the first half of the twentieth century.

Although watercolour was used in ancient Egypt and in Japan, it is the illuminated manuscripts of medieval Europe that appear to be the parent of modern watercolour painting. While the technique developed in Italy, it was the German painter Albrecht Dürer (1471-1528) who was one of the first artists to employ watercolour as a medium in its own right. During the eighteenth century in Holland, France and Switzerland the technique became more extensively used. It was in England in the eighteenth and nineteenth centuries, however, that practitioners such as Sandby, Cozens, Girtin, Cotman and Turner realised its full potential. Watercolours and drawings of the Irish School record the people and places of Ireland over almost three centuries.

Pastel

Pastel as a medium is a form of chalk, made from dry powder-coloured pigment mixed with gum arabic (a non-greasy glue) and used as a binder. It is very soft, offers a full range of colours and is made in the form of fragile sticks about a finger long. The softest pastels can give the impression of a painting, while the hardest pastels can give the effect of a drawing. One major drawback of this flexible medium is the ease with which it smudges and falls off the paper. Although pastels were first created in northern Italy in the sixteenth century, French artists did not perfect the technique, mainly used for portraiture, until the eighteenth century. The use of pastel was revived in the late nineteenth century in the work of Toulouse Lautrec. Pastel was a favourite medium of the French artist Edgar Degas (1837-1917). *Dancers in a Dressing Room*, a pastel executed on paper, with its

Eucharistic Symbols, a watercolour by Evie Hone

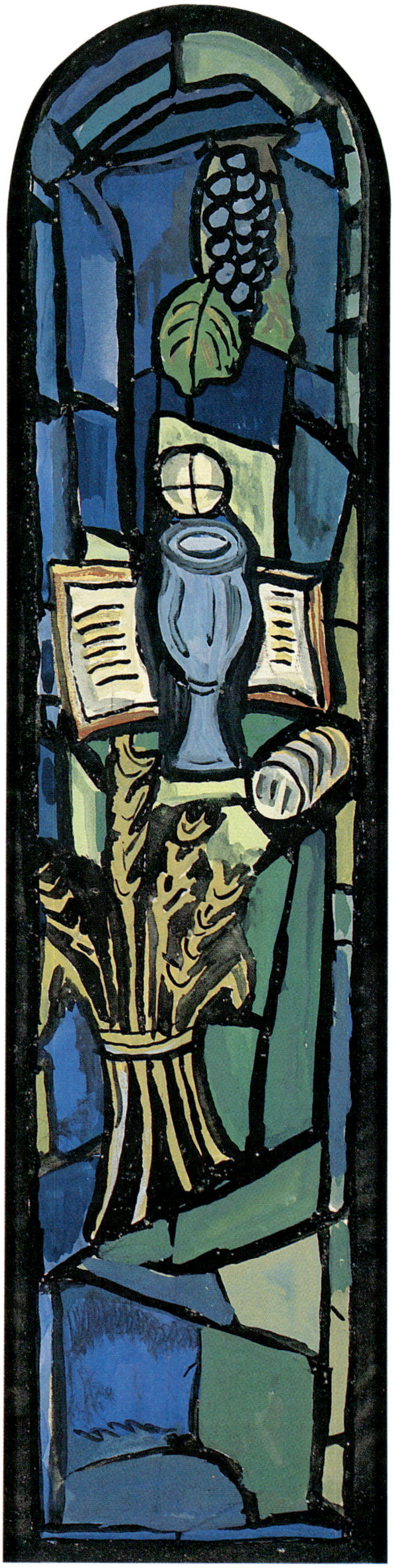

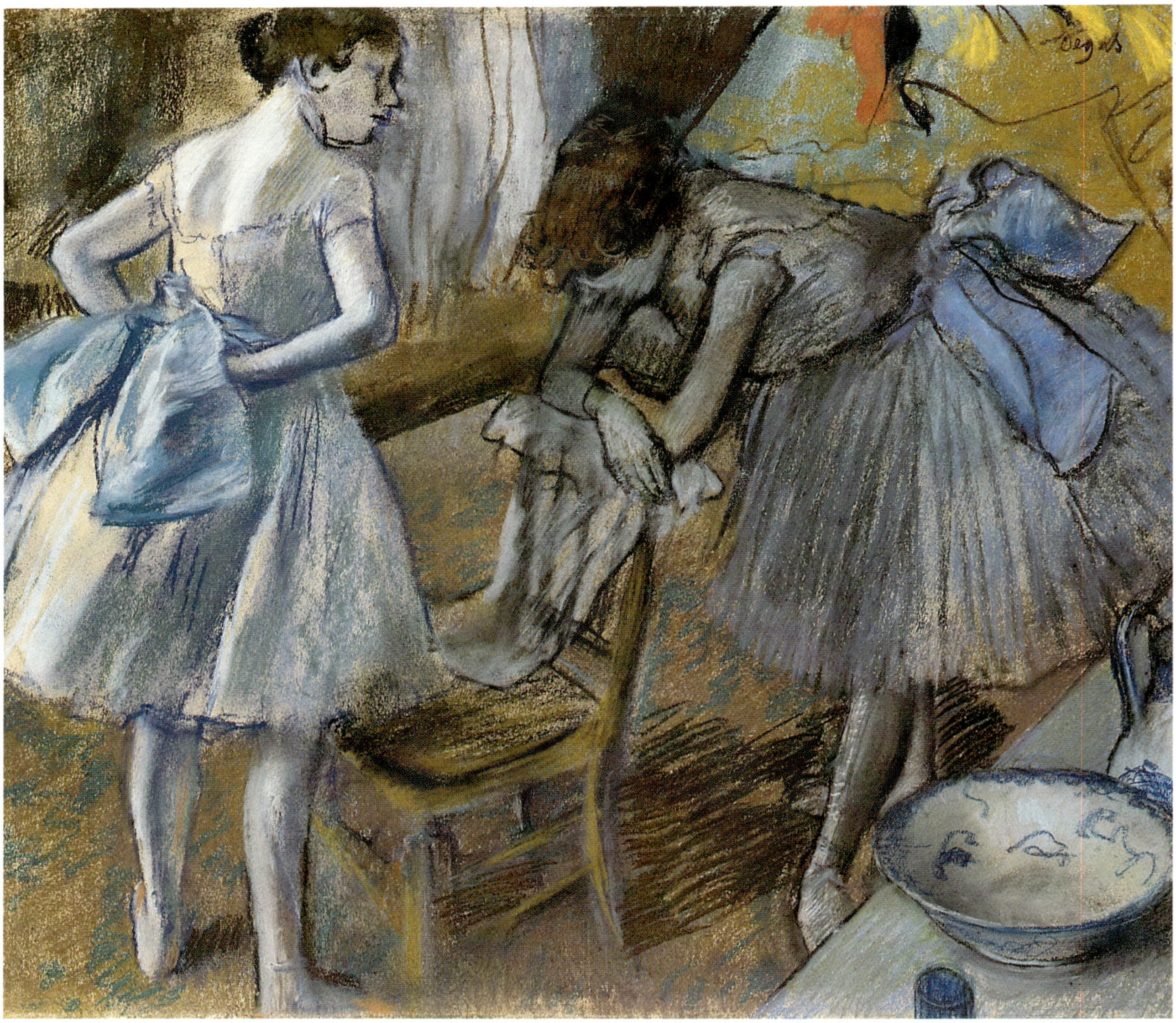

Dancers in a Dressing Room, a pastel by Edgar Degas

peculiar angular composition, reflects not just the influence of the new technique of photography on Degas, but also that of Japanese woodcut prints, then widely available in Paris. From the 1860s onwards Degas concentrated on a range of modern subjects, including ballet, café concerts, racecourses, women working and bathing. He was more interested in human figures than in the countryside, and in this he differed from his impressionist friends. Primarily a draughtsman, Degas made important technical experiments, particularly in pastel. Irish artists from the mid eighteenth century, such as Hugh Douglas Hamilton and Thomas Frye, were particularly gifted in their use of pastel.

Drawing

A drawing is by definition a mark made by hand, usually on paper. Some of the oldest artworks known are cave drawings from southern France and Spain. The Egyptians drew on papyrus, a paper-like material made from pressed plant stems, while the Irish scribes drew on parchment, made from treated calf skins. The Chinese drew on silk, their special material, and according to tradition it was the Chinese who invented paper in AD 105. The Muslims spread the knowledge of papermaking from the East through

Europe, and a page from the holy book of Islam, the Koran, shows how the Persians developed 'beautiful writing' or calligraphy into an art form.

Artists used drawing for a number of purposes. It was the first step in their training; traditionally in art schools drawing was the most important subject. Students started off by drawing copies of engravings of Old Master paintings. Then they progressed to sketching copies of Greek and Roman statues, and until they had mastered drawing they were not allowed paint. While drawing was also used for jotting down and recording ideas, one of the most important functions of a drawing was to create a work of art. All drawings are made to express the artist's own ideas, regardless of any other purpose they might serve, such as a preliminary sketch for a painting, a cartoon for stained glass, or a study for something specific like clouds, the folds of drapery or shadows on a wall. *Three Commedia dell' Arte Characters* 1955/6, by the twentieth-century Italian artist Gino Severini (1883-1966), is a good example of a drawing as a work of art in its own right. While the artist has used ink on paper to portray three musicians, the drawing is also a record, a form of self-expression, of the unique way Severini's imagination takes concrete shape. Charcoal is another drawing medium much favoured by artists because

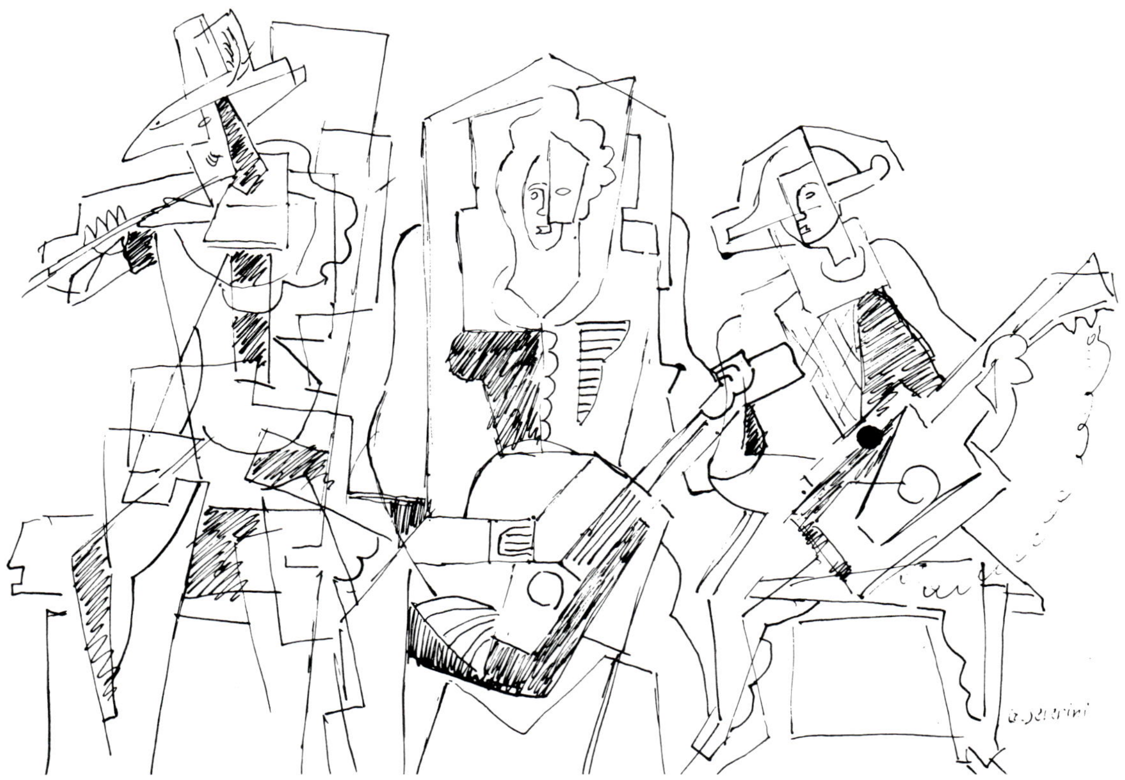

Three Commedia dell'Arte Characters, a drawing by Gino Severini

it lends itself to sensitive gradations of tone. *The Grand Canal Dock, Ringsend, Dublin* is not typical of Paul Henry's work in that it shows an industrial scene in Dublin. Henry (1876-1958), one of the most successful painters to come from Belfast, is best known for his west of Ireland landscapes. In this drawing he has rubbed the charcoal heavily to achieve darker tones and lightly for pale tones, thus exploiting the grain of the paper to good effect. The end result is a quiet, evocative and atmospheric drawing, showing the dock site replete with factory buildings, and the smoking tall chimneys, known as 'The Tramway Twins'.

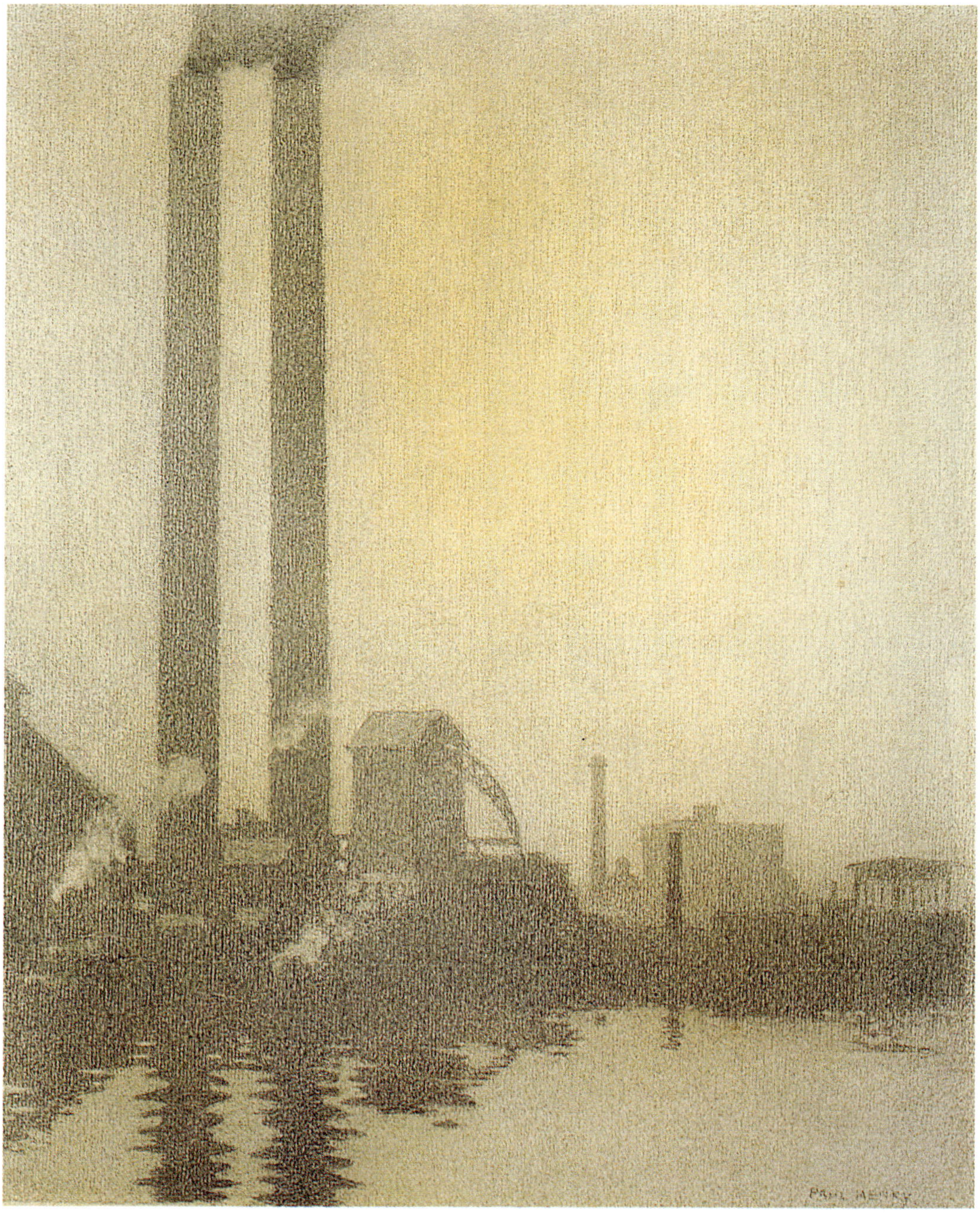

The Grand Canal Dock, Ringsend, Dublin
a charcoal drawing by Paul Henry

Irish artists first received their training at the Dublin Society Drawing Schools, which had in 1750 taken over the private drawing school of Robert West. The Society established a scheme of awarding premiums to artists. In 1740 the first Dublin Society premium was awarded to Susanna Drury for her watercolour perspectives (gouache on vellum) of the Giant's Causeway, a famous landmark on the coast of County Antrim. Pupils at the Dublin Society Schools were instructed in figure, ornamental and landscape drawing, and from this time until well into the nineteenth century most noteworthy Irish artists trained at the School. Also of influence was the annual exhibition of the Society of Artists, which took place from 1765 onwards. Nowadays artists have a dizzying array of materials to choose from when making drawings, including pencil, graphite, crayon, charcoal, chalk, pastel, pen and ink, brush and ink and felt-tipped markers.

Prints

An original print is the printed impression produced from a block, plate, stone or screen on which the artist who conceived the idea has worked. Because the artist has chosen to render the idea in 'print', it is possible to produce a number of identical images, each one an original work by the artist. Each image is called an 'impression' and the number of different impressions made is called an 'edition'. After the total number of prints in the edition has been 'pulled', the blocks, plates, stones or screens are destroyed or recycled so that no further impressions may be taken. One of the most important points about prints is that they give the artist another range of techniques for producing art, more ways of earning a living, and they bring works of art to a much wider audience. It is only a modern convention to limit an edition of prints, thus creating an increasing demand for the limited number and making them more desirable as an investment.

The finest and most prized prints are those produced in limited numbers. The basic technique of printmaking has been familiar to European artists for the last five hundred years and is thought to originate from methods used nearly fourteen hundred years ago in China. The Japanese brought the art to an extremely high standard in comparatively recent centuries. Printmaking was originally done by hand. It became popular in the centuries after the invention of the printing press, as woodblocks and lithographs became the basic form of illustration for books and newspapers. Wood engraving and lithography came into favour in the nineteenth century, being cheaper and faster methods. They allowed colour to be printed in, rather than hand-tinted later on to the print. The photographer, and more recently the computer, has overtaken the printmaker as the provider of popular images. Nowadays the printmaker has returned to the realm of the artist, producing limited numbers of original prints.

The following are some of the main printmaking methods:

a) Relief prints are most often printed from blocks of wood or pieces of lino. The non-printing areas must be cut away to leave the image in relief. The ink is applied using a pad or roller. The paper is laid on the block and the image is transferred either by using a press or by 'burnishing' (rubbing) the back of the paper with a 'baren' or wooden spoon. The terms woodcut, wood engraving, linocut and relief etching describe different types of relief prints.

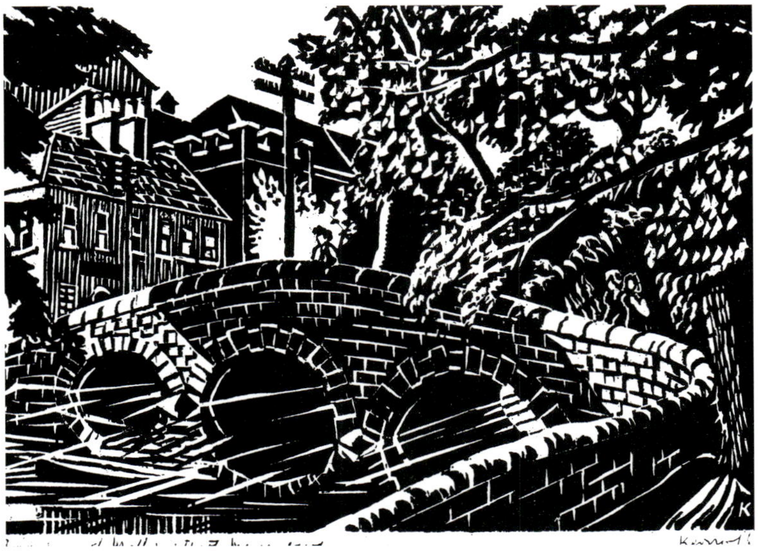

Bridge over the Mall, Westport, County Mayo, a woodcut print by Harry Kernoff

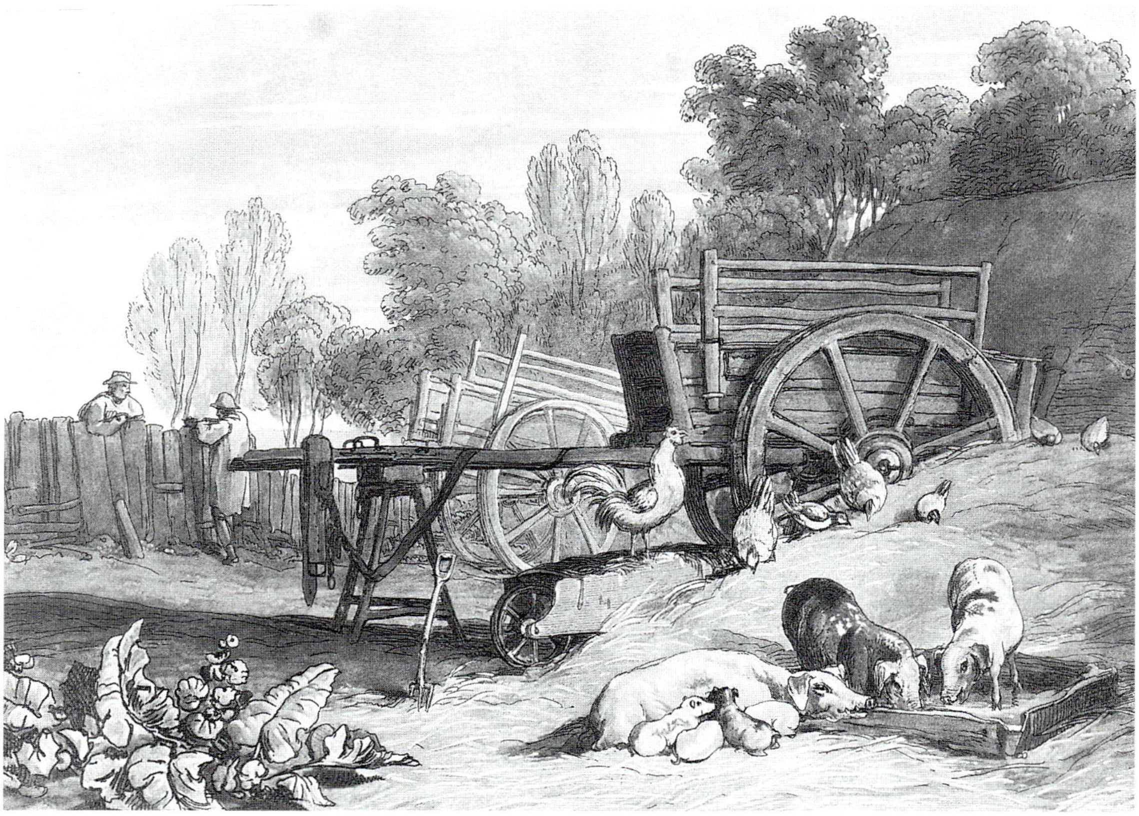

Farmyard with the Cock, an etching and mezzotint by Joseph Mallord William Turner

Woodcut is the earliest and most important of the relief printing methods, having been developed in the western world around 1400, when paper first became available. The woodcut reached a high point in the fifteenth and sixteenth centuries in Germany and Northern Europe, especially in the work of Albrecht Dürer. In the eighteenth century Japanese printmakers perfected the technique of full-colour woodcut printing, and two masters closely associated with this method are Hiroshige and Hokusai. During the late nineteenth century Japanese woodcuts were imported into Europe, where they had a strong influence on impressionist and post-impressionist artists. *Bridge over the Mall, Westport, Co. Mayo*, issued by Harry Kernoff (1900-74) in 1947, is an example by an Irish artist closely associated with woodcut printing. Kernoff lived in Dublin for most of his life, where he was associated with some of the best-known literary and theatrical figures, who appear in many of his paintings.

b) Intaglio prints. 'Intaglio' comes from the Italian word meaning to carve or incise. An etching is an example of an intaglio print. An etching is a print taken from a sheet of metal, usually copper or zinc, into which the image has been bitten with acid. In a line etching, the metal plate is first covered with an acid-resistant 'ground'. The artist draws the image through this ground, thus exposing the metal surface, and then immerses the plate in an acid bath. The acid etches away the unprotected metal, creating lines which will hold ink. The artist may use more complicated methods to create different effects, but always relies on the acid to etch the plate.

Intaglio printmaking began in the 1430s when it was realised that ink could be held in engraved lines in metal plates and could be transferred under pressure from plate to paper. Other kinds of intaglio prints are engravings, drypoints

The Phoenix Pillar, Phoenix Park, Dublin, a steel engraving by George Petrie

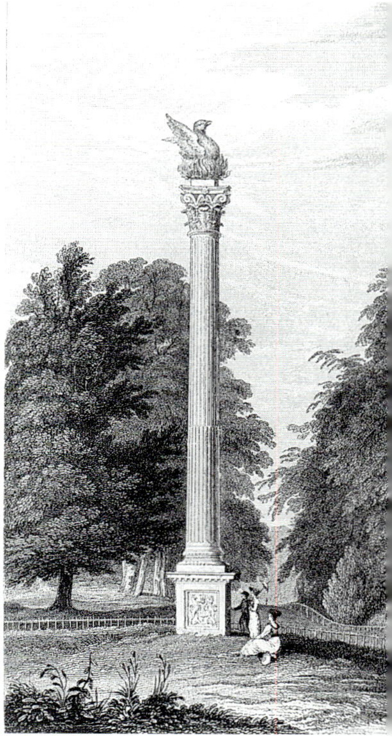

and mezzotints (here the plates are worked manually rather than with an acid). An intaglio print is printed on an etching press under tremendous pressure, so that the dampened paper is actually forced into the inked lines and textures of the plate.

Both Rembrandt and Goya were master etchers. *Farmyard with the Cock* by Joseph Mallord William Turner (1775-1851) is a superb example of a combined etching and mezzotint, published by Charles Turner in 1809 in London.

During the eighteenth century copies of well-known paintings became sought after, largely through the efforts of the English artist William Hogarth (1697-1764), who engraved and sold many copies of his paintings. This proved to be an effective means of circulating new ideas and developments in art to a wider audience. *The Phoenix Pillar, Phoenix Park, Dublin* is an example of a steel engraving by George Petrie (1790-1866), the nineteenth-century Irish topographical painter, which was published by Fisher & Co, London.

c) A lithograph (lithography means 'stone drawing') is printed from slabs of Bavarian limestone, or more recently from zinc or aluminium plates. The artist draws or paints

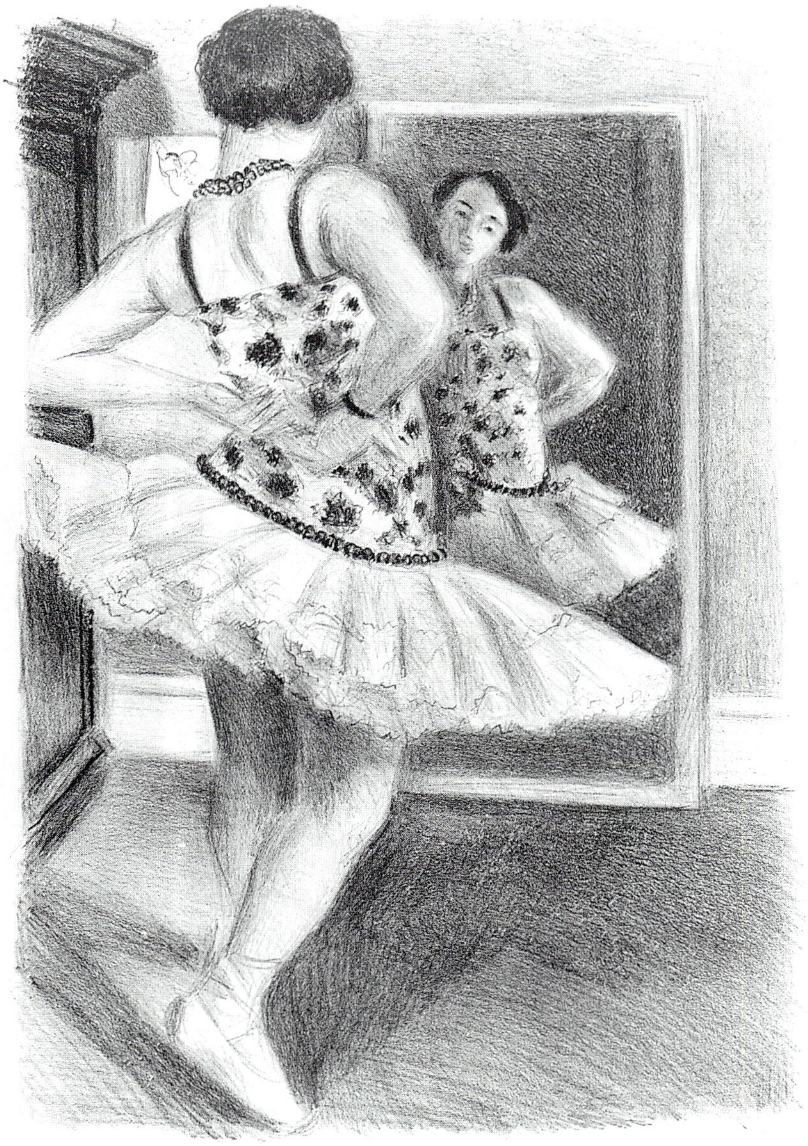

Ballet Dancer reflected in the Mirror, a lithograph by Henri Matisse

the image on the stone using a greasy crayon or ink. Then the stone is chemically treated to fix the image. In the printing of a lithograph, the stone is dampened and ink is rolled over it; the greasy areas of the image attract the ink, while the damp areas of the stone repel it. The paper is laid on the stone by means of a lithographic press, thus transferring the image to the paper.

While lithography is particularly identified with the work of Toulouse Lautrec and Edvard Munch, the National Gallery possesses *Ballet Dancer reflected in the Mirror*, a wonderful lithograph issued in 1927* by Henri Matisse (1896-1954), another twentieth-century master.

d) Screenprinting is often described as a type of stencil printmaking. Screenprints, also known as serigraphs or silkscreen prints, are printed using a screen made from a very fine fabric, originally silk, stretched over a frame; the non-printing areas are sealed with a filter or a stencil; the open areas of the mesh will print the image. The paper is placed beneath the frame and the ink is pulled along the screen with a rubber blade or 'squeegee'. The ink, passing through the open mesh of the screen, is deposited onto the paper below. Andy Warhol was a very successful screenprinter.

Some of the most prized prints in the National Gallery of Ireland are the eighteenth-century portraits which portray well-known figures of the time, including Oliver Goldsmith by G. F. Marchi, James FitzGerald, the Twentieth Earl of Kildare by James McArdell, and Frederic Prince of Wales by Thomas Frye. Other valued prints include the collection 'Views in the South of Ireland', an example of which is *The Entrance to Waterford Harbour*, issued in parts between 1795 and 1799 by Thomas Sautelle Roberts (1760-1826) in etching and aquatint.

The Entrance to Waterford Harbour, one of a series of superb prints by Thomas Sautelle Roberts

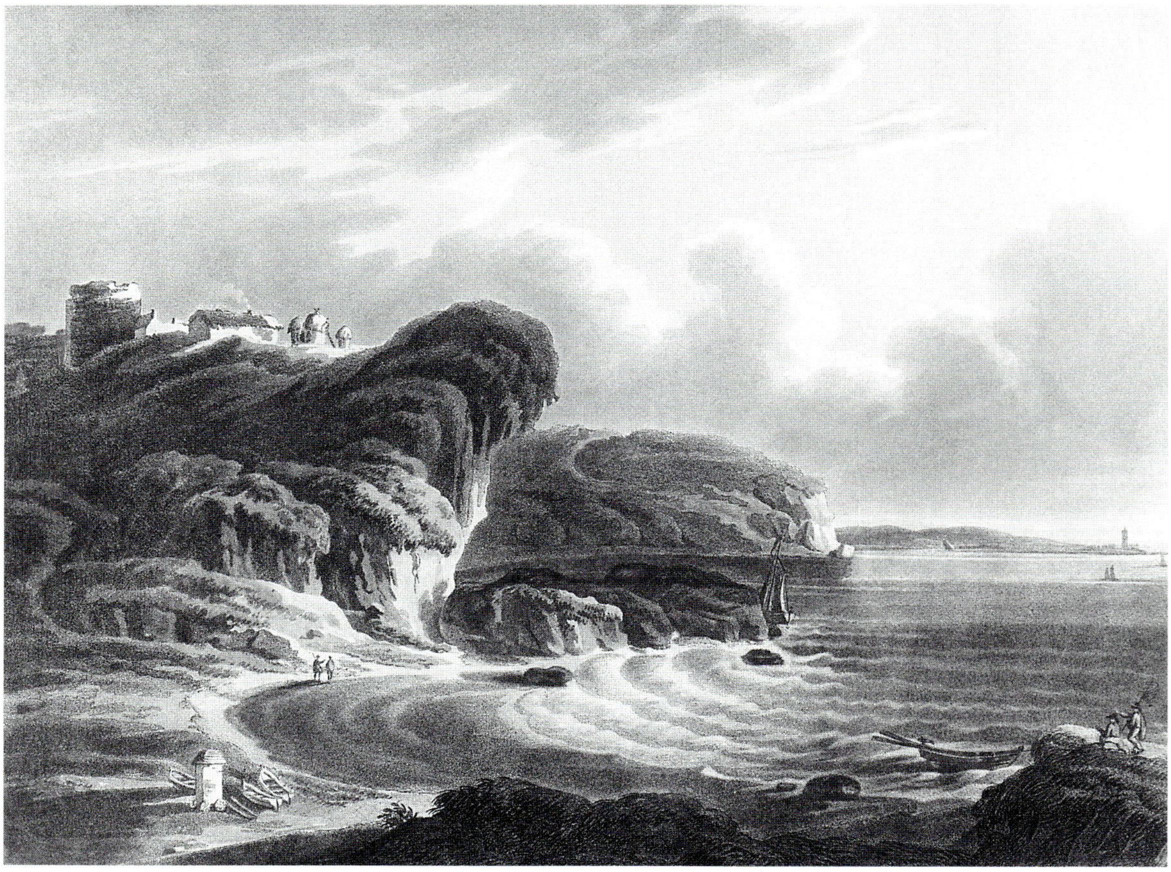

Frames

A frame is a border which helps to protect the picture and enhance its appearance. Originally borders served a protective or structural function, often around religious images that were set in large altarpieces. Frames are most frequently made of wood, but they can also be added in paint, in so-called *trompe-l'oeil* ('to deceive the eye'), at the edge of a canvas or around a fresco. Moulded plaster frames became popular in the nineteenth century and were usually gilded by applying thin leaves of gold to the frame. Panel paintings sometimes have frames made from the same piece of wood as the panel, carved to form an integral part of the work of art. Since about 1400, frames have been made separate from paintings and not many pictures keep the same frame all their life. Even a short stroll through the Gallery will show you how fashionable frames change from plain black to decorated gold, often popular during the same century. Whenever possible, the National Gallery tries to find frames to suit the size, style and age of the picture they are going to enhance.

Other information on artistic techniques may be found in the following books:

D. Carr, M. Leonard, *Looking at Paintings,* Getty Museum in association with British Museum Press, 1992

B. Gascoigne, *How to Identify Prints,* Thames and Hudson, 1986

P. Goldman, *Looking at Drawings,* British Museum Press, 1979

P. Goldman, *Prints, Drawings and Watercolours,* Getty Museum in association with British Museum Press, 1988

H. Kühn, *Conservation and Restoration of Works of Art and Antiquities,* Butterworths, 1986

G. Petherbridge, *Conservation of Library and Archival Materials and the Graphic Arts,* Butterworths, 1987

S. Smith, H. F. Ten Holt (eds.), *The Artist's Manual,* Macdonald Illustrated, 1990

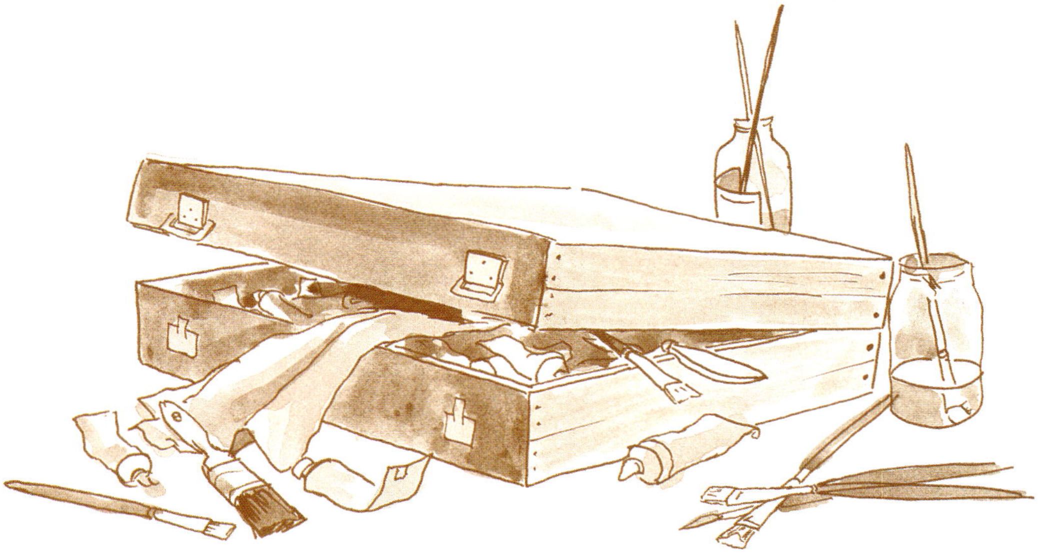

8

Create your own Museum and Exhibition

This chapter gives step-by-step instructions on how to make a classroom museum and how to mount an exhibition.

Creating a classroom museum

Students in school have a unique opportunity to combine their skills to create a classroom museum. In the process of making their own museum, students will be able to sharpen their research, data gathering, organisational and problem-solving skills, while experiencing the excitement of learning about the past through clues found close to home.

There are museums and galleries in most of the world's major towns and cities. Before the students set about creating their own classroom museum, you might suggest that they visit a local museum or historic site, paying particular attention to its content, layout and design. Encourage the students on their return to describe the museum, gallery or stately house they visited. Give them some time to think about and analyse the museum. Once all these matters have been discussed, the students will be ready to embark upon their project.

There are three elements involved in making a museum:

- selecting a subject
- collecting objects and information relating to the subject
- deciding how the objects will be arranged and displayed

The following steps should be followed by the students, under the teacher's guidance:

1. Choose a theme, such as 'The history of the school'.
2. Plan how to go about collecting the objects and information needed for the display. This is the most difficult task. It might be a good idea to form the young people into small groups and allocate a different activity to each group. The following are examples of the types of activities the students themselves might undertake in small groups:

- Set up interviews with past and present principals, the architect, board members, donors, past and present teachers and pupils.
- Visit local resource centres to gather information, e.g. the library, newspapers, a museum or gallery, town hall and planning office, the local heritage centre.

- Search out photographs of the school in its early years by contacting past pupils. Include building plans and architects' drawings.
- Advertise for other memorabilia: school reports, letters, textbooks, class projects, trophies, sports equipment and pictures.
- Hunt out old desks, chairs, blackboards, science equipment, sewing machines, maps, charts, etc to put in the museum.
- Consider seeking donations from past pupils and the local community.

3. Ask the principal for a spare room in which to house the museum.
4. Decide how the objects will be arranged and displayed on panels, tables and bookcases. Install and clearly label the exhibits, noting the name and date of the object, when it was acquired and why it is important.
5. Assign a number of students to list all the exhibits and to write a brief guide to the museum.
6. Appoint a team of students to look after publicity. This will involve making posters, typing up invitations for the official opening and writing a press release. They should advertise the posters locally, send out the invitations and contact the newspapers about the museum opening. Invite past and present pupils, teachers, parents and members of the local community to the opening reception.
7. Plan the opening day, requesting the principal to launch the museum. After the opening, have a party for all those who contributed to the project.
8. Organise the class on a rota basis so that there are students available to explain and interpret the museum and exhibits to visitors.

A further suggestion: The students might be interested in creating a local history museum. Local history is the history of a street, a neighbourhood, a city, a town, a village, a county, or even a large area such as a province, or a region such as The Midlands. Once everyone knows what a local history museum is, arrange to visit one so that the students can see for themselves how objects are displayed and interpreted for visitors.

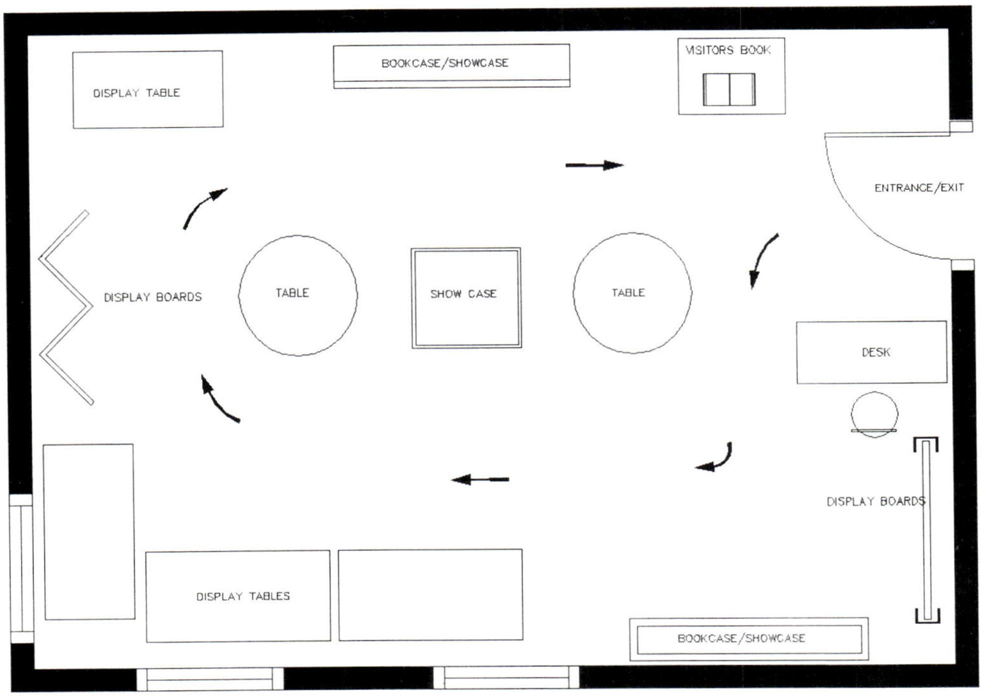

Classroom museum floor-plan (B. Drinan)

No matter where students live, or what type of community they come from, they can benefit from drawing on materials found in their own school, neighbourhood and local community to create their own exhibition. Besides gaining experience in research, hanging and mounting, writing and problem-solving, they will learn a great deal about their community, as well as the fundamentals of exhibition design.

You will need to allow plenty of time to plan the exhibition. You might suggest to the students that they visit different exhibitions, so that they can discuss details of the layout and display before they begin work on their own. Many museums and galleries mount special temporary exhibitions. To be suitable, the exhibition room must have public access, sufficient hanging space, good lighting, some form of control of the heating and humidity levels, and it must be safe and secure. The principal might book the local community hall and the students could paint the walls a neutral colour for the exhibition.

There are three key elements to an exhibition:

- selecting a theme
- acquiring objects and information relating to the theme
- deciding how the objects will be mounted and displayed

The following steps should be taken:

1. Try to select a popular subject like 'Wildlife'.
2. The students need a plan to help them go about securing works for the exhibition. Form them into small groups and assign each group a separate task. For example:

- Type up a notice outlining exhibition entry details: the name and address of the artist; the number and title of the sculptures, paintings or photographs being submitted (mounted and framed); the size and medium of the objects. Specify the entry date.
- Put notices advertising the exhibition in the library, town hall, shops, schools, church and community hall.
- Seek a local business, preferably one relevant to the subject, to finance the venture.
- Appoint a team of students to select the works to be exhibited, to plan the display, to install the exhibits, and to write and attach a label to each one. It is important that the labels are large enough to be read comfortably. Exhibits can be mounted on display board panels or set out on tables and bookcases. Decide if the pictures will be hung along the line of the top, middle or bottom of the frame, and make sure they are hung at a level that allows for easy viewing. Allocate appropriate space to each work of art. Check that the lighting is of sufficient strength for the display to be seen clearly, and that it does not cause any damage to the works of art.
- A student who is good at writing could look after the catalogue. Each entry should contain the artist's name, the name of the lender, the title of the work,

the measurements and medium, e.g. oil, watercolour, bronze or wood. The principal could write the introduction, thanking the sponsor and exhibitors, while the art teacher could write a few paragraphs on the theme. Nominate a student to photograph exhibits for the catalogue cover and for the press. The catalogue can be printed on the school computer, and the class can help with folding and stapling.

3. Display a check-list chart outlining dates and deadlines leading up to the opening.
4. Invite a prominent figure, perhaps the mayor or the sponsor, to open the exhibition.
5. Assign several students to look after the invitations and reception. Make sure the artists, business people, local community groups, teachers, parents and students all receive invitations.
6. Phone the newspapers and radio and television stations. Have catalogues, press releases and photographs ready so that the press can view the exhibition before the launch.
7. Work out a timetable so that each student takes a turn looking after the exhibits and selling catalogues. Assign one student to record the event on video for the school archives. Prior to the opening, have a party for everyone involved in the project.
8. To help create awareness of the exhibition, organise support activities, including talks for adults, tours of the display, and workshops for children.

A further suggestion: Devise an exhibition to show the transformation in Irish culture or Irish art, from the first millennium to the second millennium. Define what you mean by 'culture'. What significance will the exhibition have for the artists and the audience? Consider the type of materials to be gathered and discuss how they will be displayed and interpreted.

Exhibition Hall floor-plan (B. Drinan)

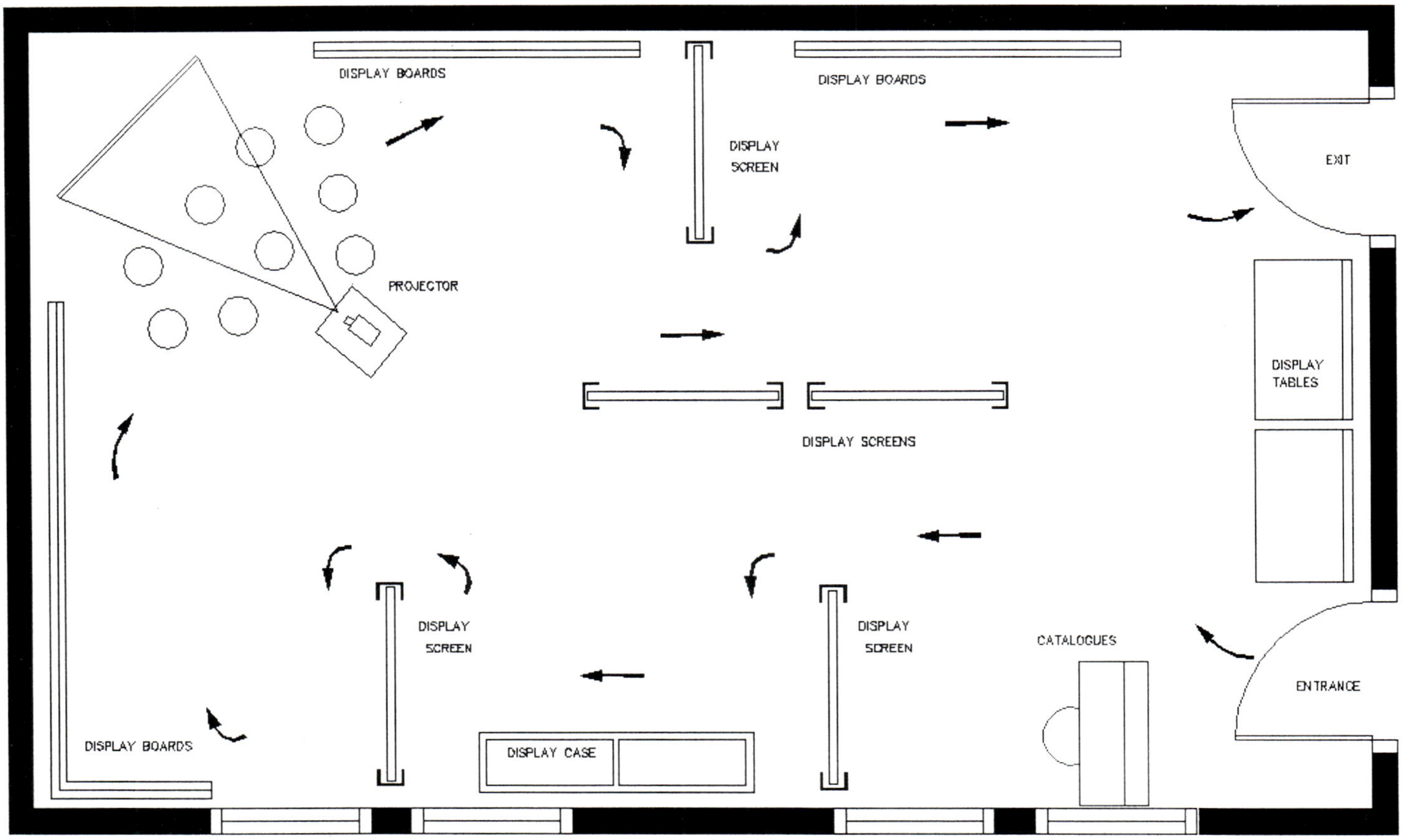

9

ART THROUGH THE CENTURIES

Fifteenth and sixteenth centuries

The Renaissance and mannerism

ITALY	
GIOTTO DI BONDONE	His work, which paved the way for the Renaissance, represented a breakthrough in the wa[y] it expressed human emotion with imagination and understanding.
DONATELLO	The most important fifteenth-century Florentine sculptor, whose work had a formative influence on Renaissance painting and sculpture.
FRA ANGELICO	A Dominican monk who decorated the convent of San Marco in Florence with a series of fifty religious frescoes.
PAOLO UCCELLO	A Florentine painter who had a particular interest in perspective and foreshortening.
MASACCIO	The first truly Renaissance artist who painted in a solid realistic style, using perspective.
PIERO DELLA FRANCESCA	A skilled mathematician who used perspective accurately in his paintings. His carefully composed works in pale, cool colours have a calm and timeless air.
GIOVANNI BELLINI	His remarkable use of colour, light and imaginative compositions made him an influentia[l] figure in fifteenth- and sixteenth-century Venice.
ANDREA MANTEGNA	A student of antiquity, his style was denoted by a decisive line, subdued colour and skille[d] use of perspective and foreshortening.
SANDRO BOTTICELLI	His extreme dependence on outline as a means of emotional expression is a summary of fifteenth-century Florentine trends. He became caught up in a religious revolution.
LEONARDO DA VINCI	A Universal Man who was an accomplished scientist, writer, inventor, engineer, architect and botanist, and one of the greatest Italian artists.
MICHELANGELO	A legendary figure who was equally gifted as a sculptor, painter, architect and poet. His emphasis on the nude human figure as a vehicle to express all the emotions a painter can depict, had enormous influence on Italian art.
RAPHAEL	He was the youngest of the High Renaissance masters and yet within ten years he had become their equal. His frescoes in the Vatican are one of the most supreme achievements of the High Renaissance.
TITIAN	A Venetian Renaissance figure with an international reputation. He was a great colourist who painted for the major courts of Europe.
AGNOLO BRONZINO	A master of the mannerist style, famed for his exaggerated poses, elegant portraits and flaw-less technique.

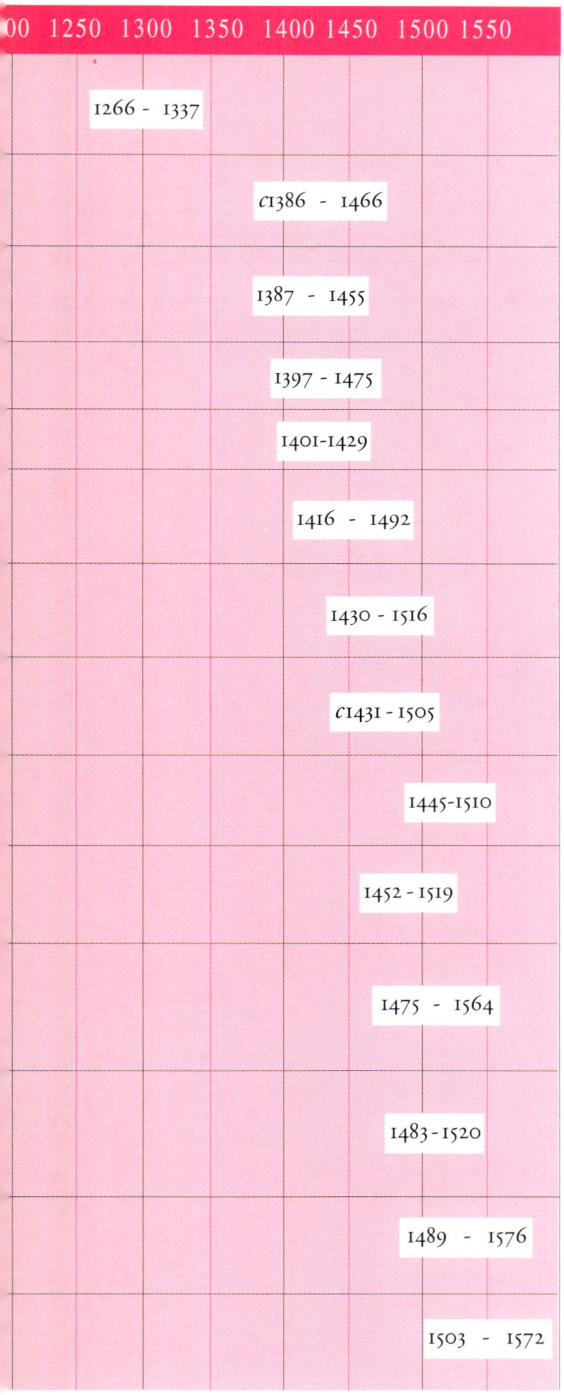

The Renaissance and Mannerism: Political and Social Background, 1400-1600

1417	The Great Papal Schism (since 1378) is settled and the Pope returns from Avignon to Rome.
1431	Joan of Arc is burned at the stake.
1446-50	Gutenberg, the German printer, invents printing with movable type.
1452	Leon Battista Alberti, Italian Renaissance architect, writes *On Architecture; On Painting.*
1469-92	Lorenzo de' Medici, 'The Magnificent', rules Florence.
1469	Ferdinand and Isabella unite Spain.
1492	Christopher Columbus discovers the Americas.
1509-47	Henry VIII reigns as King of England.
1511	Erasmus of Rotterdam, Dutch scholar and humanist, publishes *In Praise of Folly.*
1517	Martin Luther, German church reformer and founder of Protestantism, initiates his attack on Rome.
1528	Castiglione, Italian author and diplomat, writes about the Renaissance gentleman in *The Courtier.*
1532	Machiavelli, Italian politician and author, writes *The Prince.*

Fifteenth and sixteenth centuries

The Renaissance and mannerism

Netherlands	
The Limbourg brothers	Three brothers, all manuscript illuminators, whose masterpiece ***Les Très Riches Heures*** wa commissioned by the Duc du Berry.
Jan van Eyck	A major Netherlandish painter who perfected the technique of oil painting. His work is noted for its rich colours and fine detail.
Hieronymus Bosch	Horrific and fantastic visions of hell and damnation make Bosch one of the strangest painters in history.
Pieter Brueghel	Nicknamed 'Peasant Brueghel' because he depicted the lives of Flemish peasants in a sympathetic, witty and sincere manner.

Germany	
Matthias Grünewald	Strong imagination and emotional content are the hallmarks of this artist, whose masterpiece was the altarpiece at Isenheim Hospital, now in Colmar Museum in Alsace.
Albrecht Dürer	A German artist who introduced Italian Renaissance ideas to Northern Europe. His immense talent and skill can be seen in his large output of paintings, drawings, woodcuts engravings and writings on art.
Lucas Cranach	His fame rests on his detailed landscapes, expressive figures, religious and mythological pictures, as well as his portrait of Martin Luther and other contemporary figures.

France	
François Clouet	Appointed Court Painter to François I, Henry II, and Charles IX of France. Mainly know for his portrait drawings.

England	
Nicholas Hilliard	He painted exquisite miniatures that echo the delicacy, courtly grace and melancholy of t Elizabethan age.

Spain	
El Greco	A mannerist artist who was born in Crete and spent his working life in Toledo. Famed fo his elongated, elegant figures and religious imagery.

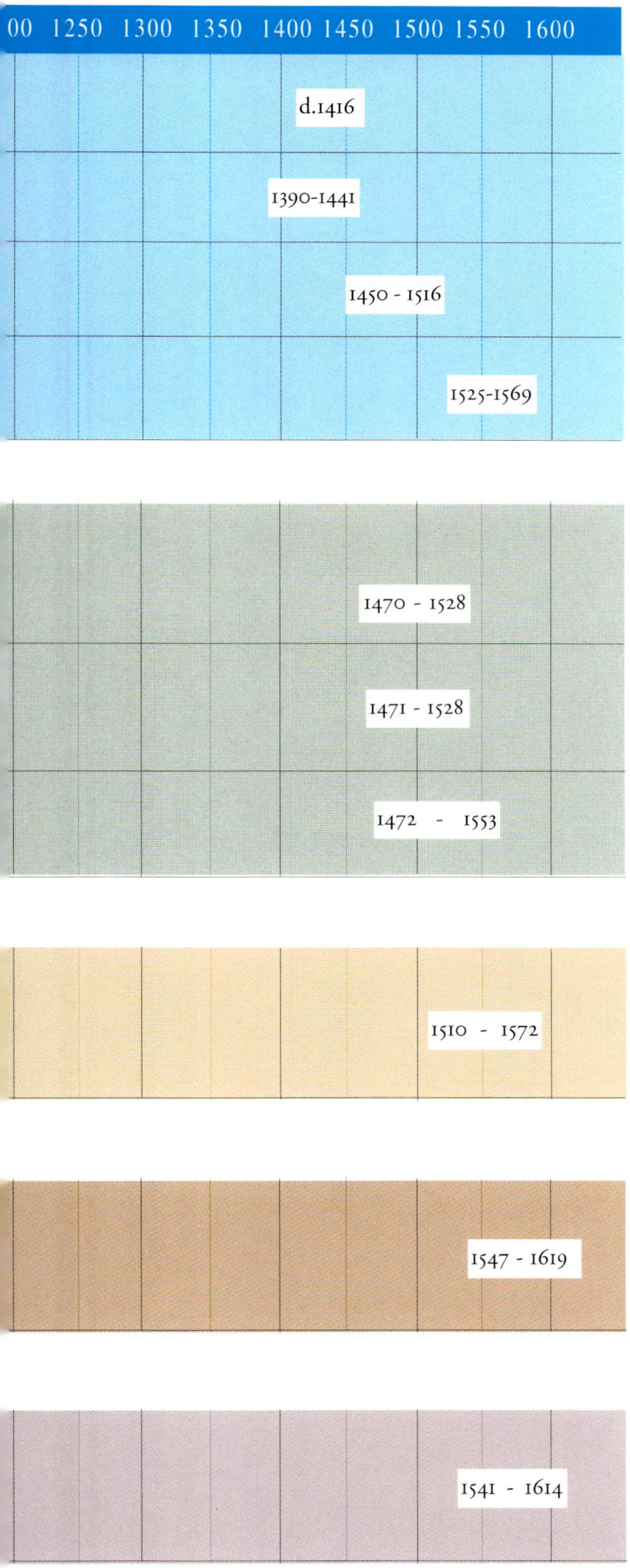

1547-84	Ivan the Terrible reigns in Russia.
1556	Charles V, Holy Roman Emperor, retires. His son Phillip II becomes King of Spain, the Netherlands and the New World.
1564-1616	William Shakespeare, English dramatist and poet.
1568	Giorgio Vasari, Italian art historian, architect and painter, publishes enlarged edition of *Lives of the Artists.*
1588	The Spanish Armada is defeated by the English.

Seventeenth and eighteenth centuries

Baroque and rococo

Italy	
Lavinia Fontana	A Bolognese portrait painter who was renowned for her ability to paint fine clothes and jewellery.
Caravaggio	A revolutionary figure in Italian art, his mature work is characterised by realism and dramatic light effects. He reputedly painted directly onto the canvas from a model, without preparatory drawings.
Bernini	The supreme artist of the baroque. The vitality of his sculpture was a key feature of the baroque period. He was also a designer and architect.
Giambattista Tiepolo	The greatest master of eighteenth-century Venetian art, he produced some of the last masterpieces of fresco painting.
Canaletto	A superb view painter. No other artist was as successful in painting Venice, its views, ceremonies and scenes of everyday life.

France	
Nicolas Poussin	The finest history painter of the seventeenth century, whose controlled compositions, rooted in history and the classical tradition, express the heroic aspects of antiquity.
Claude Lorrain	In Rome, he developed a type of idealised poetic landscape which was inspired by classical antiquity, and this had a formative influence on European painting.
Antoine Watteau	A master of the pretty, delicate rococo style, his 'fête galante' pictures displayed romantic festive scenes in a pastoral setting.
Jean-Baptiste Chardin	Considered one of the finest exponents of naturalistic still lifes and quiet domestic scenes which represented a complete contrast to the rococo painters.
François Boucher	A successful French rococo decorator and artist. He also designed for tapestries, interiors and the theatre.
Jean Honoré Fragonard	A witty and decorative rococo painter, he specialised in romantic scenes depicting courtly and ideal love. His type of rococo art was superseded by the simpler neo-classical style.

England	
William Hogarth	A painter and engraver of London life, who depicted a new view of society with his biting moral satires in works such as *The Rake's Progress.*
Sir Joshua Reynolds	A successful portrait painter in the 'grand manner', writer and lecturer, as well as being the first president of the Royal Academy.
Thomas Gainsborough	A successful portrait painter and rival to Reynolds. Landscape painting remained his real passion.

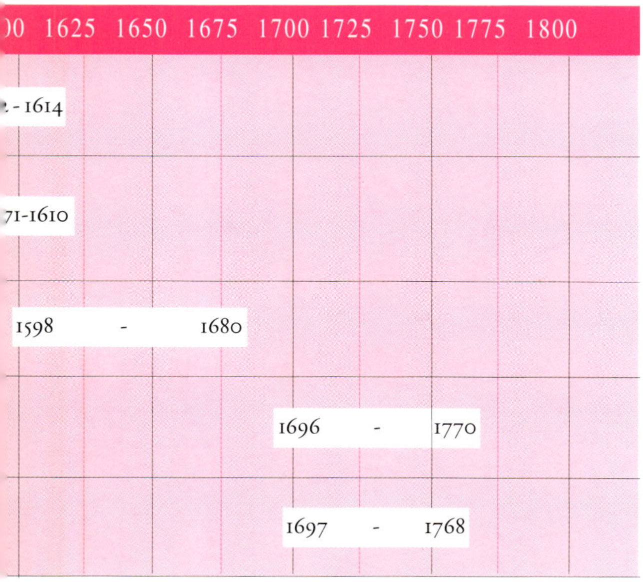

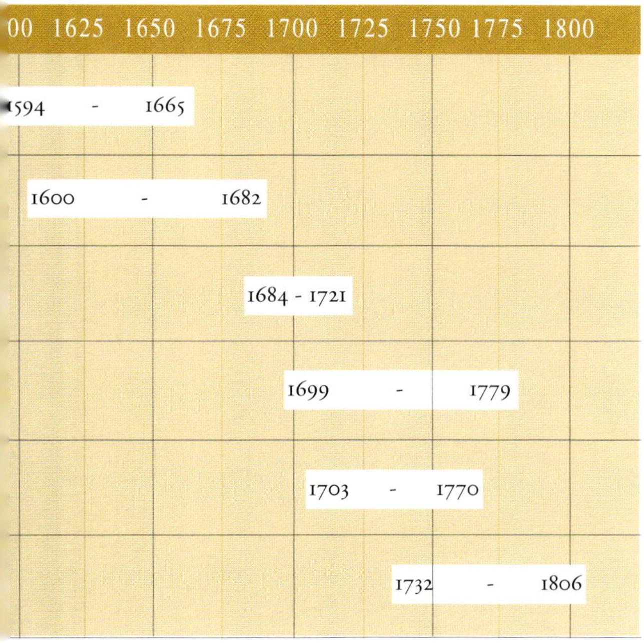

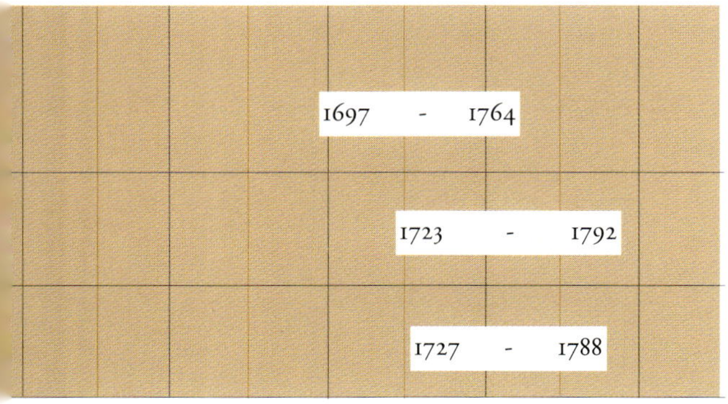

Baroque and Rococo: Political and Social Background, 1600–1800

	Catholic Counter-Reformation in Europe.
1605	Cervantes, the Spanish novelist, playwright and poet, publishes his masterpiece, *Don Quixote.*
1618-48	Thirty Years War.
1623-62	Blaise Pascal, French philosopher and mathematician.
1643-1715	Louis xiv reigns as King of France.
1646	Charles i beheaded; Commonwealth established under Oliver Cromwell.
1667	John Milton, the English poet, publishes his epic poem *Paradise Lost.*
1682-1725	Peter the Great reigns in Russia.
1694-1778	Voltaire, the French author who was devoted to tolerance, justice and humanity.
1715-1774	Louis xv reigns as King of France.
1726	Jonathan Swift, writer and Dean of St Patrick's Cathedral, Dublin, publishes *Gulliver's Travels.*
1742	Handel's great choral work, *The Messiah*, is first performed in Dublin.
1762-96	Catherine the Great extends Russia to the Black Sea.
1770-1827	Ludwig van Beethoven, German composer, who became the dominant influence in nineteenth-century music.
1774-92	Louis xvi reigns as King of France.
1775-83	American War of Independence.
1776	American Declaration of Independence.
1789-95	French Revolution.

Seventeenth and eighteenth centuries

Baroque and rococo

Netherlands	
Peter Paul Rubens	Brought the exuberance of Italian baroque to Northern Europe, creating religious and allegorical paintings for churches and palaces. A master of drama and lover of rich colour.
Frans Hals	A master portrait painter, whose rapid technique and perceptive eye could catch expressio and costumes with a few confident strokes.
Anthony van Dyck	The Flemish baroque painter of religious, landscape and mythological scenes, but most famous for his portraits of King Charles I.
Rembrandt van Rijn	An artist with a prodigious output who was outstandingly gifted as a painter, draughtsma and printmaker. His series of self-portraits, executed between 1629 and 1669, are renowne
Jan Steen	A painter who specialised in ordinary scenes of everyday life. Many of his pictures are humorous and convey a moral or message.
Jacob van Ruisdael	The finest Dutch landscape painter, who exerted a huge influence on nineteenth-century European landscape painting.
Johannes Vermeer	Considered one of the greatest painters of Northern Europe. A master of light and colour he produced works that are serene and timeless.

Spain	
Diego de Velázquez	He possessed a singular ability to capture the truth of the character and situation on canvas. Is renowned for his masterpiece ***Las Meninas***.
Murillo	The leading painter in Seville in the late seventeenth century, his works were copied and imitated in the later eighteenth and nineteenth centuries.

Ireland	
Nathaniel Hone the Elder	Dublin-born portrait painter in miniature and oils. Founder member of the Royal Acaden London. Famed for *The Conjurer*, which was an attack on Reynolds.
Hugh Douglas Hamilton	A distinguished artist who was successful in Dublin, London and Rome. Highly skilled portrait painter in oil and pastel, also known for his historical subjects.
James Barry	Cork-born, befriended by Edmund Burke, who financed his studies in Italy. Prominent eighteenth-century portraitist and painter of historical subjects in the grand manner in Lon

United States	
John Singleton Copley	A Boston painter whose early classical style gave way to romanticism. Noted for his portraits, history and genre scenes.
Benjamin West	His extraordinary scenes from history, both modern and ancient, made him a major figur in London's art world.
Gilbert Stuart	An extremely successful portrait painter, renowned for his series of George Washington portraits. Worked in Ireland between 1787 and 1793.

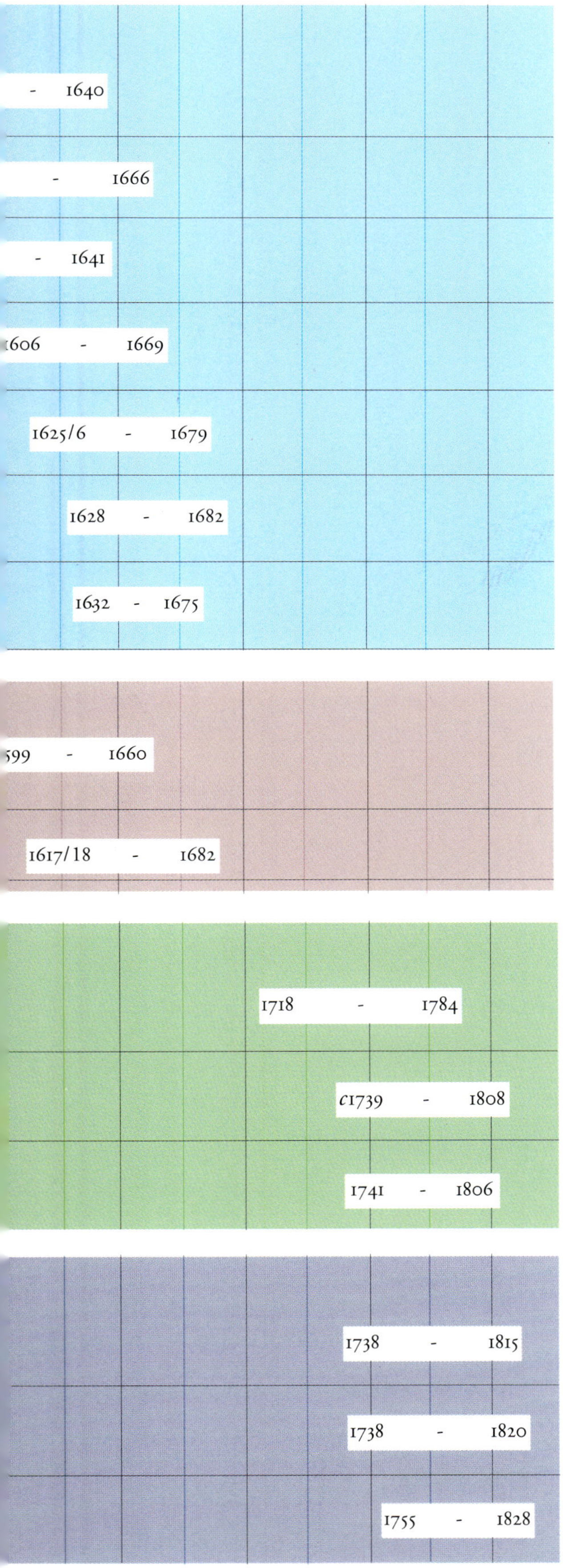

1792-1822	Percy Bysshe Shelley, the English lyric poet.
1795-1821	John Keats, English poet and leading figure of the romantic movement.
1798	William Wordsworth and Samuel Taylor Coleridge, English romantic poets, collaborate on *Lyrical Ballads.*
1799-1837	Aleksandre Pushkin, the Russian poet and writer.
1799-1815	Napoleon rules France for fifteen years.

Nineteenth century

Neo-classicism to post-impressionism

France	
Jacques-Louis David	Painter and political figure of the revolutionary and Napoleonic periods in France. Renowned for his neo-classical-style portraits.
Jean August Dominique Ingres	A pupil of David, and also a neo-classical painter. He was a superb draughtsman and his portraits and subject pictures display his passionate love of drawing.
Eugène Delacroix	With Géricault, he was labelled a romantic artist for his bold use of colour, and dramati literary and historical subject matter.
Gustave Courbet	Leader of the realist movement, who felt it was his duty to record the world as it was, without idealisation.
Camille Pissarro	A father-figure among the impressionists and a prolific artist, who painted every aspect o the French countryside.
Edouard Manet	A member of the impressionists, his *Déjeuner sur l'herbe*, painted in a brilliant and fresh technique, shocked French society.
Auguste Rodin	Celebrated and influential sculptor who combined the realistic and romantic tendencies nineteenth-century art with innovations like fragmented figures as finished works of art.
Edgar Degas	A member of the impressionists, he was a great experimenter who recorded the manners and movements of society in drawings, pastel, paintings and sculpture.
Paul Cézanne	A post-impressionist artist, known as the 'father of modern painting' because his theorie on space, form, shape and colour influenced twentieth-century art.
Claude Monet	It was from one of Monet's paintings, *Impression, Sunrise*, that the impressionist group, o which he was the leader, acquired its name.
Berthe Morisot	The first female artist to join the impressionists – the other was Mary Cassatt. Executed portraits and outdoor scenes, etchings and lithographs.
Renoir	An artist who contributed rich colour effects and solidity of form to impressionism. He more interested in figure painting than landscapes.
Paul Gauguin	An artist rebel who gave up a career in finance to paint at Pont Aven in Brittany and in South Sea islands. He had a lasting influence on twentieth-century art.
Georges Seurat	Inventor of the 'pointillist' technique, in which the paint was applied in small dots of pu colour, which blend in the eye of the viewer.

Germany	
Caspar David Friedrich	A romantic painter who expressed with brilliant clarity the mystery of nature through hi beautiful landscapes.

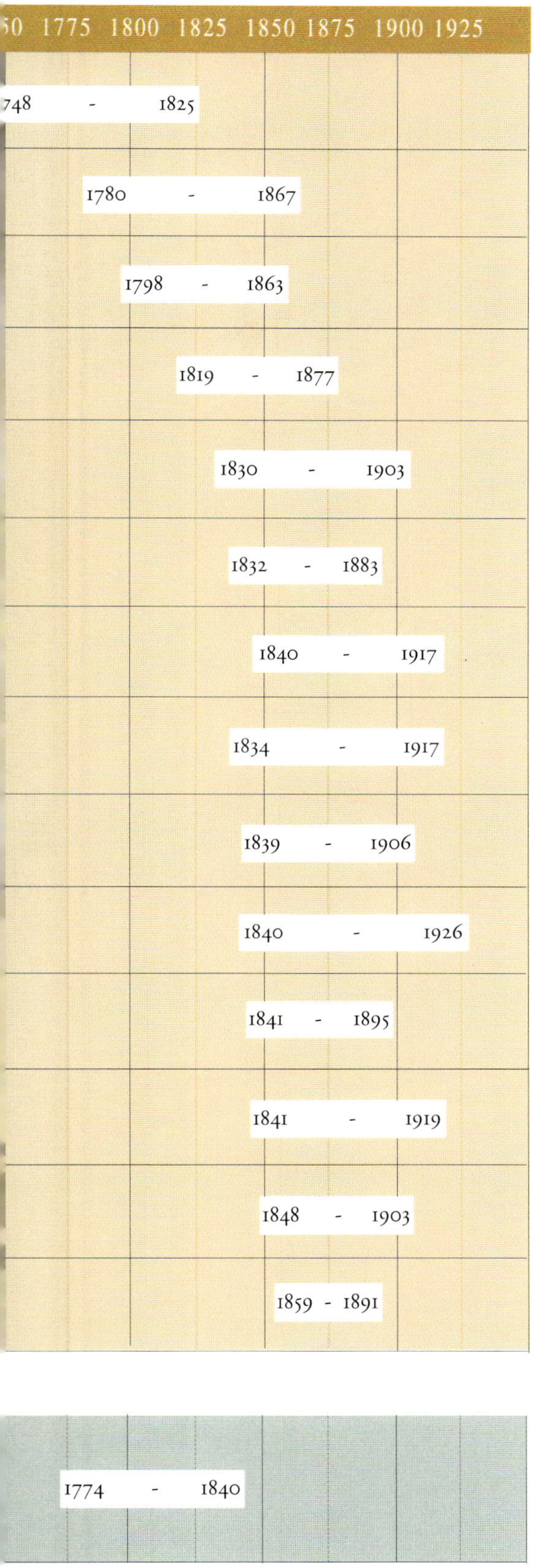

NEO-CLASSICISM TO POST-IMPRESSIONISM: POLITICAL AND SOCIAL BACKGROUND, 1800-1900

1803-69	Hector Berlioz, French romantic composer and the founder of modern orchestration.
1804	Napoleon I crowns himself Emperor of France.
1808	Goethe, German poet, novelist and dramatist, publishes his masterpiece *Faust.*
1810-49	Frederic Chopin, Polish composer and pianist.
1812	The English poet Byron establishes his reputation with 'Child Harold's Pilgrimage'.
1825	First railway completed in England.
1827	Mendelssohn, German pianist, conductor and composer, writes *A Midsummer Night's Dream.*
1829	Catholic Emancipation Act; enabled Catholics to enter parliament.
1828-1906	Henrik Ibsen, Norwegian playwright and poet.
1829	Schubert, the Austrian composer, publishes the 'Great' Symphony in C Major.
1837	John Field, Irish composer, dies in Moscow.
1837-1901	Victoria reigns as Queen of England.
1837/9	Daguerre develops a photography process in Paris.
1838	Charles Dickens, the English Victorian novelist, writes *Oliver Twist.*
1840-1902	Emile Zola, French novelist and social reformer.

Nineteenth century

Neo-classicism to post-impressionism

Spain	
Goya	A major Spanish artist. Principal painter to Charles IV of Spain, also a prolific draughtsm and printer, renowned for his series of etchings, *The Disasters of War* (1810-13).

England	
William Blake	A painter, poet and visionary who invented a highly personal mythology, verbal and visual, express his view of the world.
Turner	An innovative artist renowned for his ability to capture the atmosphere and mood of a scene. His works display dazzling accuracy and beauty.
John Constable	Admired in France for his paintings of the English landscape. His deep understanding of nature and sky studies is visible in all his famous pictures, including *The Hay-Wain*, 1821.

Ireland	
William Mulready	Born in Ennis, he settled in London, where he became a successful painter of genre subje pictures. Less well known for his superb figure drawings.
Daniel Maclise	Cork-born artist who studied at the Royal Academy schools. He became the most succes ful history painter of his day. Executed frescoes for the new Houses of Parliament.
Frederic William Burton	Celebrated watercolourist, whose best-known work was *The Meeting on the Turret Stairs.* Appointed director of the National Gallery, London, 1874-1894.

Japan	
Hokusai	An astonishingly prolific painter, draughtsman and printer whose famous views of Moun Fuji were done when he was over sixty-five.
Ando Hiroshige	A master woodcut printer, famed for landscapes, including *Rain Shower on Ohashi Bridge* in which nature is grand and the people are small.

Netherlands	
Vincent van Gogh	He evolved a highly personal style in which he tried to communicate the innermost feeli of the artist. He lived a short tragic life. His works can be seen in the Van Gogh Museum in Amsterdam.

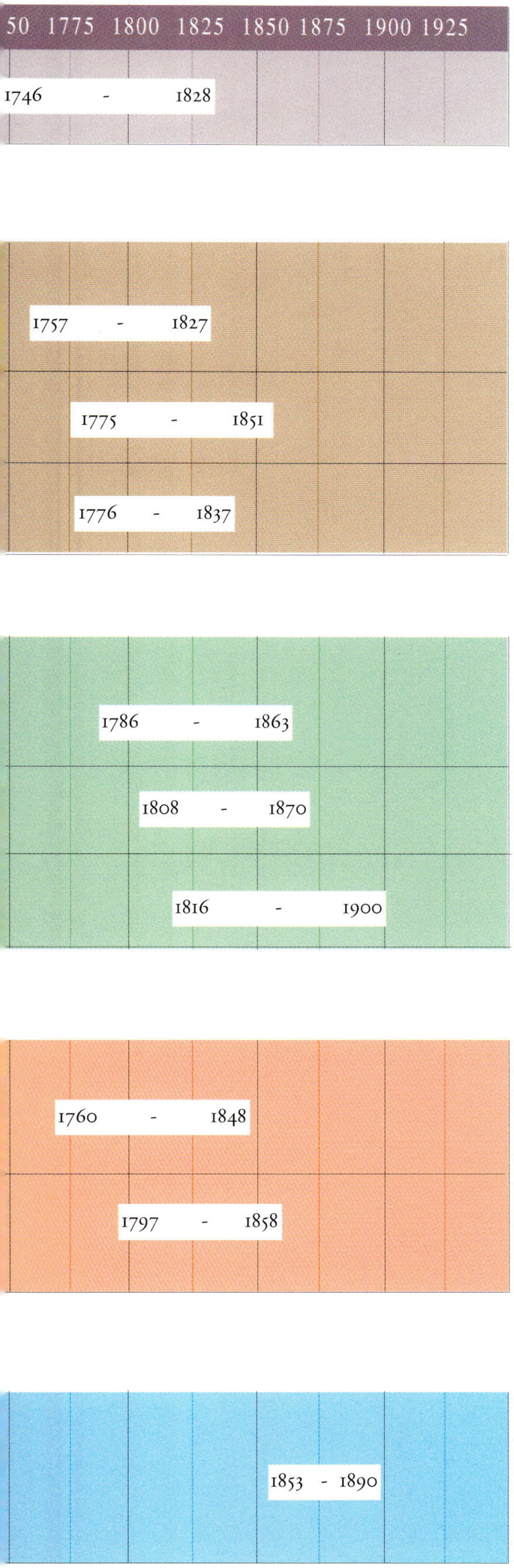

1844	Telegraph perfected by the American painter Samuel Morse, who with his assistant, Bain, invents the Morse code.
1845-50	The Great Irish Famine resulted in widespread death and emigration.
1853	Admiral Perry, the American naval officer, reopens communication between Japan and the outside world after 250 years of isolation.
1855	Walt Whitman, the American poet, publishes 'Leaves of Grass'.
1859	Charles Darwin, the English scientist, publishes *On the Origin of the Species.*
1861	Russia abolishes serfdom.
1861-5	American Civil War; 1863 Abolition of slavery.
1863-9	Leo Tolstoy, Russian novelist, writes *War and Peace.*
1867	Dostoevsky, Russian novelist, produces his major work *Crime and Punishment.*
1867-95	Karl Marx writes *Das Kapital*, the fundamental text of Marxist economics.
1870-1	Franco-Prussian War.
1876	Wagner, the German opera composer, publishes his masterpiece *The Ring of Nibelung.*
1876	The British scientist Alexander Bell patents his invention, the telephone.
1880	Charles Stewart Parnell becomes leader of the Home Rulers.
1989	W. B. Yeats, Lady Gregory and Edward Martyn found the Irish Literary Theatre.
1892	Tchaikovsky, Russian composer, writes the ballet *The Nutcracker.*
1895	Oscar Wilde's play *The Importance of Being Earnest* is published.

Nineteenth century

Neo-classicism to post-impressionism

United States	
James MacNeill Whistler	A London-based artist and printer. His paintings, influenced by Japanese art, expressed arrangements of colour, e.g. harmonies, achieved by closely relating colours and tones.
Winslow Homer	The greatest painter of New England country life, he was a leading figure in nineteenth-century American art.
Thomas Eakins	One of the best-known portrayers of the American outdoor life, including a series of wor on themes of hunting, swimming, sailing and rowing.
Albert Pinkham Ryder	An original and poetic painter, whose romantic landscapes and seascapes have a visionary and brooding quality.
John Singer Sargent	An American virtuoso portrait painter who settled in London and painted figures from th fashionable Edwardian and Georgian society.

Twentieth century

The modern movement, up to 1950

France/Italy/Holland	
Henri Matisse	Leader of the Fauves ('wild beasts') group, he was an artist who created expressive painting pure colour and joy. Also known for his sculpture, prints and coloured-paper cut-out sha
Piet Mondrian	Developed a form of abstraction called 'pure reality' based on geometric shapes, primary colours and black and white. His works are often called geometrical abstractions.
Marcel Duchamp	The exhibition of his readymades foreshadowed the 'anti-art' Dada movement. At the 191 Armory Show in New York, he showed *Nude descending a staircase*, a visual equivalent to the moving figure.
Umberto Boccioni	An Italian futurist painter, sculptor, writer and member of the group of painters called th futurists. He published the 'Manifesto of Futuristic Painters' in 1910.

Austria/Germany/Switzerland	
Gustave Klimt	A leading Austrian art nouveau painter who created flat, decorative pictures showing exot nudes. Most successful as a designer for the applied arts.
Emil Nolde	A German expressionist artist of landscapes, biblical scenes and mythology painted in a stark, distorted and emotional style. Also a noted printer.
Paul Klee	A Swiss artist and printer whose childlike poetic style he once described as 'taking a line f a walk'. An impassioned teacher and writer on art.

Norway	
Edvard Munch	An expressionist painter famous for his intense scenes of loneliness, anxiety, death and the passion between men and women.

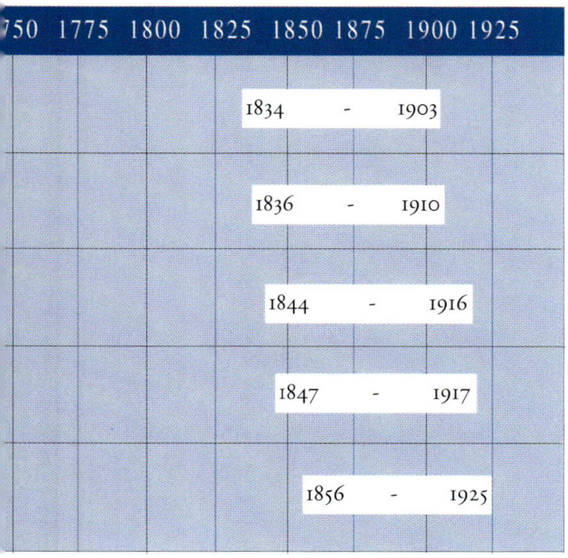

1895	Marconi, Italian pioneer, invents wireless communication.
1896	Thomas Edison, the American scientist who invented the phonograph (1877) and the electric light bulb (1879), invents motion pictures.
1898	Marie and Pierre Curie, scientists, discover radium (Nobel Prize in 1903).
1899	Sullivan, Carson Pirie Scott Department Store is completed in Chicago – a key building in the development of the skyscraper.

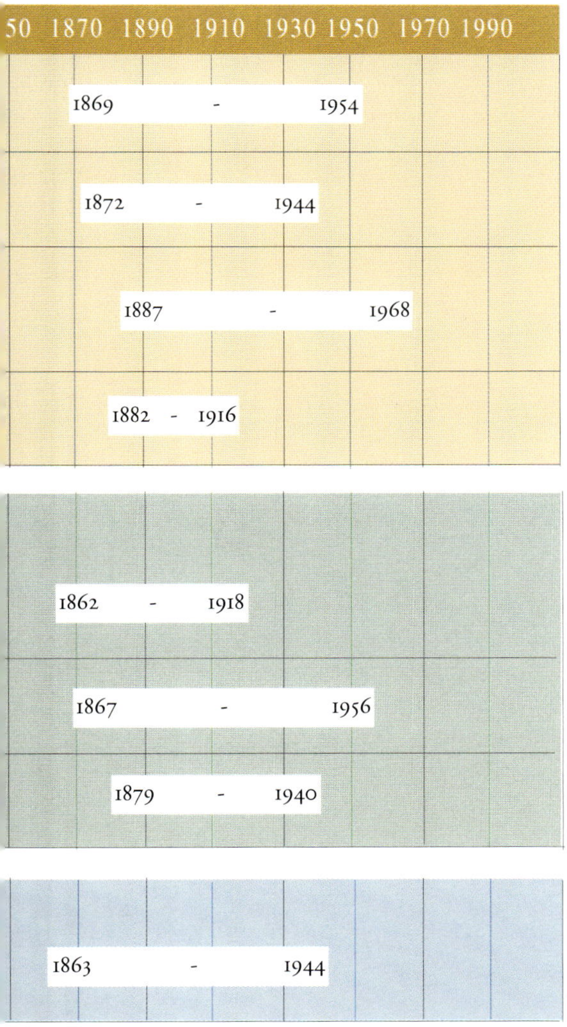

Modern Art:
Political and Social Background, 1900-50

1900	Sibelius, Finnish composer, writes the nationalistic symphonic poem 'Finlandia'.
1902	Debussy, French composer, writes the opera *Pelleas and Melisandre.*
1903	Wright brothers' first flight with power-driven aeroplane.
1905	Einstein, the German-Swiss physicist, publishes his theory of relativity.
1905-1980	Jean-Paul Sartre, French author and philosopher, leading proponent of existentialism.
1909	Mahler, Austrian composer and conductor, publishes his ten symphonies: *Song of the Earth.*
1911	Revolution in China.
1912	Schoenberg, Austrian-Hungarian composer, writes *Pierrot Lunaire.*

Twentieth century
The modern movement, up to 1950

England	
Henry Moore	The first major modern British sculptor. Famed for his sculptures of the family and the female figure, and his series of London drawings, *Underground Air Raid Shelter*, 1940-3.
Francis Bacon	Dublin-born artist of international significance. Renowned for his depiction of people as distorted figures, sometimes disturbing, often shown in three panels, as a triptych.
David Hockney	His international and popular success dates from the early 1960s, with origins in Pop Art. A figurative artist who developed a variety of styles in California. Creates prints, set desig and uses new technology.

Russia	
Wassily Kandinsky	A pioneer of abstract painting. Co-founder of the Blue Rider Group, he taught at the Bauhaus. Left Russia in 1896, and lived in Paris, Munich and New York.
Kasimir Malevich	Russian painter with an interest in national folk-art. His experiments with pure geometric painting launched suprematism. Also designed scenery and costumes.
Marc Chagall	He spent his life in exile in France and the United States painting pictures inspired by Russian folklore and mythology.

Spain	
Pablo Picasso	Painter, sculptor, draughtsman, graphic and stage designer and ceramicist, particularly associated with cubism. The great genius of twentieth-century art.
Joan Miró	Leading surrealist painter, sculptor, ceramicist and ballet designer. His works are famous f their witty imagination and wonderful colour.
Salvador Dali	Somewhat of a sensationalist. This painter, writer and illustrator made surrealism an inter nationally known style.

Ireland	
John Lavery	Belfast-born artist who achieved international renown for his society portraits and genre scenes. Appointed official war artist 1914-18, attached to the Royal Navy.
Roderic O'Conor	Ireland's first modernist painter who studied in Dublin, Antwerp and Paris. An internation figure through his association with Gauguin and the Pont Aven School.
Jack B. Yeats	Arguably the major Irish painter of the twentieth century. He began his career as an illustrator, but it was his late expressive work in colour which won him an international reputation
William Orpen	Based in London, he was one of the most successful portrait painters of this century. Appointed official war artist 1914-18. He taught a generation of Irish artists.
Mainie Jellett	Leader of the modern movement in Ireland and founder of the Irish Exhibition of Living A She developed a highly personal painting style based on cubist principles.

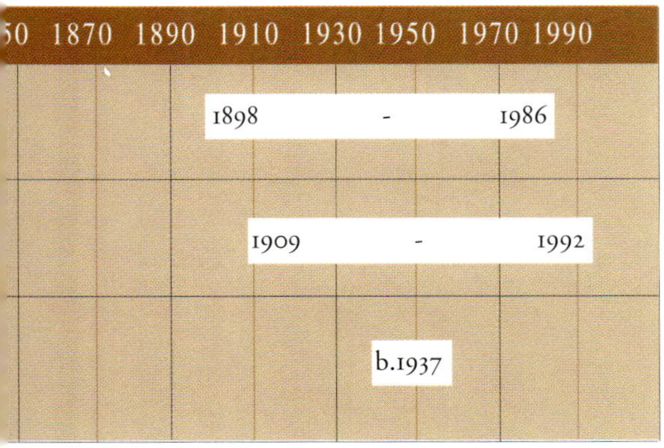

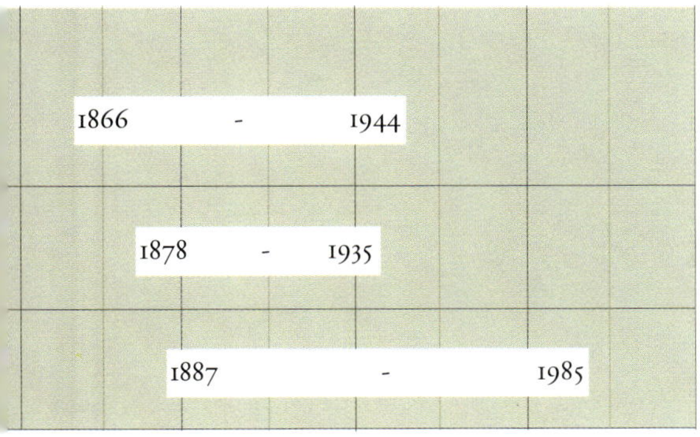

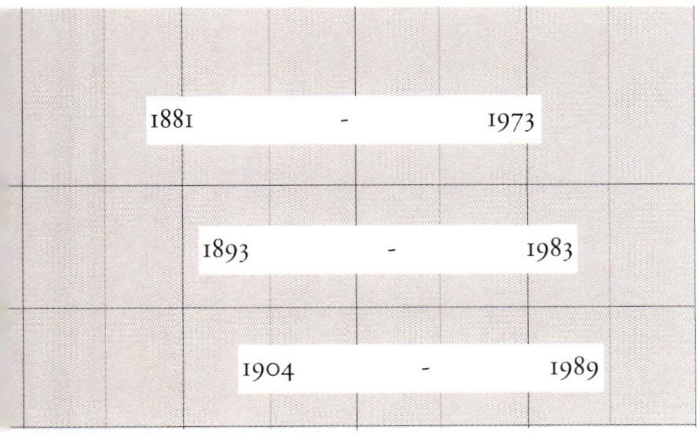

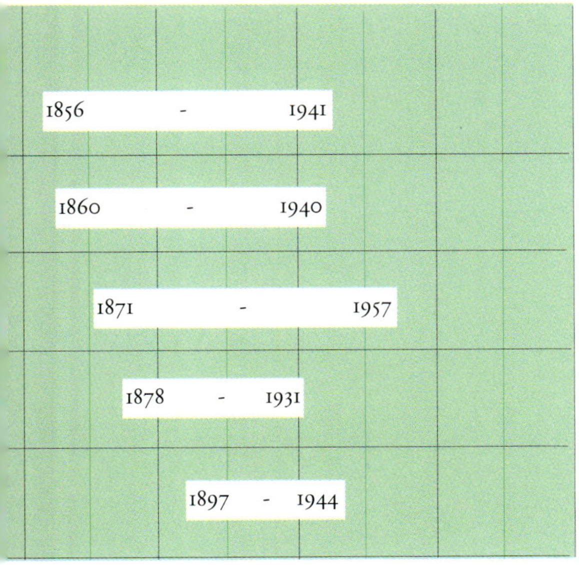

1913	Stravinsky, Russian composer, writes music for Diaghilev's ballet, *The Rite of Spring*.
1914-18	World War I (USA enters in 1917).
1915	Gandhi leads struggle for Indian Independence (1915-47) by non-violent non-cooperation.
1916	Easter Rising. Irish Republic proclaimed in Dublin.
1917	Russian Bolshevik Revolution.
1919	Bauhaus, German teaching school for the visual arts and architecture, founded by Gropius.
1921	Anglo-Irish Treaty signed resulting in the creation of the Irish Free State.
1922	Mussolini, Italian dictator and founder of fascists, becomes prime minister in 1922.
1922	James Joyce's novel *Ulysses* is published.
1923	W. B. Yeats is awarded the Nobel Prize for Literature.
1925	George Bernard Shaw is awarded the Nobel Prize for Literature.
1925	Baird, the Scottish electrical engineer, pioneers television. 1928 sees the first TV broadcasts in America.
1928	Women gain the vote in Britain.
	D. H. Lawrence, the English writer, publishes *Lady Chatterley's Lover*.
1929	Wall Street Crash. Great Depression 1929–mid 1930s.
1933	Hitler seizes power in Germany.
1936-9	Spanish Civil War. General Franco becomes head of state and government.
1938	Samuel Beckett's novel *Murphy* is published (Nobel Prize awarded in 1969).

Twentieth century

The modern movement, up to 1950

UNITED STATES	
EDWARD HOPPER	A realist painter, printer and illustrator whose works accurately depicted particular feature American city life in a sharp attractive style.
GEORGIA O'KEEFE	An artist renowned for her flower pieces, still lifes and desert landscapes of the southwest. Her style is described as 'magic-realism'; it has surrealist undertones.
ALEXANDER CALDER	Fused engineering and sculpture to produce different types of mobiles. Also a painter and illustrator of children's books.
MARK ROTHKO	An abstract painter of the New York school, his works are defined by horizontal areas of tl washes of paint, which soaked into the canvas and made bands of colour appear to float.
JACKSON POLLOCK	Leader of abstract expressionism, who abandoned conventional methods to use dripping a splashing techniques, using metallic paints and sand.
ANDREW WYETH	One of the best-known living artists in the United States, he paints in a meticulously deta naturalistic style, mostly in tempera, depicting the lifestyle and people of Maine.
ROY LICHTENSTEIN	The best-known American 'Pop Artist', famous for enlarging the strip cartoon and transforming it into powerful effective images.

SOUTH AMERICA	
DIEGO RIVERA	Mexican painter, muralist and graphic artist who was involved in left-wing politics throughout his career. He painted several monumental mural decorations. Married to Frieda Kahlo.
FRIEDA KAHLO	A Mexican realist painter who depicted her own life. An accident in youth left her in pain for life, and this partly explains the haunting complexity of her paintings.

AUSTRALIA	
SYDNEY NOLAN	Modern Australian artist famed for his Ned Kelly pictures. He painted scenes of the out-back, influenced by Australian aboriginal art, in a lyrical surrealist style.

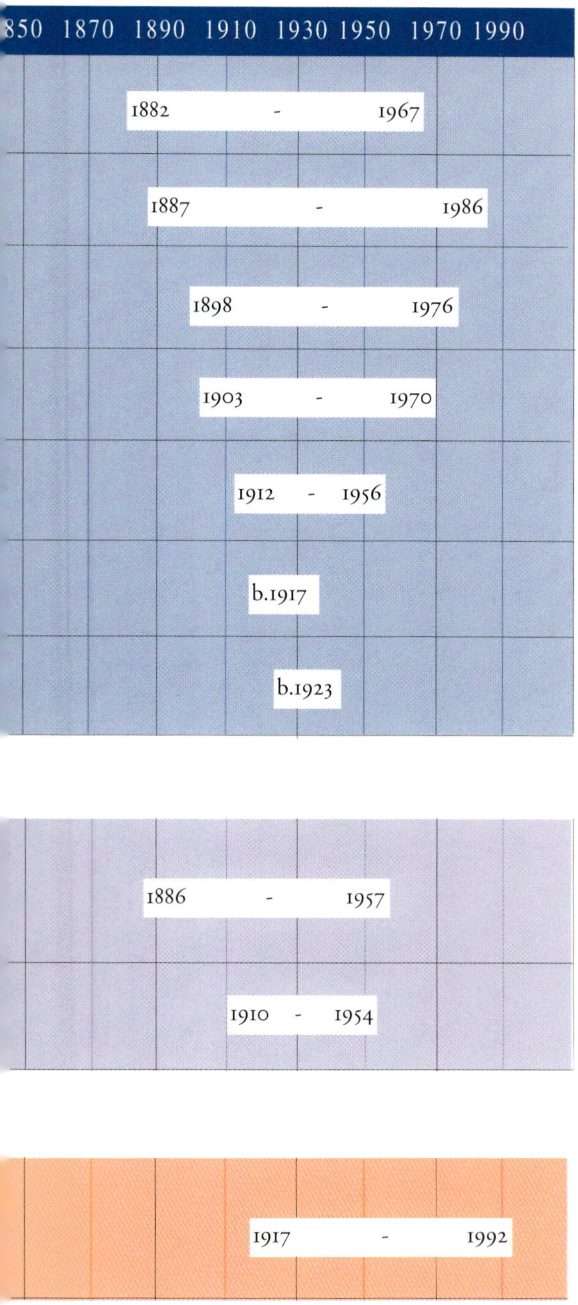

1939-45	World War II.
1940	Ernest Hemingway, American author, writes *For Whom the Bell Tolls.*
1945	Atomic bomb is dropped on Hiroshima and Nagasaki in Japan. End of World War II.
1945	United Nations Charter.
1948	The independent state of Israel is proclaimed.
1949	Ireland left the Commonwealth and became the Republic of Ireland.
1949	Faulkner, American novelist, is awarded the Nobel Prize.

Eighteenth to twentieth centuries

Irish Art

Ireland	
John Michael Wright	An English artist who visited Dublin in 1679 when he painted *The Ladies Catherine and Charlotte Talbot.* Wright may have made more than one visit to Ireland.
Garret Morphy	One of the earliest known Irish artists who was skilled at painting portraits and costume. A prolific worker celebrated for his portraits, favoured by many Jacobite families in Dublin.
James Latham	An assured and highly regarded Tipperary-born artist who studied in Antwerp. He became the finest early-eighteenth-century Irish portraitist, executing single and double portraits, such as *Bishop Robert Clayton and his wife Katherine.*
Nathaniel Hone the Elder	Dublin-born portrait painter in miniature and oils. Founder member of the Royal Academ Famed for *The Conjurer,* a subject picture that was really an attack on Sir Joshua Reynolds.
George Barret	One of the earliest Dublin Society School painters who studied under James Mannin. His superb landscape-painting skills are fully revealed in his masterpiece, *View of Powerscourt Waterfall.*
Hugh Douglas Hamilton	A distinguished artist who was successful in Dublin, London, Rome and, latterly, Dublin i the 1790s. Highly skilled portrait painter in oil and pastel, also known for his historical subject
James Barry	Born in Cork and befriended by Edmund Burke, who financed his studies in Italy. A prom nent eighteenth-century portrait painter and painter of historical subjects in the grand-mar ner in London. Died impoverished. See *Self-Portrait as Timanthes.*
William Ashford	An English-born artist who settled in Dublin and became one of the foremost landscape painters of his time. See *Panorama of Dublin from Chapelizod.* Appointed the first presiden the Royal Hibernian Academy in 1823.
Francis Wheatley	London-born artist. During his brief stay in Ireland he painted *The Volunteers Meeting in College Green,* 1779, representing a unique record of this historical event.
Thomas Roberts	The finest and most gifted eighteenth-century Irish landscape artist, who painted idealised and classical landscapes, including the *Lucan Demesne* series in the National Gallery.
William Mulready	Born in Ennis, he settled in London, where he became a successful painter of subject pictu such as *The Toy Seller,* and also landscapes. Less well known for his superb figure drawings.
George Petrie	Major topographical artist who illustrated views of Ireland in watercolour. See *The Last Circuit of Pilgrims at Clonmacnoise.* Member of the RHA, an antiquary, archaeologist and music collector.
James Arthur O'Connor	A landscape painter whose style developed from an early realistic phase, to romantic and dram ic pictures best illustrated in his scenes of County Wicklow, such as *View of the Devil's Gle*
Daniel Maclise	This Cork-born artist studied at the Royal Academy schools, did portraits and book illust tions in London and became the most successful history painter of the day. He executed frescoes for the new Houses of Parliament. See *The Marriage of Strongbow and Aoife.*
Frederic William Burton	Celebrated watercolourist, also an art historian and antiquary. Born in Corofin, he painte portrait miniatures and Irish subject pictures in watercolour. Celebrated for *The Meeting o the Turret Stairs.* Appointed director of the National Gallery, London, in 1874.

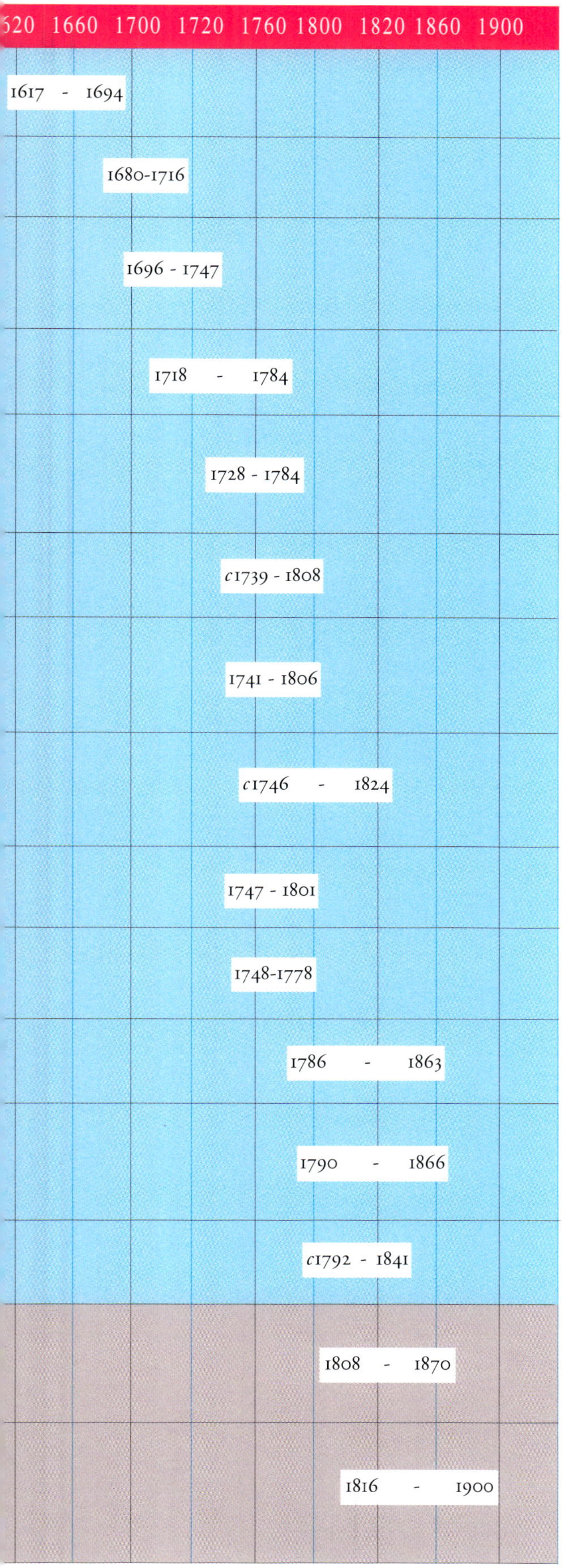

Ireland: Political and Social Background, 1700-1950

1710	George Berkeley's philosophical theory *The Principles of Human Knowledge* is published.
1726	Jonathan Swift, writer and dean of St Patrick's Cathedral, publishes *Gulliver's Travels.*
1738	Turlough Carolan (1670-1738), the chief musician of Gaelic Ireland, dies.
*c*1780	Brian Merriman, the Gaelic poet, writes *Cúirt an Mheáin Oídche.*
1791	United Irishmen founded in Belfast and Dublin.
1798	1798 Rising. Wolfe Tone (1763-98) is arrested and dies.
1800	Maria Edgeworth's novel *Castle Rackrent* is published.
1803	Unsuccessful rising organised by Robert Emmet (1778-1803).
1828	Daniel O'Connell (1775-1847) is elected MP for Clare.
1829	Catholic Emancipation Act is passed, enabling Catholics to enter parliament and hold civic and military office.
1830	William Carleton's *Traits and Stories of the Irish Peasantry* is published.
1837	John Field, composer, dies in Moscow.
1842-5	Young Irelander Movement.
1845-50	The Great Irish Famine resulted in widespread death and emigration. Population reduced by 20%.
1875	Charles Stewart Parnell (1846-91) is elected MP for Meath, and begins Home Rule movement.
1879	Land League set up by Michael Davitt (1846-1906).
1884	Gaelic Athletic Association established.
1893	Gaelic League founded by Eoin McNeill and Douglas Hyde (1860-1947).
1895	Oscar Wilde's play *The Importance of Being Earnest* is published.
1898	W. B. Yeats, Lady Gregory and Edward Martyn found the Irish Literary Theatre, which became the Abbey Theatre in 1904.

IRELAND	
JOHN HENRY FOLEY	Leading Irish sculptor who was also renowned in England and India. He had the ability t give vitality and expression to his portrait busts and public statues.
NATHANIEL HONE THE YOUNGER	He spent twenty years with the Barbizon painters in France, then returned to paint landscapes of north County Dublin, a typical example of which is *Pastures at Malahide.*
JOHN BUTLER YEATS	Artist, writer and excellent speaker, he was one of the leading Irish portrait painters of this century. Also the father of a talented family; Jack the painter, Lily the embroiderer, and Lolly the printer, skilled craftswomen who founded the Dún Emer and the Cuala Press. His other son, the poet and dramatist, is illustrated in the portrait of *William Butler Yeats.*
SARAH PURSER	Accomplished and successful portrait painter. A key figure in the development of Irish art. Among her many achievements was the establishment of the stained-glass studio, An Túr Gloine.
JOHN LAVERY	Belfast-born artist who achieved international renown for his society portraits and genre scenes. Appointed official war artist 1914-18, attached to the Royal Navy. Lavery's wife, Hazel, can be seen in the large canvas *The Artist's Studio.*
WALTER OSBORNE	Studied in Antwerp and worked in Brittany. A much loved artist, whose style combines th colour and freedom of impressionism with a genuine feeling for humanity, seen in *The Lustre Jug.*
RODERIC O'CONOR	Ireland's first modernist painter who studied in Dublin, Antwerp and Paris. An internatio al figure through his association with Gauguin and the Pont Aven School. *Farm at Lezave* depicts a scene in Finistère, Brittany.
JACK B. YEATS	The major Irish painter of the twentieth century. Born in London, his boyhood spent in Sligo observing Irish life provided the material for much of his work. He began as an illustrator but it was his late expressive work such as *The Singing Horseman* or *Grief* which won him an international reputation.
PAUL HENRY	Born in Belfast, trained in Paris. The artist most associated with a west of Ireland landscap genre, which was originally developed on Achill Island, and can be seen in *Launching the Currach.*
WILLIAM ORPEN	Based in London, he was one of the most successful portrait painters of the century, also a brilliant draughtsman. Appointed official war artist 1914-18. Over twelve years he taught a generation of Irish artists. Famed for his large satirical picture, *The Holy Well.*
WILLIAM LEECH	After training in Dublin and Paris he went on to Brittany, where he painted his most successful genre pictures, including *The Convent Garden.* Also a painter of portraits and superb flower-pieces.
HARRY CLARKE	The major Irish stained-glass artist of the century, who in his short lifetime created a body of exquisitely crafted glass. His glowing windows of rich design and highly finished detail can be seen in the Honan Chapel, Cork.
MAINIE JELLETT	Leader of the modern movement in Ireland and founder of the Irish Exhibition of Living Art. Her highly personal painting style, based on cubist principles, can be seen in *Achill Horses.*
EVIE HONE	A highly influential stained-glass artist who was descended from a dynasty of painters. He masterpiece, the east window of Eton College Chapel, illustrates her bold, expressive style. *Snow at Marlay* shows her fluid painting skills.

** The pictures listed in italics are in the National Gallery of Ireland*

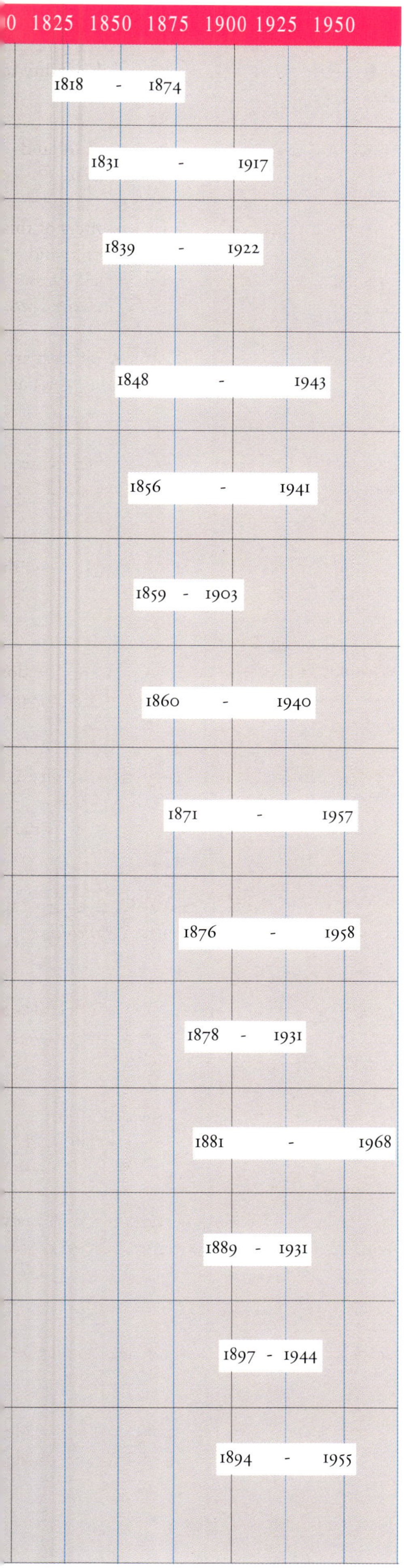

1905	Sinn Féin party formed by Arthur Griffith (1871-1922).
1907	Rioting at the Abbey opening of J. M. Synge's *Playboy of the Western World.*
1913	Irish Volunteers and Cumann na mBan founded.
1914-18	World War I. Home Rule Bill suspended.
1916	Easter Rising. Irish Republic proclaimed in Dublin. Execution of rebel leaders.
1918	Countess Markievicz, first woman elected to the British parliament, did not take her seat.
1919	First meeting of Dáil Éireann in Mansion House; De Valera elected president.
1919-21	War of Independence.
1921	Anglo-Irish Treaty signed, resulting in the creation of the Irish Free State.
1922	Provisional government formed.
	The novel *Ulysses* by James Joyce (1882-1941) is published.
1922-23	Civil War. W. T. Cosgrave's Cumann na Gael founded.
1923	W. B. Yeats (1865-1939), poet and dramatist, awarded Nobel Prize.
1925	G. B. Shaw (1856-1950), critic, novelist and dramatist, awarded Nobel Prize.
1926	Rioting at the Abbey opening of Seán O'Casey's *The Plough and the Stars.*
1932	Fianna Fáil political party, set up by de Valera in 1926, succeeds to power.
1932-8	Economic tariff war between Britain and Ireland.
1937	The new Constitution of Ireland is approved.
1938	Douglas Hyde (1860-1947) becomes president of Ireland.
	The novel *Murphy* by Samuel Beckett (1906-89) is published (Nobel Prize 1969).
1939	The poet Seamus Heaney is born in County Derry (Nobel Prize 1995).
1939-45	World War II – state of emergency declared. Ireland remains neutral.
1942	The epic poem *The Great Hunger* by Patrick Kavanagh (1904-67) is published.
1949	Ireland Act – Republic of Ireland inaugurated.
	Unesco chooses an Irish novel, *Cré na Cille* by Máirtin Ó Cadhain (1907-70) for translation into several European languages.

Glossary of Art Terms

Abstract art
Art which does not imitate or directly represent external reality. In one sense all art is abstract in that it 'abstracts' visual material from the world as perceived by the artist.

Academic art
A descriptive term for art which obeys academic 'rules', or art which originates from within an official academy. It also means history painting portrayed in the 'grand manner' subjects from classical antiquity and the Bible. Nowadays it has come to mean outdated narrative painting.

Aerial perspective
Often described as 'bird's-eye view', it is the means by which distance is rendered by using progressively paler colours.

Alla prima
To create a completed picture in one session.

Altarpiece
A religious painting composed of one or several compartments, intended to stand on or hang above an altar of a church or chapel.

Anatomy
The physical structure of the human body, including the skeleton, bones and muscles. Anatomical drawing was a key aspect of the training of many academies and was used as a way of teaching artists how to illustrate balance, form and movement and the inter-relation of the different parts of the body.

Animation
A term used to describe cartoon characters who move about freely like real people. Their movements are made up of many pictures filmed one at a time and then speeded up. There could be as many as sixty different drawings in sixty seconds of animation. Nowadays animators use computer graphics to speed things up, but when Walt Disney first began, every drawing was done by hand.

Annunciation
The occasion when the Angel Gabriel announced to the Virgin Mary that she was to conceive and give birth to Jesus, the Son of God.

Antiquity
This term usually applies to the era of Greek and Roman civilisations which ended in the fifth century AD with the fall of the Roman Empire. 'Antique' refers to objects and sculpture of antiquity.

Aquarelle
Painting which uses watercolour washes.

Aquatint
An intaglio printmaking method in which areas of tone are created by covering the plate with powdered resin. When heated, the resin melts into particles. When the plate is put into an acid bath, biting takes place around each particle, giving an irregular effect, which often appears like a watercolour wash. The strength of the acid used and the length of the etching time determines the degree of texture and tone achieved. The print is also called an aquatint.

Ascribed or attributed to
Evidence suggests that the work is by the named artist.

Atelier
A French word meaning an artist's studio.

Avant-garde
A French term now used to refer to art that is modern, experimental, innovative and way ahead of its time.

Barbizon School
A school of naturalistic landscape painting centred on the village of Barbizon in the forest of Fontainebleau near Paris, between 1830 and 1860.

Binder
A liquid medium, for example oil for oil paint or gum arabic for watercolour, which is mixed with colour pigment to make paint stick to a surface.

Bodycolour
A water-soluble pigment that is opaque as opposed to transparent. By mixing lead white or Chinese white with watercolour, the artist produces bodycolour. Turner is an example of an artist who made extensive use of bodycolour, usually with watercolour.

Brightness
The intensity of any given colour.

Bronze
A type of metal made from copper and tin, used for making tools and sculptures. The word also means a statue or object cast in bronze.

Calligraphy
The art of fine handwriting or letter forming.

Camera obscura
Italian words meaning 'dark room'. It is a box-like device that uses a lens to project an image onto a glass screen, which can then be traced.

Canvas
A course woven material, usually linen or cotton, on which artists paint.

Caricatures
These are funny pictures of political or other well-known figures, whose most recognisable features are exaggerated by being drawn much larger than normal, to make them look humorous or ridiculous.

Cartoon
A full-size preparatory drawing ready for transfer onto a canvas, panel, wall or tapestry. The enlargement is done by squaring up the drawing in proportion to the original, and transferring it in sections. The word 'cartoon' nowadays describes different kinds of illustrations, all of which rely on strong design for their effect. The drawings are bold with clear lines, and this type of art is called graphic art. Cartoon strips or comic books are stories told in pictures.

Catalogue
A list of works of art often accompanying an exhibition. A *catalogue raisonné* is a complete scholarly catalogue of an artist's work.

Chiaroscuro
An Italian word for 'light-shade'. The term is used to describe exaggerated contrasts of light and shade in paintings or drawings, notably in the work of Caravaggio.

Classical
Refers to works of art inspired by or modelled on the art of ancient Greece or Rome. Also applies to art that is based on logical and reasoned principles and deliberate composition.

Collage
A French word meaning 'pasting' or 'gluing'. It is used to describe a work of art made by pasting bits of paper, fabric or materials onto a background.

Composition
The manner in which the various elements in a picture are organised.

Computer art
Art that is generated electronically, that is, from within a computer.

Conversation piece
A small group-portrait in oils in which the sitters are shown engaged in conversation, usually indoors. These paintings were particularly popular in eighteenth-century England.

Cruciform
In the shape of a cross.

Design
The planned arrangement of the elements in a picture (line, shape, form, colour, texture and space), often called composition. Also the preliminary drawing or design for a picture.

Diptych
A painting, usually an altarpiece, made up of two hinged panels.

Donor
The person who commissions a work of art. The term is usually used when a portrait of the donor is included in the work of art.

Drypoint
An intaglio printmaking technique in which a metal point is used to draw onto a metal plate, raising a thin residue of metal, called a 'burr'. This leaves a soft, velvety line when the plate is printed. The greatest exponent of the technique was Rembrandt. The print is also called a drypoint.

Easel
An upright stand used by artists to hold the canvas or panel.

Engraving
A process, used by printmakers, of cutting lines into wood block or metal plate with a sharp tool called a burin. These prints are called engravings.

Etching
A method of printmaking whereby the plate is first coated with an acid-resistant substance, then the image is cut into the substance with a sharp needle. Finally the etched plate is immersed in acid, which 'bites' into the cut image. This method of printmaking reached a high point in the seventeenth century in the work of Rembrandt. These prints are called etchings.

Fake
A copy of an artwork made with the intention of pretending to be the original.

Fauvism
A short stage in the development of early-twentieth-century painting, led by Henri Matisse and André Derain. Because the artists created pictures painted in bold, clashing colours, full of distortions and flat decorative patterns, the critics called them 'Les Fauves', the wild beasts.

Fête galante
A French term meaning 'courtship party'. The term was coined by the French Academy to describe Watteau's reception piece for membership of the Academy, *The Pilgrimage to the Island of Cytheria* (1717), a painting representing a masquerade on the theme of love.

Focal point
The centre of interest in a picture.

Foreground
That part of the painting which is closest to the viewer, usually the lower area of the composition.

Foreshortening
A method of producing forms on a two-dimensional surface so that they appear to project or recede from the picture plane.

Form
The suggested shape or solidity of objects in a work of art.

Fresco
An Italian word meaning 'fresh'. It is a way of painting on a newly plastered wall, using colour pigments mixed with water, so that the paint is absorbed and becomes part of the wall's surface.

Genre painting
A type of picture representing ordinary subjects engaged in everyday life.

Gilt/gilding
The application of a thin film of gold leaf to a painting, frame or other surface.

Glaze
A transparent film of paint.

Golden section
Also called the 'golden mean', it is a system of proportions developed by the ancient Greeks which establishes a harmonic ratio between two unequal parts of a painting. The Golden Section was thought to be the perfect ratio because it involves only three measurements.

Gouache
Poster paint or opaque white added to watercolour paint.

Grand tour
An extensive tour of the Continent, with Rome as the focal point, undertaken by English and Irish aristocrats who wished to perfect their languages, view the splendours of Rome and absorb the culture acquired by foreign travel. Many collected works of art and antiquities for their family estates, thereby spreading the taste for Italian culture. The First Earl of Milltown acquired his famous collection in the mid eighteenth century on the Grand Tour of Italy. It was subsequently bequeathed to the National Gallery in 1902.

Graphic art
A term used to describe all forms of printmaking.

Grisaille
Grisaille comes from the French word meaning grey. A painting, often a preparatory underpainting or sketch in grisaille means it is exclusively done in tones of grey. It is used on decorative cycles to imitate sculpture and architectural ornament and similar *trompe l'oeil* effects

Ground
The first layer/undercoat to cover completely the canvas or panel prior to painting. See also 'primer'.

Highlight
A term used to describe an area of particular importance in a picture.

Horizon line
This is where the sky and earth appear to meet. The horizon line is drawn across the picture corresponding to the artist's eye-level. The vanishing point is where parallel lines appear to meet on the horizon line.

Icon
A Greek word *eikon*, meaning an ideal portrait, likeness or image. An icon is a sacred panel painting of Christ or one/several of the saints, the practice of which evolved in the Greek Orthodox Church and in Russia in the fifth century.

Iconography
The study by art historians of the story, images and symbols in works of art.

Idealised
Something that is represented in an ideal or perfect form rather than naturally.

Illumination
Hand-drawn decoration or illumination of manuscripts with coloured pictures, initials, patterns or borders, usually used during the Middle Ages.

Impasto
An Italian word describing paint applied thickly to a canvas or panel.

Landscape painting
Emerged in seventeenth-century Holland and France as a subject in its own right. It is a painting showing a view out of doors, usually in the country.

Life-drawing
Drawing the human figure from a live model.

Life-model
A person who poses in a studio, to be drawn by an artist.

Linear perspective
The means by which an artist creates an impression of depth by using imaginary lines that meet at a point in the distance called the vanishing point. It is also a method whereby figures meant to be seen in the distance are shown as being smaller than those meant to be seen close up.

Lithography
A printing process based on the principle that oil and water never mix. Lithography uses a greased surface for printing as opposed to an engraved surface.

Masterpiece
The term is usually applied to an artist's finest work, or to an exceptionally fine work of art.

Media
The materials in which an artist works, e.g. tempera, or the technique which he/she uses.

Medium
The materials the artist uses to make a work of art, e.g. pencil, crayon, paints, inks. It also means the substance, e.g. oil, gum or egg, used to mix the colour pigments.

Mezzotint
An intaglio printmaking method in which the metal plate is first roughened all over with a sharp tool called a 'rocker' to create a pattern of 'burrs', which prints a deep, velvety black. The artist scrapes down the burr to achieve the lightness of tone required. The main feature of the process is that the artist works from dark to light, from a black ground to highlights. The technique was particularly popular in eighteenth-century England. The print is also called a mezzotint.

Middle Ages
The period in Europe between the end of the Dark Ages and the Renaissance, from about the sixth to the fourteenth centuries. It is usually called the medieval period.

Miniature painting
A very small painting, usually a portrait, painted on ivory, parchment or vellum. The term originally came from illuminated manuscripts.

Modernism/Modern art
In art history the term tends to refer to the period from the 1870s onwards which produced a progressive style of art that broke with and rejected earlier modes of expression.

Moral
Concerned with a sense of right and wrong.

Mosaic
Decoration found on walls and floors, used by the ancient Greeks and Romans onwards. It consists of small pieces of coloured marble, tiles, glass or stone fixed to the surface with cement.

Mural
A large wall painting or decoration. A mural is usually painted directly onto the wall or on panels attached to the wall.

Mythology
A fictitious legend or tradition, mostly accepted as historical. Usually involves the beliefs of a people concerning their origins, deities, heroes and the universe. Mythological painting generally describes pictures whose subject matter is classical mythology treated in an elevated and ennobling way.

Narrative painting
Painting which tells a story. It also describes a form of nineteenth-century salon painting in which narrative played the key role.

Naturalism
An attempt to show figures, objects and the setting in a realistic way. In art it refers to imitating the appearance of the everyday world through minute observation of the natural world.

Oil paint
Paint made by mixing colour pigments with linseed oil.

Old Master
Mostly used to describe distinguished artists from an earlier period, in particular the Renaissance.

Palette
A surface made out of hardwood, with a thumb hole, on which the artist lays out and mixes colours.

Papier mâché
Paper mixed with paste and modelled when moist.

Pastel
A fragile stick of colour made from pure dry pigments used for 'painting' on paper. It is often used to describe pale colours in general. A pastel is also a finished artwork.

Patron
A patron is a person who buys or commissions a work of art.

Pentimento
An Italian word which means 'repentance' or change of mind. It is a term used to indicate repainting or overpainting of a picture by the artist in the course of its execution.

Perspective
Artists create an illusion of depth and space by using perspective. It is a method of showing three-dimensional objects on a two-dimensional flat picture surface, one of its main principles being that parallel lines converge to a single point (vanishing point) on the horizon.

Pigment
The actual colour used in paint, originally from natural sources, but now almost exclusively chemically formed. Raw colour, usually powder, which when mixed with a liquid, e.g. oil or water, forms paint.

Plein air
The French word for 'open air' is usually used for artworks that are, in part or wholly, painted outdoors. The artists of the Barbizon school were early exponents and their methods influenced the younger impressionists.

Pointillism
A technique of applying paints in small regular dots of pure colour so that when viewed from a distance, the colours appeared to blend. The French artists Georges Seurat and Paul Signac developed it in the nineteenth century.

Portrait
A painting that records the likeness of a particular person.

Predella
An Italian word for the series of small paintings that form the lower section of large altarpieces. The predella usually has narrative scenes from the lives of the saints who are represented on the panels of the altarpiece above.

Pre-Raphaelite Brotherhood
A group of mid-Victorian English painters who during the 1850s wished to recapture the directness and simplicity of Italian painting before Raphael. The seven founder members were William Holman Hunt, Dante Gabriel Rossetti, John Everett Millais, James Collinson, Frederick Stephens, Thomas Woolner and William Michael Rossetti. Although not a member, Ford Madox Brown was associated with the group. The movement was intensely literary. The artists used an elaborate form of symbolism and painted in strong colour on a wet white ground, which gave their pictures a brilliant quality.

Primary colours
Red, yellow and blue are primary colours and they can be mixed to make other colours. Orange, green and purple are secondary colours. A secondary colour is made by mixing two primary colours, e.g. yellow and blue make green.

Primer/priming
The primer or ground is the surface to which paint is applied, or the preparation of that surface for painting. It consists of a preliminary coating of ground applied to a panel or canvas in order to produce a smooth sealed surface. Painters used the traditional primer of 'gesso', consisting of chalk mixed with glue and water.

Profile
A side view of the face.

Proportion
The relationship of one part to another and of these parts to the whole.

Quattrocento
The Italian for 'four hundred' refers to the fifteenth century in Italian art.

Quill
A pen made from a feather.

Recession
The illusion of depth in a painting, created through perspective.

Relief
A raised surface. Sculpture that is carved or modelled and projects from a background. Bas-relief, also called low relief, projects only slightly, as on a coin.

Replica
An exact copy of an artwork, usually made by or supervised by the original artist.

Reproduction
A copy of a work of art produced by a machine.

Royal Academy
A society founded in London in 1768 to encourage the teaching of painting, sculpture and design in England.

Royal Hibernian Academy
Since its foundation in 1823, it has fostered and encouraged the development of the fine arts in Ireland through the establishment of the Academy schools and their annual exhibition.

Royal Ulster Academy of the Arts
A society founded as a sketching club in 1878 and reconstituted as the Royal Ulster Academy of the Arts in 1951, to provide a forum for painters, sculptors and architects to exhibit annually.

Scale
The size of a drawing in relation to the object being drawn.

Sculpture
A three-dimensional work of art created by carving, modelling or, more recently, by constructing or arranging materials.

Seascape
A scene featuring the sea.

Self-portrait
A portrait of an artist by him or herself.

Sfumato
An Italian word meaning 'smoke'. A method of applying thin transparent layers of paint so that the transition from one colour to another is done gradually and smoothly so as to be imperceptible – the colours blending as if they were smoke. The effect is to make objects or the landscape appear to recede into the distance. Notable in the work of Leonardo da Vinci.

Shade
The degree of darkness or depth of colour.

Silhouette
An image showing an outline of a figure created by cutting the image out of black paper or by colouring it black.

Sitter
The subject of a portrait.

Sketch
A rough drawing, painting or outline recording an idea, often made as a preliminary study for a composition.

Still-life painting
A painting or drawing of fruit, flowers, game or household objects. True still life is concerned with the representation of intimate objects of the day-to-day world for its own sake, free from any symbolic function.

Stretcher
The wooden frame over which the canvas of an oil painting is stretched. The corner joints of the stretcher are so designed that a triangular wedge may be tapped in to adjust the tautness of the canvas.

Studio
The artist's workroom.

Style
A system of signs used to enhance meaning, whatever the art or its medium. The distinguishing characteristics, e.g. technique, subject matter, treatment, by which an artist or a period is identified.

Support
The surface on which a painting is made, such as canvas, wood panel, paper or ivory.

Symbolism
A sign or design which is accepted as standing for or meaning something else. It is also a movement in literature, art and architecture from the mid 1880s through to the First World War.

Symmetry
The balance or harmony between parts.

Tempera
A quick-drying painting medium made from mixing coloured ground pigments with an emulsion of egg yolk. An important technique for panel painting in Europe.

Tondo
Italian for 'round' – a circular painting, drawing or sculpture. Circular paintings were fashionable in Italy in the mid-fifteenth century.

Tone
The variation of brightness in a colour.

Triptych
A painting, usually religious, on three separate but related panels, hinged together, consisting of a central section and two wings.

Trompe l'oeil
It is a French word for 'fool the eye'. A type of illusionism, a *trompe l'oeil* is a painting or a detail of a painting that deceives the viewer. The subject of the painting is shown in such a realistic and natural way that the viewer is 'tricked' into thinking it is three-dimensional.

Vanishing point
An imaginary point on the horizon line where parallel lines appear to meet.

Veduta
An Italian word meaning 'view'. *Veduta* is a drawing or a painting of a place, usually a town or a city. *Veduta ideata* is an imaginary view, while *Capriccio* is often architecturally accurate but fantastic in its composition. Panini and Piranesi, Canaletto and Guardi are the best-known vedutisti. Leading eighteenth-century view painters Panini, Canaletto and Guardi catered for the wealthy classes, who purchased their works on the 'grand tour' of Italy.

Vellum
Paper made from animal skin.

Visionary
A spiritual person, someone who has visions of another life.

Volume
Form that implies dimensions in length, breadth, depth and weight.

Wash
A flat, thin layer of ink or watercolour applied with a brush.

Watercolour
A method of painting in which colour pigments are mixed with water and glue.

Woodcut
A relief printmaking method in which a shape is carved from a block of wood leaving a raised image between the carved areas. The surface is covered with ink, paper is pressed onto the surface, and the print is produced from the inked raised surface. The prints are also called woodcuts.

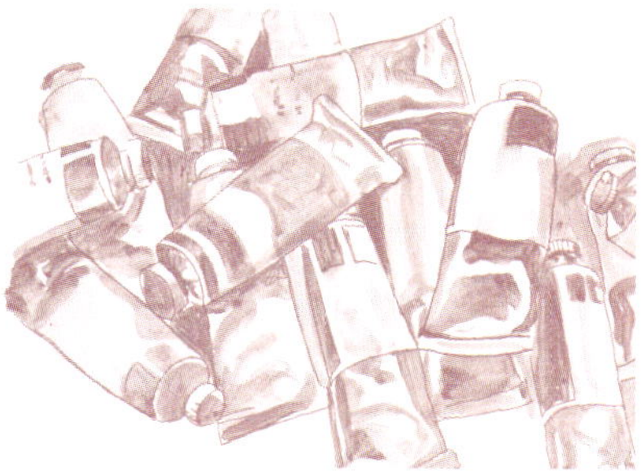

Suggestions for further reading on Irish art

General Irish art

B. Arnold. *A Concise History of Irish Art.* Thames & Hudson, 1969
A. Crookshank and Knight of Glin. *The Painters of Ireland 1660-1920.* Barrie & Jenkins, 1978
A. Crookshank and Knight of Glin. *The Watercolours of Ireland.* Barrie & Jenkins, 1994
B. Fallon. *Irish Art 1830-1990.* Appletree Press, 1994
P. Harbison, H. Potterton & J. Sheehy. *Irish Art and Architecture.* Thames & Hudson, 1987
B. P. Kennedy. *Irish Painting.* Town House and Country House, 1993
B. P. Kennedy and R. Gillespie (Eds). *Ireland – Art into History.* Town House and Country House, 1994
S. B. Kennedy, *Irish Art*, Gill & Macmillan, 1997
S. B. Kennedy, *Irish Art and Modernism.* Institute of Irish Studies, 1991
R. Knowles. *Contemporary Irish Art.* Wolfhound Press, 1982
P. Larmour. *The Arts and Crafts Movement.* Friars Bush Press, 1994
K. McConkey. *A Free Spirit Irish Art 1860-1960.* Antique Collectors Club & Pyms Gallery, 1990
W. Ryan Smolin, E. Mayes & J. Rogers (Eds). *Irish Women Artists.* National Gallery of Ireland, 1987
J. Sheehy. *The Rediscovery of Ireland's Past – The Celtic Revival 1830-1930.* Thames & Hudson, 1980
T. Snoddy. *A Dictionary of Irish Artists in the Twentieth Century.* Wolfhound Press, 1996
A. Stewart. *Royal Hibernian Academy of Arts; Index of Exhibitors 1826-1976.* Manton Publishing, Dublin. Vol 1 1985, Vol 2 1986, Vol 3 1987
W. Strickland. *A Dictionary of Irish Artists.* 2 Vols. 1913. Reprinted Irish Academic Press, 1989

Irish artists

B. Arnold. *Mainie Jellett and the Modern Movement in Ireland.* Yale University Press, 1991
B. Arnold. *Orpen: Mirror to an Age.* Jonathan Cape, 1991
R. Bennington. *Roderic O'Conor.* Irish Academic Press, 1992
M. Bourke. 'Frederic William Burton; Painter, Antiquarian and Art Historian', *Éire-Ireland. Journal of Irish Studies,* Minnesota, 1991
M. Bourke. 'Portrait of Evie Hone in her Studio by Hilda van Stockum', *Studies.* Summer 1997
J. Campbell. *The Irish Impressionists in Ireland, France and Belgium.* National Gallery of Ireland, 1984
J. Campbell. *Mary Swanzy.* Pyms Gallery, London, 1986
J. Campbell. *Frank O'Meara.* Hugh Lane Municipal Gallery of Modern Art, 1989
J. Campbell. *Nathaniel Hone the Younger.* National Gallery of Ireland, 1992
A. Crookshank. *Mildred Anne Butler.* Town House/National Gallery of Ireland, 1992
C. Crouan. *Maurice MacGonigal.* Hugh Lane Municipal Gallery of Modern Art, 1991
D. Ferran. *Leech: An Irish Painter Abroad.* National Gallery of Ireland, 1996
N. Gordon Bowe. *The Life and Work of Harry Clarke.* Irish Academic Press, 1989
N. Gordon Bowe, D. Caron & M. Wynne. *Gazetteer of Irish Stained Glass 1903-63.* Dublin 1988
F. Greenacre. *Francis Danby.* Tate Gallery, London, 1988
J. Hutchinson. *James Arthur O'Connor.* National Gallery of Ireland, 1985
S. B. Kennedy. *Paul Henry.* Town House/National Gallery of Ireland, 1991
A. Le Harivel. *Nathaniel Hone the Elder.* Town House/National Gallery of Ireland, 1992
K. McConkey. *Sir John Lavery.* Cannongate Press, Edinburgh, 1993
A. Maher and C. de Courcy. *Fifty Views of Ireland.* National Gallery of Ireland, 1985
K. O'Brien. *Harry Kernoff RHA.* Martello. Spring 1990
A. O'Connor. 'James Latham: Two Portraits', *Burlington Magazine,* Vol 116, March 1974
J. O'Grady. *The Life and Work of Sarah Purser.* Four Courts Press, 1996
R. Ormond and J. Turpin. *Daniel Maclise 1808-70.* Arts Council of Great Britain, 1972
M. Pointon. *Mulready.* Victoria and Albert Museum, London, 1986
W. L. Pressly. *The Life and Art of James Barry.* Yale University Press, 1981
H. Pyle. *Yeats: Portrait of an Artistic Family.* National Gallery of Ireland, 1997
H. Pyle. *Jack B. Yeats: a Biography.* London, 1970
RHA. *Sean Keating.* Royal Hibernian Academy, Dublin, 1989
J. Sheehy. *Walter Osborne.* National Gallery of Ireland, 1983
J. White. *Gerard Dillon. An Illustrated Biography.* Wolfhound Press, 1994
M. Wynne. *Irish Stained Windows.* Eason, 1977
M. Wynne. 'Thomas Roberts 1748-78', *Studies,* 1977
M. Wynne. 'Thomas Frye', *Burlington Magazine,* London, Vol 124, 1982
M. Wynne. *Fifty Irish Painters.* National Gallery of Ireland, 1983

Index of Artists

(whose work is included in this book and exhibited in the National Gallery of Ireland)

Note: See the General Index for page references

Index
Note: numerals in italic refer to the illustratons

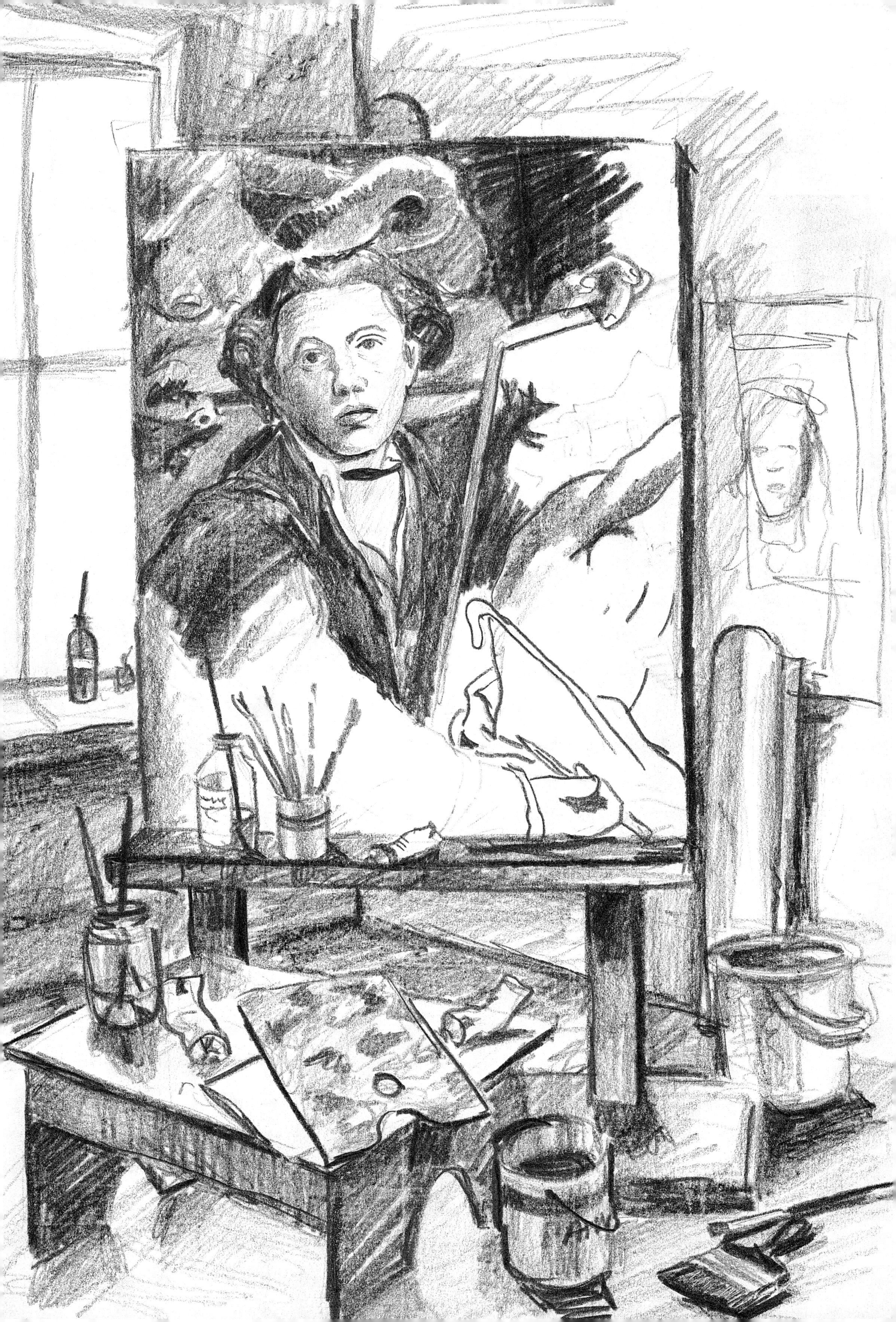